Contents

Researching the Police in the 21st Century

Researching the Police in the 21st Century

International Lessons from the Field

Edited by

James Gravelle
Head of Policing and Security, University of South Wales, UK

Colin Rogers
Professor of Police Science, University of South Wales, UK

Editorial matter and selection © James Gravelle and Colin Rogers 2014
Individual chapters © Respective authors 2014

All rights reserved. No reproduction, copy or transmission of this
publication may be made without written permission.

No portion of this publication may be reproduced, copied or transmitted
save with written permission or in accordance with the provisions of the
Copyright, Designs and Patents Act 1988, or under the terms of any licence
permitting limited copying issued by the Copyright Licensing Agency,
Saffron House, 6–10 Kirby Street, London EC1N 8TS.

Any person who does any unauthorized act in relation to this publication
may be liable to criminal prosecution and civil claims for damages.

The authors have asserted their rights to be identified as the authors of this work
in accordance with the Copyright, Designs and Patents Act 1988.

First published 2014 by
PALGRAVE MACMILLAN

Palgrave Macmillan in the UK is an imprint of Macmillan Publishers Limited,
registered in England, company number 785998, of Houndmills, Basingstoke,
Hampshire RG21 6XS.

Palgrave Macmillan in the US is a division of St Martin's Press LLC,
175 Fifth Avenue, New York, NY 10010.

Palgrave Macmillan is the global academic imprint of the above companies
and has companies and representatives throughout the world.

Palgrave® and Macmillan® are registered trademarks in the United States,
the United Kingdom, Europe and other countries.

ISBN 978–1–137–35746–5 hardback
ISBN 978–1–137–35747–2 paperback

This book is printed on paper suitable for recycling and made from fully
managed and sustained forest sources. Logging, pulping and manufacturing
processes are expected to conform to the environmental regulations of the
country of origin.

A catalogue record for this book is available from the British Library.

A catalog record for this book is available from the Library of Congress.

Figures and Tables

Figures

Tables

Preface

The origins for this book lay in a discussion that took place in my office at the University of South Wales with my fellow editor, Dr James Gravelle. Having published numerous articles together, both nationally and internationally, and conducted much research and many evaluations for the police, we regularly discussed the past, present and the future changing landscape of policing across the world. The drive for evidence-based policing, coupled with the introduction of the new College of Policing, Police and Crime Commissioners and of course the need for austerity in delivering public services such as the police, led us to the conclusion that research into, and on behalf of, the police was in need of closer consideration.

Questions we posed each other in our discussions related to such topics as access into the police organisation itself, confidentiality of information, informed consent and the role of the culture of the police. Widening our thoughts introduced us to considering research that involved police and their partners and the various topics that could be considered.

Realising that many books on researching the police were, in some senses, actually books that focussed on research methodology, we decided to try and bridge that gap by introducing a book that considered real-life research methods employed by researchers, both inside and outside the police organisation. This real-life approach would, we realised, highlight the many problems of researching the police and criminal justice agencies. However, it would also allow the reader to witness how the particular researchers, working on a number of different topics, negotiated their way through these problems to ensure their research was built upon sound, ethical and valid methods. Consequently, this book, entitled *Researching the Police in the 21st Century: International Lessons from the Field*, has been written with that in mind. It is believed that the chapters in this book will be of great use to those conducting research and evaluations into the police and their partners and provide possible templates for others to use in real-life situations, whilst also allowing the student to use the examples provided in the various chapters as a learning aid. The future of policing appears to be that of a drive for professionalisation, reliant upon a bank of professional knowledge underpinned by good-quality research. We believe that this volume will assist in that quest.

Acknowledgements

It is customary for editors in works such as this to thank certain individuals for their help and work in its production. We can see no reason why this should not apply for this volume!

Many thanks go, we feel, to the contributing authors of this volume who all readily agreed to undertake the work on the various chapters. Their enthusiasm for their individual work has been inspirational, and the odd requests for amendments were cheerily met and attended to within the strict time limits set by the editors.

Many thanks should also go to Harriet Barker and Julia Willan, the staff at the publishers, who have guided us with their support.

Finally, a very special thank you to loved ones who are always the unsung heroes of such projects. To Alison and Alice – Diolch unwaith eto!! and Anna, thank you for your unwavering support.

Contributors

Editors

James Gravelle works at the International Centre for Policing and Security at the University of South Wales, UK. He previously worked for the University of Glamorgan as a consultant and Research Assistant (RA) and regularly carried out research on behalf of Police Services. Research for the police includes work on Tasking Demand Management Units (TDMUs), community intelligence and the use of volunteers. As a Fellow of the Higher Education Academy, James has been involved in planning, writing and development of material within higher education on areas such as 'policing in the big society', 'knowledge management', 'policing in the financial crisis', 'the use of intelligence' and 'the impact of terrorism on policing'.

Colin Rogers is the first Professor of Police Science appointed by the University of South Wales, UK. He is a former police officer having served with the South Wales police for 30 years, retiring in 2003 at the rank of Inspector. During his police service, he undertook his academic qualifications and was appointed part-time lecturer in Criminology at the University of Glamorgan, UK. He was appointed as a senior lecturer at the Centre for Police Sciences in May 2004, and later became a Principle Lecturer, before being awarded his Readership in Police Sciences in 2010. Professor Rogers is also Visiting Professor at Charles Sturt University, Sydney, Australia. He is the author and co-author of nine books on policing and police-related matters and has published nearly 200 articles in both practical and academic journals, both nationally and internationally.

Contributors

John Foust began his career in law enforcement as a police officer in New Mexico in 1978. In the early 1990s, he transitioned into police education and training. He served as the Director of Police Training at both Western New Mexico University and at the Del Mar Regional Police Academy (Corpus Christi, Texas). In 2007, he accepted a position with the Metropolitan Police Department in Washington, DC. He currently works as a Special Assistant to the Chief of Police. In that capacity he researches critical issues to policing, monitors department-wide activities and keeps the chief appraised of events and activities. Additionally, he is a faculty member of the University of Maryland System. As an Adjunct Associate Professor, he teaches criminal justice. John is a research student at the University of Glamorgan, where he pursues his doctorate in Police Science.

Bernhard Frevel is a Senior Lecturer at the University of Applied Science for Public Administration of North Rhine-Westphalia and Professor at the University of Münster, Germany. He studied educational science, sociology, psychology and political science in Siegen and Cologne (1982–1986), was awarded his doctorate in Social Science at the Fern Universität Hagen (1993) and received his venia legendi for political science in Münster (2009). He also taught at the German Police University. He works and researches on different aspects of Police Science, especially crime prevention, security governance and the organisation of police.

Amanda Milliner studied Police Science at the University of Glamorgan, UK, graduating with a 1st class honours degree for her work on marginalised groups and is now undertaking a PhD after receiving funding to undertake the study. Amanda has previously worked for the University of Glamorgan as a Research Assistant (RA), spending time researching the police organisation on issues relating to vulnerable groups. More recently, Amanda worked as a lecturer in Criminology and Police Science, specialising and focusing on vulnerable, marginalised and hard to reach groups in relation to policing. In recent years, Amanda has published articles for academic journals aimed at both international and national audiences. Amanda's current research interest involves community engagement, with particular focus on improving the current interface between the police and vulnerable/marginalised members of society. Amanda regularly attends national and European conferences to present her findings.

Louise Skilling is currently undertaking a PhD, researching how communities in Kenya can build their resilience to improve their safety. She has served as a police officer with West Midlands Police. She obtained her MSc ('Street Girls and Their Vulnerability to HIV Infection in Freetown, Sierra Leone') from Coventry University, UK. Louise has researched groups at risk of HIV infection in South Sudan on behalf of Population Services International (PSI) and for the past five years worked for Mines Advisory Group (MAG) as their Senior Community Liaison Advisor monitoring and evaluating their programmes globally in conflict and post-conflict settings; during this time, she contributed to the 'Sourcebook on Socio-Economic Survey' produced by Geneva International Centre for Humanitarian Demining (GICHD).

Garry Thomas is a doctoral candidate at the Centre for Police Sciences, University of Glamorgan, UK. He is also a former police officer with South Wales Police retiring in 2012 at the rank of Inspector after 30 years' service. Garry entered the police service with an honours degree in Applied Chemistry (1981). During the course of his police service, he attained a Master's degree in the Study of Security Management (1996) and published an article in relation to the security management of enterprise parks. In addition to his operational duties with South Wales Police, he was also a Basic Command Unit Crime and Disorder Manager and was involved in the introduction of Police Schools Liaison Officers, Drug and Alcohol Arrest Referral Schemes and Neighbourhood Policing throughout South Wales. He was also a member of and provided secretarial services to the All Wales Regional Neighbourhood Policing Practitioners Group between 2005 and 2008. Garry was seconded to the National Policing Improvement Agency at the rank of Chief Inspector between 2008 and 2010, where he was a Field Officer for the South West Region of England.

About This Book

Each chapter of this book considers methodical issues surrounding research, particularly focusing on researching police organisations, their partners and their function. As part of each chapter, authors have highlighted particular challenges along with potential strategies for overcoming such difficulties, which it is hoped will be of benefit for future researchers.

Further, the chapters will explore definitions, scenarios and best practice guidelines to ensure that robust, good-quality research methods can be disseminated. Therefore, each chapter begins with a brief synopsis of the research undertaken providing readers with context and an overview of methods used as part of the study, whilst including a section of 'lessons learned', highlighting key points made throughout the research, thus providing the reader with a best practice guide that is easy to read, evaluate and put into practice.

Chapters

The first chapter provides the reader with an overview of police research. Specifically, Colin Rogers and Garry Thomas suggest that research around policing has changed significantly to meet the needs and aspirations of a changing police service, along with continually shifting political dimensions and landscapes. In addition, the chapter looks at the relationship that exists between police and academic research, before considering current developments in police research.

In Chapter 2, Colin Rogers examines a specific community safety crime prevention partnership as it attempted to reduce recorded crime and disorder, whilst also hoping to reduce fear of crime. It includes a consideration of such approaches as zero tolerance policing style, consultations with community and high-visibility policing. As the researcher worked within the police organisation involved in the research, Colin explored the challenges and complexities associated with the need to remain neutral and not influence or prefigure the outcome of the research. This specific chapter explores covert observations providing the researcher with a number of ethical challenges and decisions.

Chapter 3 examines the change in police resources deployment through the introduction of a Demand Management Unit. It analysed the work carried out by the unit as it attempted to rationalise the delivery of policing services to the public. James Gravelle discusses the role of the 'outsider/insider' approach as he explores the implications of such reform within the confines of the increasing pressure on the already finite policing resources, utilising a mixed methods approach.

The main aim of Chapter 4 is to explore and describe the impact community intelligence has on local policing. Here, Garry Thomas explores the extent to which Community Intelligence supports policing initiatives, within the context of the National Intelligence Model (NIM). Using a mixed method approach, and from the unique position of being an 'insider' at the beginning of the research and an 'outsider' upon its conclusion, Garry evaluates the value of such intelligence, including its use, evaluation and application to assist in the delivery of police services to the public.

Chapter 5 considers a research project entitled 'Cooperative Security Policy in the City' and designed as a study based on comparative case studies with intra- and inter-comparison using a multilevel triangulated method. Bernhard Frevel evaluated Crime Prevention Partnerships in Germany using a varied methodology, including problem-centred interviews, analysis of documents, statistics (socio-demography, socio-economy, crime data), quantitative network analysis, participatory observation and surveys.

In Chapter 6, John Foust discusses the methodological approach employed for critical analysis of the police union's or association's effect on management decisions in the United States, England and Wales. This chapter discusses key points and issues relative to the research process. First, it introduces a discussion on motivation, purpose and the development of the research question. Subsequently, research strategies and methods in general are explored and the methods utilised for this particular research are described and explained. This chapter further considers the process and rationale for the selected methods and addresses specific issues that are relative to the topic at hand.

Amanda Milliner in Chapter 7 discusses the interaction between the police and disadvantaged groups, focussing specifically on adults with learning difficulties. The chapter considers how a greater appreciation of the current engagement process between the police and potentially marginalised and vulnerable sections of the community will improve police legitimacy. Given the sensitive nature and the significance of this research study, validity and reliability, confidentiality and anonymity, are explored in some depth.

Chapter 8 discusses the research methods for investigating 'street girls' involved in prostitution and their vulnerability to HIV/AIDS infection. Here this research suggests ways in which the police and their partners, including the public health community, can inform and educate these young vulnerable women about HIV/AIDS. Carried out in Freetown, Sierra Leone, Louise Skilling investigated using a qualitative multi-method approach having to deal with the difficulties of ascertaining the 'identity' of the 'insiders' and the definitional debates surrounding the term 'street girls'.

In Chapter 9, Colin Rogers considers some of the important and significant lessons that can be drawn from carrying out important research such as that explored by the various authors in this book. In addition, he highlights and illustrates some of the problems associated with research in general and with an organisation such as the police in particular. The chapter provides not only an appraisal of the problems faced by all of the contributors but also how they overcome these problems, thus allowing for future police and criminal justice researchers to learn and apply important lessons.

1
Research on Policing: Insights from the Literature

Garry Thomas, Colin Rogers and James Gravelle

1.1 Introduction

Policing in England and Wales is facing challenges and undergoing significant changes as a drive for professionalisation of police and the creation of a body of police knowledge to support the concept of policing as a profession is under way. In support of these changes, such institutions as the College of Policing are attempting to inculcate into the police force the concept of evidence-based practice, founded on quality research, including academic and practitioner-based research and evaluations.

However, research on policing remains an emotive subject, particularly when discussing what should be researched. Initiated in the United States in the early 1950s and in the United Kingdom in the 1960s, research on policing has gone through many stages of development and has been undertaken and supported by a variety of different institutions (Reiner, 1989; 1992; 2010). Researching the police is particularly interesting due in part to the unique position, power and privilege the state bestows on the organisation. The unique culture that exists within the police organisation makes the challenge of research even greater, offering commentators and researchers a rare opportunity to investigate and get in close to this powerful institution. The political landscape in which the police operate also adds to the sense of importance and as policing does not exist within a political vacuum, this makes the topic of policing a dynamic and sensitive area for research. Additionally, in the context of the increasing financial problems, combined with finite resources and ever-growing demands on the public police, issues surrounding expenditure, budgets, costing and performance targets play an integral part in today's police services across the globe. This remains a primary concern for many senior police officers, politicians and others involved in policy making and service delivery. This chapter considers lessons and insights from police research undertaken in the past and also that being currently undertaken, in order to provide some idea of where this topic will lead us to in the future.

1.2 Past developments in the research on policing

Reiner (1989; 1992; 2010) suggests that research on policing practically commenced in the United Kingdom at the start of the 1960s with a change in the politics associated with the police and theoretical developments in disciplines such as criminology, sociology and law. He credits Michael Banton with being the first British academic to carry out empirical research on policing in his study entitled 'The Policeman in the Community' (Banton, 1964). Reiner (1992: 439–441) gives Banton's (1964) research numerous plaudits, including a 'significant starting point', a 'pioneering sociological study', a 'central research strategy', the 'study was ahead of its time' and 'path breaking'. Banton's (1964) research was quite rare not only in being the first empirical research, but also as it provided a comparison between policing in the United Kingdom and the United States.

Research on policing in the United States was already being pioneered by sociologist William Westley (1953; 1956; 1970), with his studies on police occupational culture, which focussed on police violence and secrecy (McLaughlin, 2007; Greene, 2010). Further, between 1965 and 1967 President Lyndon B. Johnston (1908–1973) established the Commission on Law Enforcement and the Administration of Justice (under Executive Order 11236) (Katzenbach, 1967) to extensively research all aspects of crime and law enforcement in the United States and to provide funding for future research (Rojek et al., 2012). As Punch (2010: 155) points out, at this time all eyes were on the United States, as the United States was seen as 'the land of research, publications, and innovation – but also of violence, discrimination, and corruption in policing', and thus all aspects of policing 'good and bad' were open to research.

Reiner (1989; 1992; 2010: 11–12) suggests that there have been four stages in the development of the research on policing since the 1960s, namely *consensus, controversy, conflict* and *contradiction*.

The *consensus* stage commenced in the 1960s, when research such as Banton's (1964) tended to support the police, emphasised what was good about policing and what could be learned from the successes in policing. Banton (1971; 1973; 1975) was also responsible for organising three seminars in the 1970s at the University of Bristol on 'The Sociology of the Police', which were influential in evaluating the research of the time and deciding on the future themes for academic sociological research on policing in the United Kingdom.

The *controversy* stage appeared during the late 1960s and early 1970s when the research became more critical of police practices (and malpractices), and academic researchers began to take a greater interest in policing, particularly in its limitations. Smith and Morgan (1989: 235) argue that 'research has cast serious doubt on the effectiveness of traditional policing strategies'. However, Greenhill (1981) suggests that research of an organisation's practices adds a degree of professionalism to that organisation and increases its status. Brogden and Shearing (1993) and Chan (1996; 1997) support this view and suggest that professionalism changes organisational culture and has a positive impact on accountability.

The *conflict* stage occurred during the late 1970s and early 1980s, as policing and politics merged, and critical and radical criminology as well as Marxist academic research flourished. This period also saw resurgence in the quest for police accountability and governance. Morgan (1989a; 1989b) argues that research on policing is an important function in holding the police to account. However, MacDonald (1987: 5) advises that the drive for accountability has 'forced research back onto the organisational agenda'. Brown (1996) suggests that the findings of the research undertaken during the *controversy* and *conflict* stages resulted in the development of some hostility between the police and academic researchers, and difficulties in researchers' gaining access to police staff and data. A problem also highlighted by MacDonald (1987) and Laycock (2001: 1), who maintain that 'Practitioners and researchers have operated in different universes for a long time'.

The *contradiction* stage of the late 1980s coincided with the growth of realism, and in particular, 'left realism' as advocated by Lea and Young (1984). Left realism contradicted the view of the Home Office's preference for 'administrative criminology' (Cornish and Clarke, 1986) and the 'right realism' of Wilson (1975). Since the 1980s, the concept of realism has changed the focus on policing towards greater police effectiveness and crime control, and seen the introduction of policing initiatives such as problem-oriented policing and intelligence-led policing (Reiner, 2010). Brown (1996) suggests that in contrast to the previous two stages, academic research was now required by police managers to ensure that the service they provided was efficient, effective and economical. Research was also seen as a useful tool to challenge reform and to stimulate innovation (Weatheritt, 1986). Therefore, it was also important that the research was valid, reliable and objective (Hibberd, 1990). In the current era, Reiner (2010: 13) argues that 'The driving paradigm for most police research now is clearly *crime control*'.

Reiner (1992: 444–456) initially suggested that there were 'eight distinct types of institutions supporting research on policing in Britain', namely, Academic Institutions, Research Councils and Foundations, Government Organisations, Internal Police Research, Independent Research Organisations, Pressure Groups, Journalists and Private Enterprise. However, Reiner (2010: 9–11) later reduced this to four sources of police research, namely, *Academic Research, Official Police Research, Think Tanks and Independent Research Organisations* and *Journalists*.

Academic Research was generally undertaken by academics at *Academic Institutions* such as universities and other higher education establishments. During the 1980s, centres specialising in police studies appeared within these institutions offering undergraduate and postgraduate degree courses in criminal justice and police studies. Reiner (1992; 2010) observes that up until the 1980s, nearly all the published research on policing was undertaken by academics from disciplines such as criminology, sociology, psychology and law.

Official Police Research includes research undertaken by Government Organisations and Internal Police Research. *Government Organisations* historically involved in research on policing include the Home Office Research Unit, the Home Office Research and Planning Unit (HORPU), the Home Office Police Research Group (PRG), the Home Office Research, Development and Statistics (RDS) Directorate and the Home Office Science Group. Reiner (1992: 448) suggests that during the *conflict* stage in the development of research mentioned above, there was an 'extensive development of local government research on policing'. The period after 1981 saw the creation of a number of local authority police monitoring groups whose attention was focussed on researching the activities of their local police, particularly in relation to police accountability. This research brought some local authorities into direct conflict with the chief constables for their areas. However, after the introduction of the Crime and Disorder Act, 1998 (Home Office, 1998), most of the local government research on policing has been undertaken in conjunction with the police and focussed on partnership policy issues (Reiner, 2010). Other statutory organisations such as the Audit Commission (1990a; 1990b; 1993) have also conducted research on policing, particularly in relation to performance management and efficiency.

Internal Police Research generally falls into two main categories: national and local research. National internal police research is normally undertaken by bodies affiliated to the Home Office, such as the Scientific Research and Development Branch (SRDB), which was formed in 1963 as a direct result of Recommendation 44 from the Royal Commission on the Police: Final Report: 'We recommend the establishment of a central unit, under the general direction of the chief inspector of constabulary, with responsibility for planning and research (paragraph 241)' (Willink, 1962: 144). The SRDB was mainly staffed by seconded police officers and scientists, who conducted research on operational policing issues and technical equipment, and liaised with police forces around the country. The seconded officers were later to form the Police Research Services Unit (PRSU), whose role was to act as a liaison between the scientists of the SRDB and the police service (Weatheritt, 1986). More recently the National Policing Improvement Agency (NPIA), Research, Analysis and Information (RAI) Unit (now part of the College of Policing), has carried out research nationally on behalf of police forces throughout the United Kingdom. Local internal police research is normally undertaken by small research and planning units, which are generally staffed by police officers and police support staff. Their role was mainly administrative and involved evaluation of certain police initiatives. The research they produced was rarely critical of their force and was used to 'support a preferred course of action rather than analysing the necessity for it and the results of it' (Weatheritt, 1986: 19). However, Weatheritt (1986) does concede that improvements have been made, as internal staff gained more research expertise and advice was sought from external experts. The Government's New Public Management (NPM) initiative (Barton and Barton, 2011) of the early 1980s, with its emphasis on economy (value for money), efficiency and effectiveness, also encouraged the police service to undertake good-quality research to improve its performance (Weatheritt, 1986). More recently, research undertaken by internal police research units follows current academic research principles and produces objective, valid and reliable research findings (Dawson and Williams, 2009; Stanko, 2009).

Think Tanks and Independent Research Organisations also include Reiner's earlier 'Research Councils and Foundations', 'Independent Research Organisations' and 'Pressure Groups' (1992: 444–456). *Research Councils and Foundations* appeared during the 1980s and were funded either by the government or by charitable organisations interested in undertaking research on policing. The Economic and Social Research Council (ESRC) is one of seven government-funded research councils in the United Kingdom and supports research on policing and the wider criminal justice system. The Nuffield Foundation is an example of a charitable trust that is financially and politically independent, financed from its own investment portfolio and supports research on policing.

Independent Research Organisations such as the Police Foundation was established in 1980 as a self-funding independent charity. 'The Police Foundation is the only independent think tank focused entirely on developing knowledge and understanding of policing and crime reduction and challenging the police service and the government to improve policing for the benefit of the public' (Police Foundation, 2013). Other independent research organisations that undertake research on policing include the Policy Studies Institute (PSI) and the influential Policy Exchange (Loveday and Reid, 2003; Boyd, 2012).

Pressure Groups concerned with political issues and, in particular, civil liberties, have been involved in monitoring and researching the police since their inception, mainly focussing on police accountability. Liberty (formally the National Council for Civil Liberties) established the Civil Liberties Trust (formally the Cobden Trust) in 1963 to undertake research on its behalf in the field of civil liberties. Another group that conducts research on policing under a statutory obligation is the Equality and Human Rights Commission (EHRC) (formally the separate Equal Opportunities Commission, the Disability Rights Commission and the Commission for Racial Equality, and their counterparts in Wales, Scotland and Northern Ireland). The EHRC operates under the remit of promoting and monitoring human rights and protecting, enforcing and promoting equality in relation to 'age, disability, gender, race, religion and belief, pregnancy and maternity, marriage and civil partnership, sexual orientation and gender reassignment' (Equality and Human Rights Commission, 2013).

Journalists have also carried out research on policing, which generally involves observational studies in relation to police corruption, police tactics and policing practices and other matters not subjects of research by academics.

Although omitted from Reiner's (2010) revised sources of police research, *Private Enterprise* is also responsible for funding research on policing by academics, particularly in relation to business crime (Reiner, 1992: 455–456). This has expanded in recent years with the increase in the number of private security companies providing policing services that were traditionally provided by the police service.

In addition to the four sources of police research outlined above by Reiner (2010), Brown (1996: 180–186) suggests that there are also four types of research investigators, which she identifies as *Inside Insiders, Outside Insiders, Inside Outsiders* and *Outside Outsiders*. These terminologies are used as a framework when considering researchers' contributions to this book.

Inside Insiders research investigators would come under Reiner's (2010) *Official Police Research* source and in particular the category of *Internal Police Research* and sub-category of local internal police research (Reiner, 1992). Internal or in-house (inside) research on policing is generally undertaken by police officers or police support staff (insiders) from within their own police force. *Inside Insiders* have received quite a lot of criticism from academics in the past, with their research findings being regarded as 'foregone conclusion' research (Weatheritt, 1986: 19). Brown (1996) suggests that internal police researchers have very little research experience, and their research is seldom scrutinised by academics or published in academic journals. However, she does recognise that as more police officers and staff attain higher education qualifications, for example, to become university graduates or undertake post-graduate studies, their experience of research is improving. Punch (2010: 157) argues that most senior police officers in the United Kingdom now have a degree; several have more than one degree, and he has been 'impressed with their knowledge and academic ability' as 'smart cops'.

Outside Insiders are those who are generally regarded as former police officers and staff who become academics and conduct research on policing, such as Holdaway (1979; 1983; 1989; 1991; 1996; 1997; 2009) and Young (1991). Heslop (2012: 525) regards Holdaway as a pioneer in the research on policing and describes his study as the 'most ground-breaking ethnographic studies of the occupational culture of the British police ever undertaken', particularly as Holdaway conducted his field work covertly as an *inside insider*, before leaving the police service in 1975. Individuals in this group have an intimate inside knowledge of policing, but as academics are still viewed with some suspicion because they now operate outside the police culture. Brown (1996) also suggests that *outside insiders* include police officers and staff seconded to national organisations, such as Her Majesty's Inspectorate of Constabulary (HMIC) or Home Office research departments or units, that research and externally examine individual police forces. Members of this group are often criticised for following government dictates and their research efforts are concentrated on management and organisational issues, particularly in relation to performance management.

Inside Outsiders are categorised as professional research investigators working within the internal research departments of police forces, such as the Metropolitan Police Service, Strategic Research and Analysis Unit (SRAU) or professional researchers commissioned by police forces to undertake research or consult on a particular issue. Dawson and Williams (2009: 375) assert that the SRAU provides the Metropolitan Police Service with quality bespoke research with the aim of improving 'organisational learning' and providing evidence on which 'decision making can be grounded' whilst still working within a police culture.

Outside Outsiders are described as professional academics who undertake research on policing on behalf of academic institutions, government organisations, think tanks, independent research organisations and even private enterprises. They are individuals who are independent of, and do not receive funding from, the police service. Journalists, whether academics or not, may also fit into this category.

Innes (2010: 128) appears to support Brown's proposal of four types of research investigator (1996) and offers four relationships under which research on policing is conducted: *Research by the police, Research on the police, Research for the police* and *Research with the police.*

Research by the police is very similar to the *inside insiders* researcher above, with research being conducted internally by the police without the direct support of academics. This research is generally analytical, producing information and intelligence products from crime and performance data.

Research on the police is conducted by academics on a policing topic, with little input from the police on the design and conduct of the research. This may be compared to the *outside outsiders* researcher above.

Research for the police involves the police commissioning research on a specific policing topic, which is managed by a professional academic researcher. This relationship has comparisons with the *inside outsiders* researcher above.

Research with the police is undertaken as part of a collaborative partnership between police staff and academic researchers to find a solution to a specific policing problem or issue. This relationship would involve collaboration between *inside insiders* and *outside outsiders* to the benefit of both the police staff and the academic researchers. *Research with the police* appears to be gaining renewed interest and momentum in relation to the current and future development of evidence-based policing (Sherman, 1998; 2009; Bullock and Tilley, 2009; Lum et al., 2011).

1.3 Police and academic research

Police and academic collaborative relationships is not a new concept. In 1987, MacDonald (1987) produced a paper commissioned by the UK Police Foundation entitled 'Research and Action in the Context of Policing: An Analysis of the Problem and a Programme Proposal'. He was aware of the *conflict* in the 1970s and 1980s between the police and academic researchers when conducting social research on policing in an attempt to improve social action and referred to this conflict of interest as the 'dialogue of the deaf' (MacDonald, 1987: 1 – See Appendix A1 for MacDonald's 'Preamble – An Interpretation of the Brief'). MacDonald (1987: 1) advocated promoting 'collaborative rationality in the cause of better policing in a democratic society'. He also identified that research on policing was becoming more politically driven, often moving away from critical independent research towards government consultancy. The research process itself was also shifting towards evaluative research and in particular the evaluation of policing policies and practices. MacDonald (1987: 11) recognised that academics sometimes referred to evaluation as 'dirty research, sometimes unscientific', but also acknowledged that academic research could not divorce itself from the 'complexity of social life'. Evaluative research afforded researchers the opportunity to influence policy and practice, and MacDonald (1987) developed an engagement model for academic researchers to collaborate more closely with their government and police clients. Laycock (2001) agrees with the principles of MacDonald's (1987) arguments and suggests that the police should be involved in setting the research agenda in partnership with academic researchers. She also proposes that academic researchers should consider interim reports, as police practitioners need timely results from the research in order to take action.

MacDonald's (1987) paper has prompted a number of relatively recent research articles, which build on the theme of collaboration and a 'dialogue of the deaf' (Bradley and Nixon, 2009; Johnston and Shearing, 2009; Buerger, 2010; Cordner and White, 2010; Fleming, 2010; 2012; Foster and Bailey, 2010; Innes, 2010; Lunt et al., 2010; Marks et al., 2010; Murji, 2010; Scott, 2010; Stephens, 2010; Wuestewald and Steinheider, 2010; Fyfe and Wilson, 2012; Guillaume et al., 2012; Henry and Mackenzie, 2012; Steinheider et al., 2012).

The first of these articles by Bradley and Nixon (2009: 423–424) acknowledges the 'critical police research tradition' (Reiner, 1992; 2010) and the 'policy police research tradition' (MacDonald, 1987), but advocates a third 'intimate and continuous' collaborative partnership police research tradition as a means of ending the 'dialogue of the deaf'. This is similar to the *research with the police* relationship suggested by Innes (2010). Indeed Innes (2010) and other authors acknowledge Bradley and Nixon's (2009) contribution to the debate. It would appear from the above that *outside insiders* may have a role to play in fostering this relationship of collaborative partnership, by forming a conduit between the police and academia. However, Punch (2010: 159) argues that the 'dialogue of the deaf' is not the problem that it once was between the police and academia: 'Rather it is one of short-sighted, populist-oriented governments who want the police organization to be a servile agency that is institutionally deaf'.

1.4   Current developments in research on policing

The debate on what research should be undertaken in relation to policing began in earnest in the 1960s. Banton (1964; 1971; 1973; 1975) commenced this process in the United Kingdom, with further contributions from Holdaway (1979; 1983), whilst in the United States the Commission on Law Enforcement and the Administration of Justice was established for this purpose (Katzenbach, 1967). More recently, Brown (1996: 177–178) has suggested that there are four main functions of research on policing, which may be summarised as follows: to hold the police to account; to measure the professionalism of the police; to ensure economy (value for money), efficiency and effectiveness in policing; and to prepare for changes in policing. Similarly, Laycock (2001: 2) suggests that there are three reasons for good police research: the current focus on outcomes, the professionalisation of policing and evidenced-based problem solving. But Skogan and Frydl (2004: 328–331) suggest that research on policing should be focussed on 'Enhancing Crime Control Effectiveness', 'Enhancing the Lawfulness of Police Actions', 'Enhancing the Legitimacy of Policing', 'Improving Personnel Practices', 'Fostering Innovation', 'Assessing Problem-Oriented and Community Policing', 'Responding to Terrorism' and 'Organizing Research'.

Mazeika et al. (2010: 521–522) conducted a review of the research on policing literature for the period 2000–2007 to establish exactly what was being researched. This included publications in police journals, criminal justice journals, non-criminal justice journals, government journals and books. They identified four research typologies: 'Theoretical/Discussion Research', 'Descriptive Research', 'Correlate Research' and 'Outcome Research', and 29 subject sub-categories under the following six research category headings: 'Organization of Police', 'Attitudes and Behavior', 'Accountability and Misconduct', 'Police Strategies', 'Citizen Satisfaction' and 'Measurement'. 'Citizen Satisfaction' and 'Measurement' both appeared as a subject sub-category and a research category heading. (See Appendix A2 for a list of the six research categories and 29 subject sub-categories.)

(1) Theoretical/discussion research: general discussions of issues or theories in policing; may reference empirical research of others, but does not conduct any analyses.

(2) Descriptive research: description of implementation or process; typically narrative; may include judgments of efficacy, but is not supported by primary research.

(3) Correlate research: survey or secondary data analysis that does not evaluate a specific policy, program or tactic, but rather assesses correlates or typologies.

(4) Outcome research: empirical analysis evaluating a policy, program or tactic.

(Mazeika et al., 2010: 521)

Mazeika et al. (2010: 520–524) found that the number of publications had increased from 456 in 2006 to 522 in 2007, an increase of 66 publications. The main increase being in the publication of police-related books, which rose by 48.3% from 2006 to 2007. Their study also included the trends in police research from 2000 to 2007. These trends indicated that 'police strategies' was the most popular research category, amounting to 37.4% of the total. This was followed by the research category of 'organization of police', which saw the greatest increase between 2005 and 2007 to a high of 33%. Outcome-based research declined by 32.6% in 2007 after experiencing five years of growth in previous years. There was also a decrease in research focussed on the sub-category of community policing and perhaps surprisingly a decrease in the amount of research published in police journals. Similar annual reviews had previously been undertaken for the literature published between 2000 and 2006 by Beckman et al. (2003; 2004; 2005), Gibbs et al. (2006), Varriale et al. (2007), Telep et al. (2008) and Bartholomew et al. (2009).

One other very important aspect of the research on policing to be considered is that of *sensitive research on policing*. Sieber and Stanley

(1988: 49) define socially sensitive research as 'studies in which there are potential consequences or implications, either directly for the participants in the research or for the class of individuals represented by the research'. Lee (1993) and Lee and Renzetti (1993) criticise this definition in that it concentrates on the consequences of the research and not the technical and methodological issues, and it does not specify the kind of consequences or implications to be considered. Lee (1993: 4) offers an alternative definition of sensitive research as 'research which potentially poses a substantial threat to those who are or have been involved in it'. Lee and Renzetti (1993) provide a third definition, which relates to a sensitive topic and is similar to the definition of sensitive research offered by Lee (1993) above:

> a sensitive topic is one that potentially poses for those involved a substantial threat, the emergence of which renders problematic for the researcher and/or the researched the collection, holding, and/or dissemination of research data.
>
> (Lee and Renzetti, 1993: 5)

Unfortunately, neither Lee (1993: 4) nor Lee and Renzetti (1993: 5) specify what they consider to be a 'substantial threat'. However, Lee and Renzetti (1993) do suggest that the threat posed should at least be moderate, but more often the threat will be severe and the threat can be problematic for both the researcher and the participant.

Lee (1993: 4) suggests that these threats fall into three broad categories, which may be summarised as follows: *Intrusive threats* when dealing with issues that are 'private, stressful or sacred'; *Threats of sanction* where information that may be 'stigmatizing or incriminating in some way' is revealed; and *Political threats* when referring to the 'vested interests of powerful persons or institutions, or the exercise of coercion or domination'.

Lee and Renzetti (1993: 5) argue that it is not the topic itself that makes the research sensitive, it is the 'relationship between the topic and the social context within which the research is conducted', as what is threatening to some may be innocuous to others.

1.5   Future developments in research on policing

The College of Policing was established in 2012 and officially launched on the 4th February 2013 as a professional body for policing, to understand its needs, identify what works, share knowledge, develop, maintain and test standards, enable professional development and, via its Research Analysis and Information (RAI) Unit, forge links with academics (College of Policing, 2013b). For example, the ESRC and the College of Policing, RAI Unit, are collaborating on five police research projects to determine the evidence available to inform policymakers and practitioners. The five projects chosen for research are as follows: (1) 'How knowledge is shared – Exploring the use of the police service's social media platform POLKA'; (2) 'What's going on out there? Mapping police-related research activity in the UK'; (3) 'Understanding "Evidence-Based Policing" – How does the police service need to change?'; (4) 'Mapping what we know about policing'; and (5) 'The role of research evidence in national standards for policing' (ESRC, 2013: 1–2). It can be seen from the above that the national drive for the future of policing in the United Kingdom is towards evidence-based policing.

Weisburd and Neyroud (2011: 1) propose a new paradigm of 'Police Science', which builds on evidence-based policing policies and seeks to radically reform 'the role of science in policing'. This model would require the ownership of police science research to pass from universities to police agencies, with universities operating from police centres and the partnership led by a large public research institute. Reference is made to the National Policing Improvement Agency (NPIA) fulfilling this role in the United Kingdom, whilst recognising that the NPIA was due to be phased out by the current coalition government, as a result of their austerity measures. The new College of Policing has taken on some of the responsibilities of the now defunct NPIA, particularly in the area of police science and education, and already has a research function within its RAI Unit. Weisburd and Neyroud (2011: 12) also draw comparisons with medical and educational evidence-based science models (Sackett et al., 1996; Slavin, 2002), a concept supported by Sherman (1998). However, Thacher (2001: 409) argues that the medical model approach 'could undermine other important aspects of policing' and not address 'the full range of police concerns'.

Gravelle and Rogers (2011) observe that in times of austerity, there is a danger that the police may distance themselves from academic collaborations and high-quality independent, external and robust research and revert to in-house research in an attempt to save money. This may result in a number of unintended and detrimental consequences for the police in relation to issues such as partnership working, public confidence, training, professionalism and style of policing. Innes (2010: 128) agrees and suggests that in times of crisis it is even more important to have a greater understanding of policing – research can act as a 'mirror' reflecting the 'complex realities of policing' or as a 'motor' providing the 'engine for change and improvement'.

1.6 Conclusion

Research on policing has seen many stages of development since the 1960s, including consensus, controversy, conflict and contradiction, and more recently crime control, with research focussing on policing strategies, the organisation of policing and evidence-based policing. In her speech to the College of Policing on the 24th October 2013, the Home Secretary, Rt. Hon. Theresa May, MP, was quite clear that she expected the research on policing to be directed towards evidence-based policing to reduce crime.

> The College will work with universities to collect and review evidence on the effectiveness of different strategies and practices for reducing crime. The knowledge of what works – and what doesn't – will be shared with Police and Crime Commissioners [PCCs] and the police, and with the public as well. This will help the police become an organisation where practice is always based on evidence rather on habit. The answer to the question: 'Why do we do this?' will never be – 'Because we always have done it that way'. It will be 'Because this is what the evidence tells us works best'.
>
> (May, 2013)

The College of Policing has already identified over 40 academic institutions, mainly universities, that are conducting relevant ongoing policing-related research at master's degree level and above (College of Policing, 2013a) There is a danger here that research on policing could become totally embroiled in evidenced-based crime control policing and that research funding would only be made available to researchers who were willing to comply with central government direction. Punch (2010: 158) argues that research on policing should not just concentrate on 'policy-relevant' research, but should include research that allows the police to come under external scrutiny and fears that 'governments will impose a one-sided, crime control model which seriously distorts policing'.

Whilst the merits of conducting evidence-based crime control research on policing are impressive, cognisance should also be given to research on other aspects of policing. If not, research on policing could return to what Reiner (2010) describes as the *consensus* stage of research, which was prevalent in the 1960s.

References

Audit Commission. (1990a) *Effective Policing: Performance Review in Police Forces*, Police Paper Number 8 (December 1990), London: Audit Commission.

Audit Commission. (1990b) *Footing the Bill: Financing Provincial Police Forces*, Police Paper Number 6 (June 1990), London: Audit Commission.

Audit Commission. (1993) *Helping With Enquiries: Tackling Crime Effectively*, London: HMSO.

Banton, M. (1964) *The Policeman in the Community*, London: Tavistock.

Banton, M. (1971) 'The Sociology of the Police', *Police Journal*, 44: 227–243.

Banton, M. (1973) 'The Sociology of the Police II', *Police Journal*, 46: 341–362.

Banton, M. (1975) 'The Sociology of the Police III', *Police Journal*, 48: 299–315.

Bartholomew, B., Gibbs, J., Mazeika, D., Ahlin, E., Joseph, P. and Miller, N. (2009) 'Trends in Police Research: A Cross-Sectional Analysis of the 2006 Literature', *Police Practice and Research: An International Journal*, 10(4): 383–407.

Barton, L.C. and Barton, H. (2011) 'Challenges, Issues and Change: What's the Future for UK Policing in the Twenty-First Century?' *International Journal of Public Sector Management*, 24(2): 146–156.

Beckman, K.A., Gibbs, J.C., Beatty, P.D. and Canigiani, M. (2005) 'Trends in Police Research: A Cross-Sectional Analysis of the 2002 Literature', *Police Practice and Research: An International Journal*, 6(3): 295–320.

Beckman, K.A., Lum, C., Wyckoff, L. and Wall, K.L.-V. (2003) 'Trends in Police Research: A Cross-Sectional Analysis of the 2000 Literature', *Police Practice and Research: An International Journal*, 4(1): 79–96.

Beckman, K.A., Wyckoff, L., Groff, E.R. and Beatty, P.D. (2004) 'Trends in Police Research: A Cross-Sectional Analysis of the 2001 Literature', *Police Practice and Research: An International Journal*, 5(2): 165–189.

Boyd, E. (2012) *Policing 2020: What Kind of Police Service Do We Want in 2020?* London: Policy Exchange.

Bradley, D. and Nixon, C. (2009) 'Ending the "Dialogue of the Deaf": Evidence and Policing Policies and Practices – An Australian Case Study', *Police Practice and Research: An International Journal*, 10(5–6): 423–435.

Brogden, M. and Shearing, C.D. (1993) *Policing For a New South Africa*, London: Routledge.

Brown, J. (1996) 'Police Research: Some Critical Issues', in Leishman, F., Loveday, B. and Savage, S. (Eds) *Core Issues in Policing*, London: Longman, 179–190.

Buerger, M.E. (2010) 'Policing and Research: Two Cultures Separated by an Almost-Common Language', *Police Practice and Research: An International Journal*, 11(2): 135–143.

Bullock, K. and Tilley, N. (2009) 'Evidence-Based Policing and Crime Reduction', *Policing: A Journal of Policy and Practice*, 3(4): 381–387.

Chan, J.B.L. (1996) 'Changing Police Culture', *British Journal of Criminology*, 36(1): 109–134 (Winter 1996).

Chan, J.B.L. (1997), *Changing Police Culture – Policing in a Multicultural Society*, Cambridge: Cambridge University Press.

College of Policing. (2013a) *Policing and Crime Reduction Research Map.* Available at: http://www.college.police.uk/en/researchmap.htm [Accessed: 14 November 2013].

College of Policing. (2013b) *What We Do.* Available at: http://www.college.police. uk/ [Accessed: 14 November 2013].

Cordner, G. and White, S. (2010) 'The Evolving Relationship Between Police Research and Police Practice', *Police Practice and Research: An International Journal*, 11(2): 90–94.

Cornish, D.B. and Clarke, R.V. (Eds) (1986) *The Reasoning Criminal: Rational Choice Perspectives on Offending*, New York, NY: Springer-Verlag.

Dawson, P. and Williams, E. (2009) 'Reflections from a Police Research Unit: An Inside Job', *Policing: A Journal of Policy and Practice*, 3(4): 373–380.

Economic and Social Research Council. (ESRC) (2013) *College of Policing*, Swindon: ESRC.

Equality and Human Rights Commission. (2013) *About Us.* Available at: http:// www.equalityhumanrights.com/about-us/ [Accessed: 15 November 2013].

Fleming, J. (2010) 'Learning to Work Together: Police and Academics', *Policing: A Journal of Policy and Practice*, 4(2): 139–145.

Fleming, J. (2012) 'Changing the Way We Do Business: Reflecting on Collaborative Practice', *Police Practice and Research: An International Journal*, 13(4): 375–388.

Foster, J. and Bailey, S. (2010) 'Joining Forces: Maximizing Ways of Making a Difference in Policing', *Policing: A Journal of Policy and Practice*, 4(2): 95–103.

Fyfe, N.R. and Wilson, P. (2012) 'Knowledge Exchange and Police Practice: Broadening and Deepening the Debate Around Researcher-Practitioner Collaborations', *Police Practice and Research: An International Journal*, 13(4): 306–314.

Gibbs, J.C., Beckman, K.A., Miggans, K. and Hart, M. (2006) 'Trends in Police Research: A Cross-Sectional Analysis of the 2003 Literature', *Police Practice and Research: An International Journal*, 7(4): 337–361.

Gravelle, J. and Rogers, C. (2011) 'Research and Policing in Times of Austerity', *Police Journal*, 84(3): 222–233.

Greene, J.R. (2010) 'Pioneers in Police Research: William A. Westley', *Police Practice and Research: An International Journal*, 11(5): 454–468.

Greenhill, N.J. (1981) 'Professionalism in the Police Service', in Pope, M.D. and Weiner, N. (Eds) *Modern Policing*, London: Croom Helm.

Guillaume, P., Sidebottom, A. and Tilley, N. (2012) 'On Police and University Collaborations: A Problem-Oriented Policing Case Study', *Police Practice and Research: An International Journal*, 13(4): 389–401.

Henry, A. and Mackenzie, S. (2012) 'Brokering Communities of Practice: A Model of Knowledge Exchange and Academic-Practitioner Collaboration Developed in the Context of Community Policing', *Police Practice and Research: An International Journal*, 13(4): 315–328.

Heslop, R. (2012) 'A Sociological Imagination: Simon Holdaway, Police Research Pioneer', *Police Practice and Research: An International Journal*, 13(6): 525–538.

Hibberd, M. (1990) *Research and Evaluation: A Manual for Police Officers*, London: Police Foundation.

Holdaway, S. (Ed.) (1979) *The British Police*, London: Edward Arnold.

Holdaway, S. (1983) *Inside the British Police: A Force at Work*, Oxford: Blackwell.

Holdaway, S. (1989) 'Discovering Structure: Studies of the British Police Occupational Culture', in Weatheritt, M. (Ed.) *Police Research: Some Future Prospects*, Aldershot: Avebury.

Holdaway, S. (1991) *Recruiting a Multi-Racial Police Force*, London: HMSO.

Holdaway, S. (1996) *The Racialisation of British Policing*, Basingstoke: Macmillan.

Holdaway, S. (1997) *The Experience of Black and Asian Police Officers*, Basingstoke: Macmillan.

Holdaway, S. (2009) *Black Police Associations: An Analysis of Race and Ethnicity Within Constabularies*, Oxford: Oxford University Press.

Home Office. (1998) *Crime and Disorder Act 1998*, London: The Stationery Office.

Innes, M. (2010) 'A "Mirror" and a "Motor": Researching and Reforming in an Age of Austerity', *Policing: A Journal of Policy and Practice*, 4(2): 127–134.

Johnston, L. and Shearing, C. (2009) 'From a "Dialogue of the Deaf" to a "Dialogue of Listening": Towards a New Methodology of Policing Research and Practice', *Police Practice an Research: An International Journal*, 10(5–6): 415–422.

Katzenbach, N. deB. (1967) *The Challenge of Crime in a Free Society: A Report by the President's Commission on Law Enforcement and Administration of Justice*, Washington, DC: United States Government Printing Office.

Laycock, G. (2001) 'Research for Police: Who Needs It?' *Australian Institute of Criminology, Trends and Issues in Crime and Criminal Justice*, 211: 1–6.

Lea, J. and Young, J. (1984) *What Is To Be Done About Law and Order*, Harmondsworth: Penguin.

Lee, R.M. (1993) *Doing Research on Sensitive Topics*, London: Sage.

Lee, R.M. and Renzetti, C.M. (1993) 'The Problems of Researching Sensitive Topics: An Overview and Introduction', in Renzetti, C.M. and Lee, R.M. (Eds) *Researching Sensitive Topics*, London: Sage.

Loveday, B. and Reid, A. (2003) *Going Local: Who Should Run Britain's Police?* London: Policy Exchange.

Lum, C., Koper, C. and Telep, C. (2011) 'The Evidence-Based Policing Matrix', *Journal of Experimental Criminology*, 7(1): 3–26.

Lunt, N., Shaw, I. and Fouché, C. (2010) 'Practitioner Research: Collaboration and Knowledge Production', *Public Money and Management*, 30(4): 235–242.

MacDonald, B. (1987) *Research and Action in the Context of Policing: An Analysis of the Problem and a Programme Proposal*, London: The Police Foundation.

Marks, M., Wood, J., Ally, F., Walsh, T. and Witbooi, A. (2010) 'Worlds Apart? On the Possibilities of Police/Academic Collaborations', *Policing: A Journal of Policy and Practice*, 4(2): 112–118

May, T. (2013) *Speech Given by Home Secretary Theresa May to the College of Policing on 24th October 2013*, London: Home Office.

Mazeika, D., Bartholomew, B., Distler, M., Thomas, K., Greenman, S. and Pratt, S. (2010) 'Trends in Police Research: A Cross-Sectional Analysis of the 2000–2007 Literature', *Police Practice and Research: An International Journal*, 11(6): 520–547.

McLaughlin, E. (2007) *The New Policing*, London: Sage.

Morgan, R. (1989a) 'Police Accountability, Current Developments and Future Prospects', in Weatheritt, M. (Ed.) *Police Research: Some Future Prospects*, Aldershot: Avebury/Police Foundation.

Morgan, R. (1989b) 'Policing by Consent: Legitimating the Doctrine', in Morgan, R. and Smith, D. J. (Eds) *Coming to Terms with Policing*, London: Routledge.

Murji, K. (2010) 'Introduction: Academic-Police Collaborations – Beyond "Two Worlds" ', *Policing: A Journal of Policy and Practice*, 4(2): 92–94.

Police Foundation. (2013) *Improving Policing and Reducing Crime*. Available at: http://www.police-foundation.org.uk/ [Accessed: 15 November 2013].

Punch, M. (2010) 'Policing and Police Research in the Age of the Smart Cop', *Police Practice and Research: An International Journal*, 11(2): 155–159.

Reiner, R. (1989) 'The Politics of Police Research in Britain', in Weatheritt, M. (Ed.) *Police Research: Some Future Prospects*, Aldershot: Avebury/Police Foundation.

Reiner, R. (1992) 'Police Research in the United Kingdom: A Critical Review', in Tonry, M. and Morris, N. (Eds) *Modern Policing, Crime and Justice*, Volume 15, Chicago, IL: University of Chicago Press, pp 435–508.

Reiner, R. (2010) *The Politics of the Police* (4th ed.), Oxford: Oxford University Press.

Rojek, J., Alpert, G. and Smith, H. (2012) 'The Utilization of Research by the Police', *Police Practice and Research: An International Journal*, 13(4): 329–341.

Sackett, D.L., Gray, J.A.M., Rosenberg, W.M.C., Haynes, R.B. and Richardson, W.S. (1996) 'Evidence Based Medicine: What It Is and What It Isn't', *British Medical Journal*, 312(7023): 71.

Scott, M.S. (2010) 'Policing and Police Research: Learning to Listen, With a Wisconsin Case Study', *Police Practice and Research: An International Journal*, 11(2): 95–104.

Sherman, L.W. (1998) *Evidence-Based Policing (Ideas in American Policing)*, Washington, DC: Police Foundation.

Sherman, L.W. (2009) 'Evidence and Liberty: The Promise of Experimental Criminology', *Criminology and Criminal Justice*, 9(1): 2–28.

Sieber, J.E. and Stanley, B. (1988) 'Ethical and Professional Dimensions of Socially Sensitive Research', *American Psychologist*, 43(1): 49–55.

Skogan, W.G. and Frydl, K. (Eds) (2004) *Fairness and Effectiveness in Policing: The Evidence*, Washington, DC: The National Academies Press.

Slavin, R.E. (2002) 'Evidence-Based Education Policies: Transforming Educational Practice and Research', *Educational Researcher*, 31(7): 15–21.

Smith, D.J. and Morgan, R. (1989) 'Developing Themes in Policing Research', in Morgan, R. and Smith, D.J. (Eds) *Coming to Terms with Policing*, London: Routledge.

Stanko, E.A. (2009) 'Improving Policing Through Research', *Policing: A Journal of Policy and Practice*, 3(4): 306–309.

Steinheider, B., Wuestewald, T., Boyatzis, R.E. and Kroutter, P. (2012) 'In Search of a Methodology of Collaboration: Understanding Researcher-Practitioner Philosophical Differences in Policing', *Police Practice and Research: An International Journal*, 13(4): 357–374.

Stephens, D.W. (2010) 'Enhancing the Impact of Research on Police Practice', *Police Practice and Research: An International Journal*, 11(2): 150–154.

Telep, C.W., Varriale, J.A., Gibbs, J.C., Na, C. and Bartholomew, B. (2008) 'Trends in Police Research: A Cross-Sectional Analysis of the 2005 Literature', *Police Practice and Research: An International Journal*, 9(5): 445–469.

Thacher, D. (2001) 'Policing Is Not a Treatment: Alternatives to the Medical Model of Police Research', *Journal of Research in Crime and Delinquency*, 38(4): 387–415.

Varriale, J.A., Gibbs, J.C., Ahlin, E.M., Gugino, M.R. and Na, C. (2007) 'Trends in Police Research: A Cross-Sectional Analysis of the 2004 Literature', *Police Practice and Research: An International Journal*, 8(5): 461–485.

Weatheritt, M. (1986) *Innovations in Policing*, Beckenham: Croom Helm.

Weisburd, D. and Neyroud, P. (2011) *Police Science: Towards a New Paradigm*, Cambridge, MA: Harvard Kennedy School and National Institute of Justice.

Westley, W.A. (1953) 'Violence and the Police', *American Journal of Sociology*, 59(1): 34–41.

Westley, W.A. (1956) 'Secrecy and the Police', *Social Forces*, (March 1956), 34: 254–257.

Westley, W.A. (1970) *Violence and the Police: A Sociological Study of Law, Custom, and Morality*, Boston, MA: MIT Press.

Willink, Sir Henry. (1962) *Royal Commission on the Police: Final Report* (Command 1728), London: HMSO.

Wilson, J.Q. (1975) *Thinking About Crime*, New York, NY: Vintage.

Wuestewald, T. and Steinheider, B. (2010) 'Practitioner-Researcher Collaboration in Policing: A Case of Close Encounters', *Policing: A Journal of Policy and Practice*, 4(2): 104–111.

Young, M. (1991) *An Inside Job: Policing and Police Culture in Britain*, Oxford: Clarendon.

2

Researching the Police – Zero Tolerance and Community Safety

Colin Rogers

Research methods involved

1. Quantitative

Questionnaire survey and data statistical analysis

2. Qualitative

Covert observational fieldwork, documentary and policy analysis

About this research

This particular research examined a community safety crime prevention partnerships attempt to reduce recorded crime and disorder in a particular location while also attempting to reduce fear of crime. It included such approaches as zero tolerance policing style, consultations with community and high-visibility policing. The research aims were as follows:

1. To determine what effect the initiative had for specific targets of reducing recorded crime and the fear of crime within the chosen area.
2. To examine the effectiveness of the partnership approach with particular reference to the culture and organisational structure of the police. This research was conducted between 1999 and 2002.

2.1 Introduction

Researching social life is partly about having the right knowledge; for instance, how to design samples, when to take field notes and how to analyse data; and partly about practical skills: how to lay out questionnaires, how to get access to historical archives and how to get the co-operation of an interviewee.

Gilbert (1995: xi)

Gilbert (1995) highlights a very important point for any research of this nature – a good research is a mixture of several research methodologies. Unfortunately, this diversity of approach and the results that are produced have not been at the forefront of policing in this country for some time. Research into the activities of the police in this country over the past decade or so has tended towards providing mainly managerial information in the never-ending pursuit of cost effectiveness. In part, this should come as no surprise, since the activities of the police were actively linked to Home Office National Key Objectives. Further, individual police forces are required to provide 'force wide' objectives, which are those agreed with the local police authority (now Police and Crime Commissioner), and local objectives, ostensibly formulated after consultation with the local community. In truth, however, these objectives are very similar and overlap one another to a great extent. However, one important aspect of policing today revolves around partnership policing and community safety (Home Office, 1998a).

Consequently, because of this preoccupation with managerial concepts, both internally and externally to a large extent, research into the police and other areas of the criminal justice system has lacked what Reiner (1992) believes to be a link to social theory and has lacked a diverse approach.

2.2 Chosen methods

A matter of personal preference and style, taking account of practical possibilities and restrictions, available resources and the objectives of the research in many cases, dictates the choice of an approach to any research. This research into the concept of community safety and zero tolerance type policing would have been difficult to complete if it relied upon quantitative methods alone. Further, bearing in mind Gilbert's (1995) words on what constitutes 'good' research, a number of methods of research were utilised, including fieldwork where possible, and postal questionnaire surveys providing primary sources of statistics as well as use of secondary data in the form of longitudinal crime statistics. Choosing this multi-approach course of action, however, meant that one of the main research instruments involved would be me, particularly in the fieldwork element of this research and this in itself would provide a challenge. The specific role of me within the organisation involved in the research was to prove crucial to the evaluation of the initiative under study. The drive to remain neutral and not influence the outcome of the research findings was a difficult but necessary task. The specific area of covert observations provided me with a number of ethical decisions that are discussed later, as are the methods used to try and remain detached.

The study was completed over a four year period. This period enabled me to have prolonged participation in the daily lives and routines of the particular groups under study, and assisted in developing empathy with the norms and behaviour of the people involved in the study. It also provided me with the opportunity to become involved in social relationships with the participants within the scope of the research as well as data for study.

Some fundamental problems arise in the area of police research. One of the main obstacles in any research involving people is the difficulty in gaining access to their particular way of life. This was overcome, first, by my location in the police organisation and by the use of people who voluntarily offered me information from the various agencies within the crime prevention partnership involved in the initiative. Further, my experiences in the field over a considerable period of time helped me in compiling field notes on the subject.

2.3   Designing the research

The design for the research therefore consisted of several methodologically distinct approaches to evidence collection:

1. Covert participant observations of the interactions between police officers, other agencies such as the local authority and its crime prevention 'arm', the community safety organisation, and the public.
2. A comparative 'before-and-after' study of the impact of the initiative using responses to a postal questionnaire survey designed to obtain data on individuals' perceptions of levels of crime within the community. This also includes the initiative's impact upon issues that make up perceptions of fear of crime, and the level of confidence displayed towards the local policing agencies.
3. Secondary statistical data derived from the various census surveys and other data obtained from such surveys conducted by the British Crime Survey, the South Wales Police and other agencies operating

within the research area, including records published by official bodies.

Methods that are more overt were also used, such as interviews with members of the public during the initiative in order to gauge their response to the partnership approach to crime reduction. However, by engaging in such an activity, I would have put myself into the public arena, and by doing so, would have openly shown those involved in delivering the initiative that they were being studied. This in turn may have had a dramatic effect upon the individual members of the partnership involved in the day-to-day execution of the initiative, particularly the police who, it is alleged, are renowned for closing ranks when under scrutiny (Reiner, 2000).

Before discussing these methods individually, it is necessary to discuss several important areas of the research including the ethical considerations involved, access, privacy and informed consent.

2.4 Ethical considerations

The area of covert participant observation employed as part of this research provided some of the greatest ethical problems, and it is this area, and how these problems were overcome, that is explored in this section.

Several commentators have provided definitions of covert participant observation and in order to understand some of the criticisms levelled at this type of research, it may prove helpful to examine them. Bulmer (1982: 4) defines it as:

> Research using participant observations methods, where the researcher spends an extended period of time in a particular research setting, concealing the fact that he/she is a researcher and pretending to play some other role.

Lee (1995: 143) simply puts it this way:

> When research participants are not aware that they are being studied.

In regard to carrying out this particular research, it did not take me long to realise that each component of the area of human interaction under study – the police, the community and partnership, and zero tolerance type policing – presents its own unique problems. The first of these problems is access.

Access

One of the areas of concern was one of the main organisations under study, the police. The closed culture of the police has been high-lighted by recent authors (Bradley, 1998; Reiner, 2000) whereas previous researchers have commented on the reaction of the police to overt research (Holdaway, 1984). Indeed, as pointed out by Glover and Rushbrook (1987), many workers react in differing ways when they are aware that they are under observation.

Holdaway (1984) believes that any effective research strategy in this area would have to pierce the protective shield of the police if it were to be successful. During his research into police malpractices, for example, Punch (1985: 216) soon found that

> People were lying to me, or spreading misinformation. I also glimpsed the 'informal' system of manipulation at work... Clearly my informants had been less than open and knew a great deal more than they were prepared to tell me.

Having been a police officer for 28 years, this researcher knew from his own experiences how protective the culture of the police service could be when it sees itself under scrutiny. There does indeed exist a wide disparity between the public presentation of police work and, to use Goffman's (1990) analogy, the backstage reality. It was this backstage reality that needed to be explored in conjunction with the way people are dealt with by the police, and the interactions that take place between the different agencies when delivering a partnership approach to community policing and the so-called 'zero tolerance' style policing.

Reynolds (1982: 185) seems to sum up the position of covert research quite succinctly. He says:

> For some types of deviant or illegal behaviour it may be the only way to develop accurate descriptions that are not affected by deliberate distortions, biased recollections or outright denial.

By conducting this type of research, therefore, it is hoped that the problem of reactivity could be avoided (Lee, 1995). In essence, because individuals do not know they are being studied, research participants do not feel incensed by the research and do not change their behaviour even though to outside eyes it may be regarded as deviant. Indeed, covert research is often said to offer an inside view of those being studied. In order to carry out part of the research, therefore, it seemed that the only way forward was to adopt a covert participant observer style.

Field research is about observing the world as a stranger (McNeil, 1990). One has to consider the world strange, to try and separate oneself from getting embroiled in the 'happening', the event being observed. The element of objectivity is thus maintained.

There is a danger that participant observers may get too close to their subject and risk 'going native'(Punch, 1985) and therefore not objective enough for research. It could be argued, however, that in many circumstances, covert research is impossible unless one is already a member of the organisation to be studied. To a certain extent, as Punch (1985) points out, single person research often entails easy access, low intrusiveness in the area to be studied and a high capacity for personalised relationships (Hammersley, 1993).

However, any organisation that is part of, and represents, the power structure in a society is naturally reluctant, perhaps, to let people see exactly what occurs during its interactions with society (Holdaway, 1984). Despite Reiner's (1994) belief that the police and academics have come closer together over the years, gaining access to the subject under research from the police perspective may have proved difficult (if not impossible) owing to the 'natural' suspiciousness of the police to being studied. Defensive as police are to criticism, the research could be viewed as another attempt to discredit the police or even provide false good results to please political masters, by 'another sociologist' or a 'do gooder'. This highlights another problem. It is possible in research of this nature to suffer censure of notes and findings, to have certain conditions attached to their use, or conceivably have influence brought to bear in an effort to include certain items. This position, of course, would have been intolerable for the successful completion of this research. Access to this research arena, then, could be fraught with problems. It was a conscious decision, therefore, to conduct the studies as covertly as possible.

Privacy

Privacy is related to personal freedom in the sense that certain aspects of the self are seen as inviolable, or subject to discussion only under the most restricted conditions. Warwick (1982), when discussing Humphreys' (1975) 'Tea Room Trade', raises the question of how far the social scientist can intrude into the inner reaches of the self without jeopardising freedom. Here Warwick concludes that Humphreys intruded much too far into the lives of the men he observed and studied, as they indulged in homosexual activities in public toilets.

However, while the argument that all individuals have the right to privacy is strong, perhaps it should be qualified when applied to the police (Holdaway, 1984). The police are said to be accountable to the rule of law, a constitutional feature, which restricts their right to privacy but which they also neutralise by the maintenance of a protective occupational culture. When such an institution is highly secretive and protective, its members, it could be argued, restrict any right to privacy they already have. It is crucial that they are researched, and the covert researcher of the police has to be reminded that he/she is working within an extremely powerful organisation, which requires that its public and private practice be revealed on the basis of first-hand observation. In this research, I found it necessary to remind myself of the invasion, to some extent, of people's privacy.

From discussions conducted with individuals in this research, it was discovered that by far the majority were in favour of being spoken to, although some stipulated the guarantee of anonymity. Some even indicated that they did not care if they were identified, although they were always treated with the same careful anonymity as everyone else.

Information, along with field notes, was jealously guarded under lock and key. In conclusion, it was still felt that the covert participation method was one of the primary ways of seeing the interaction among individuals, agencies and community in their natural settings, and the police reaction to it, which is of vital importance for this research.

Informed consent

In covert participation observation, the participants of research have no opportunity to give their informed consent to being studied. Voluntary informed consent is an ongoing, two-way communication process between participants and the investigator, as well as a specific agreement about the conditions of the research participation (Seiber, 1992: 26). Lee (1995) therefore asserts that covert research violates important ethical principles. In particular, they negate the principle of informed consent, since research participants in covert studies cannot refuse their involvement. But informed consent is, practically speaking, unworkable as some sort of observational research. Punch (1985) states that if participants are aware that they are being investigated, this would prevent obtaining uninhibited responses and making unconstrained observations through covert research. If strictly applied, there is a danger that such a belief would abolish a great deal of participant observation research, while, ironically, serving to protect the powerful.

Reynolds (1982) believes that informed consent is but one procedure for demonstrating respect for the rights and welfare of participants. Other procedures may be used to demonstrate these. For example, anonymity, full disclosure following research or treatment with respect. A full and formal informed consent may in fact provide only a marginal contribution to protecting the rights of the participants.

One suggested answer to the ethical problems presented by covert research is that of the development of a code of ethics. Reynolds (1982) suggests that what is needed is to encourage the development of principles and standards to guide the implementation of covert participant observation, i.e. the establishment of a code of ethics. Such a focus, of course, reflects the hope that there are universal yet specific moral and ethical principles that will serve as a satisfactory guide for all time.

However, it is debatable whether a code of ethics would be suitable for this type of research. It could severely restrict access and as such would have a major impact on the type and amount of research material that could be used. As Punch (1985) points out,

> If I employed BSA and ASA codes of ethics in fieldwork, it would have destroyed my research.
>
> (Punch, 1985: 219)

Rather than using a fixed code of ethics, I decided to follow Punch's suggestion and make use of 'situation ethics' of the field, in which I was obliged to act responsibly and make up my own mind in the light of professional codes of ethics and the specific circumstances in which I faced. Therefore, a professional code of ethics is beneficial as a guideline that alerts researchers to the ethical dimensions of their work, particularly prior to entry into the research arena. Again, it has to be stated that this is the stance undertaken with this research. Several times the research method prompted ethical decisions about whether or not to record actual events that could possibly harm individuals and on other occasions lead to their identification. These decisions, while resolved at the time, still cause me to reflect upon them.

2.5   The question of validity

Flexibility in relation to the theoretical and substantive problems encountered in field research is the hallmark of a good researcher.

However, as Burgess (1993) points out, this may lead to the research work being branded as subjective, biased and impressionistic. The question of validity is one that often confronts the field researcher. As Webb (1966: 172) puts it, 'If reliability is the initial step of science, validity is its necessary stride.'

One solution to this problem, which is encouraged throughout this research, is that of a multiple approach to field strategies or, to use the term found in most literature on the subject, 'triangulation.' (Burgess, 1993). Triangulation in this sense refers to the use of a number of different data sources and to a number of different accounts of events. As such, details of how various interpretations of 'what happens' are assembled from different physical, temporal and spatial situations. To overcome the problem of validity, it was resolved to use a multiple approach to the research, by combining several methods in order to validate the findings. Burgess (1993) refers to this type of triangulation as 'methodological triangulation'. This involves 'within method', or the same method used on different occasions and 'between methods' when different methods are used in relation to the same object of sampling for triangulation purposes. Burgess (1993) discusses the problem of researchers conducting work objectively within their own society and asks the question: how far can sociologists understand their own society? Objectivity assumes the independence of the knower and the known. An important goal of a method is to limit whenever possible the effects of researcher bias where bias is defined to be a deviation from some empirical truth or fact (Hammersley, 1993).

2.6   Objectivity

In the area of police work, objectivity can particularly be a problem. As Punch (1985), in his study of police activity in Amsterdam, suggests, one of the main problems with being a covert participant observer is that of the danger of 'going native'. This was a major area of concern for this research, with my background in the police service. To assist in this area, it was decided to attempt something slightly different: something that was outside the normal way of doing things, that would constantly be a reminder to be objective in the research and observations. Several sticky-back notices were placed at various places where only I could see them. Inside the door of the personal locker, which had strictly limited access and opened at least twice a day, inside the top drawer of the desk, which was locked during absence and constantly in use when at work, and inside the cover of the notebook used for recording notes taken in the field, were placed the words:

THINK LIKE AN ALIEN

These notes greatly assisted in maintaining objectivity and were a reminder to observe the world not only as a police officer, but also as a person determined not to 'go native' and jeopardise the research. It was found that after a short time, at every incident or meeting concerned with this research, these words were recalled, which enabled the matters under consideration to be scrutinised far more objectively than would otherwise have been the case.

With regard to the compilation of field notes, there are several accounts of researchers' hastily made excuses to visit the toilet and other secret hideouts in order to scribble coded messages, which they later rewrote fully into their journals (Holdaway, 1984; Hobbes, 1992; Fielding, 1995). Here I felt that my location and access was a great advantage. The bureaucratic nature of the police service is such that to see a police officer not writing when in the police station, or at the scene of an incident, is rare. The police service operates under a system of highly visible and centralised authority, with each rank member looking to a number of ranks above him/her to whom work must be referred. The amount of time and effort spent attending to regulations and procedures, and therefore the paperwork, increases. The Constable is instructed to commit to writing an account of a large number of his/her encounters, and Sergeants and Inspectors are overwhelmed with the resultant paperwork. Indeed, it seems that the paperwork involved inside the police service often draws comment from both inside and outside the police occupation (Bradley, 1998).

To this end, I was constantly scribbling away in a small book chosen to look similar to the regulation police pocket book. This drew no comment from colleagues or any individuals present in the research arena. These notes were then placed into a journal at home the same day.

In relation to the choice of carrying out part of this study by means of fieldwork, Rose (1991: 129) sums up the reasons for adopting this method of research. The major successes of this approach often lie in the fact that it concentrates on research involving social organisations and on looser-knit social groups, where the focus of the enquiry is the here and now of group dynamics, the ideology or world view of the group or a specific process or experience.

2.7   Use of official statistics

One of the main sources of data concerning the particular area in which this research took place was the various official statistics, mainly published by central government. These included such documents as the Census returns, Social Trends publications, various Home Office publications and other documents. They contain demographic data referring particularly to the socioeconomic background of the area under investigation.

The sheer volume of material that is collected on a routine basis by the government and its agencies provides a rich resource for the social researcher to analyse. However, there is a temptation to use such databases without due consideration to their weaknesses, as well as strengths. Official statistics, for example, often employ unexamined assumptions about social life, which researchers, if not cautious, can inherit and reproduce in their studies. They are not social facts but social and political constructions, which may be based upon the interests of those who commissioned the research in the first place. Before using such statistics, I therefore needed to understand how they were constructed. A large part of this research utilises the recorded crimes in the particular geographical area subject to the implementation of zero tolerance type policing. Therefore, it seems only right to discuss the construction of crime figures.

Williams (1994) reveals that the statistics collected by the police are a poor indication of the full extent of criminal activity in the United Kingdom. There are a number of reasons for this. Although the police detect some crimes for themselves, such as drug-related offences and public order offences, the majority of offences come to light because the victim(s) report them. Furthermore, some crimes may never come to light. The police may not record all the activities that are reported to them, or may not record them as crimes, e.g. they may be recorded as lost goods instead of being stolen. During the course of this particular research, the Home Office guidelines in relation to the recording of offences changed, requiring the police to record all crimes with different injured parties as separate crimes, thus notionally increasing the number of criminal offences occurring within certain categories of crimes such as theft of and from vehicles and assaults. For the purpose of this research, therefore, I had to maintain a dual system of recorded crimes in order to compare recorded crimes in the geographical location over a long period of time. Also, there are many crimes that are not controlled by the police but fall under the auspices of some other authority such as

Customs and Excise. It could be argued, therefore, that official statistics are a better reflection of society's attitude towards crime and criminals rather than an objective measure of criminal behaviour.

Due to my location within one of the major organisations involved in the particular partnership initiative, I could easily access the official statistics used to record any effects the inputs had. Indeed, I was the primary person responsible for the collection of recorded data and their dissemination to partnership leaders. The primary sources of statistics used to measure the possible effects of the initiative were as follows:

- Recorded crime statistics for the area concerned.
- The number of situational crime prevention fittings such as 'home-safe' fittings carried out.
- The number of neighbourhood watch schemes established.
- The number of positive media articles published by the local press following partnership press releases.
- Demographic information provided by census returns.

2.8 Control site

In order to address the area of causality, particularly in the area of crime statistics, a comparison was made with a control site from within the same police division. This site was chosen as it roughly equates with the site under investigation and was an area that had not received any significant change in policing before or during the period of this initiative. Also, the location of the control site was some distance from the initiative area. In order to address the question of possible displacement, shifting of crime or a diffusion of benefits from the initiative area to surrounding areas, a statistical analysis of recorded crime in these areas was undertaken.

All of these sources, while readily available, have their strengths and weaknesses, and there is a temptation to use such databases without considering this fact. Much of the success claimed for this partnership scheme revolved around the reduction of recorded crime over the 12-month period of the initiative. In view of this, therefore, it seems appropriate to discuss how these statistics were compiled.

2.9 The questionnaire survey

To assist in establishing what effect, if any, the introduction of zero tolerance type policing and other partnership inputs achieved upon the fear of crime and the community perceptions of the police and crime and disorder within the area under study, a before-questionnaire survey and an after-questionnaire survey were conducted. The before and after survey designs (McNeil, 1990) have been developed in an effort to overcome the disadvantage of not being able to determine the true cause and effect. However, it cannot be legitimately argued that all the before and after differences are attributable to the experimental variable that is being investigated until it can be ascertained that without it, such changes would not have occurred or would have been smaller or different. It is always possible that some changes in the expected direction may take place even without the impact of the experimental variable.

Several other research methods were considered as an alternative to gather information about the initiative, particularly with regard to individuals' fear of crime. The approach involving semi-structured interviews with individuals from within the research area initially proved an attractive proposition. By using this technique, the interviewer can clarify questions and the presence of the interviewer can encourage participation and involvement. However, the interviewer would need to be extremely skilled in this type of research, needing to establish what material collected would be irrelevant to the research. In-depth interviews are difficult to record without using a voice recorder and usage of such a machine brings with it different sorts of problems including inhibition and ethical considerations. Interpretation of the data collected could also be considered a difficult task and subject to subjectivity on my part, while respondents may feel that their answers are not anonymous and are less forthcoming or open.

Consideration (albeit brief) was also given to conducting a street survey inside the geographic location of the initiative. This would mean me locating myself in a known location such as a shopping area in an attempt to interview individuals at random to seek their views. This process is often used in market research to determine individual's views on certain products and services. The immediate problem for this researcher was how to inform the respondent of the basis for the research while not making them aware that it was being carried out by a police officer, which may or may not have influenced their opinions, particularly about questions relating to levels of police visibility. It was considered that it would have been unethical and dishonest to lie about one's interest in the research and professional background. Further, there were practical considerations regarding this type of research, research that quickly assisted in reaching the conclusion, that this form of research was not a viable option on this occasion.

These included the fact that it is difficult to engage individuals in the type of stop-and-question sessions that would have been required. The process would have been extremely time-consuming, and perhaps what is even more important is that there was no way to ensure that samples were representative of the population in general. It would also have been virtually impossible to verify the reliability of answers obtained by revisiting individuals one had met in the street and whose identity was not known or could not have been established. Ultimately, having considered several options, it was decided that the way to obtain the information required in this research was by way of postal questionnaire survey.

However, there are also problems associated with the questionnaire-type survey. If people are aware that they are participating in a survey or an experiment, they may become more alert or aware, and may develop expectations about the outcome. Further, with all the extra attention they are receiving, they may try to respond 'extra well' (the so-called Hawthorne effect) (McNeil, 1990). As Oppenheim (1996) points out, all too often, surveys are carried out on the basis of insufficient design and planning, or on the basis of no design at all. During this research, it was realised quite early in the initial phases of the initiative that the instrument that was to be used would need careful planning and testing if meaningful results were to be obtained. Williams (1994: 71), while pointing out the usefulness of surveys in criminological research, highlights some of the major deficiencies of this research method. These include:

(i) Respondents may be mistaken about crimes, particularly less serious ones, which gives undue weight to serious crimes and reduces the usefulness of the survey as an indicator of the real level of criminality.

(ii) Respondents may be mistaken about when the incident occurred. They may be therefore including incidents that occurred before or after the relevant dates, or may exclude items that occurred within them.

(iii) Respondents may remember an incident but not wish to reveal it to the survey, e.g. a sexual offence, which the respondent found embarrassing.

(iv) Respondents may not fully understand the question, or may not consider that an incident falls within the terms of the question.

(v) Better educated respondents are more likely to recall relevant events and this may give the survey a respondent bias.

As can be seen, a survey of this type runs the risk of having certain inevitable inaccuracies, which are beyond my control. On balance, it is argued, the inaccuracies are thought to undercount offences rather than over-count them (Skogan, 1986). However, the advantages of running this questionnaire survey lie in the fact that in general it was cost effective to run, with administration costs revolving around postage and photocopying. When dealing with sensitive or confidential information, the anonymity of self-completion questionnaires can be an advantage. It must of course be reinforced to the respondent that the questionnaire is anonymous, and this was clearly stated on the instrument. Consequently, by adopting the approach of complete confidentiality, it meant that follow-up letters reminding individuals to return uncompleted questionnaires could not be adopted.

2.10   The questionnaire

It was acknowledged that questionnaires do not emerge fully fledged. They have to be created, adapted, fashioned and developed to maturity after many abortive test runs. In fact, every aspect of a survey has to be tried out beforehand to make sure that it works as intended, as each survey presents its own problems and difficulties and neither expert advice nor spurious orthodoxy is a substitute for a well-thought-out approach involving organised pilot work. As Hibberd and Bennett (1990) rightly point out, producing a questionnaire, if it is done properly, is complicated, as there are many factors to consider. A good questionnaire should be such that the respondent would be able to understand it in the way the author wanted it to be understood. In other words, the question must state clearly what it means, and not confuse the respondent in any way. Second, the respondent must be told clearly what to do, which questions to answer, which to miss out, how to answer them and so on. Misleading instructions can be as bad as misleading questions. Finally, the questionnaire must show consideration for the respondent. Ultimately, the respondent is actually providing time to complete and return the questionnaire. In recognition of this, the instrument should be made as clear and easy to complete as possible. Consequently, it is important to ensure that the questionnaire, as a goal-centred instrument, which enables the collection of information needed for analysing a specific research question, should arise from the problem definition. In this instance, the main research question revolved around the concept of fear of crime and this in itself poses many concerns and problems.

2.11 Measuring fear of crime

While any social study presents particular problems and difficulties, a study involving the concept of 'fear of crime' presents additional complexities. The idea that contextual variables might explain individuals' behaviour grew out of the social control perspective formulated in the 1920s by the Chicago school sociologists (Lewis and Salem, 1986). This approach, while a general social theory and at the same time a theory of social problems, concentrates on the impact of social disorganisation through incivility and disorder within the community. Consequently, 'Fear of Crime' is a generic term used to describe fear of incivility, those offences defined by law as criminal and any other type of behaviour deemed deviant. It is this point that presents a major problem in designing a survey to measure this concept. The term itself, in the British context at least, is a label given to anxieties and worries about becoming a victim of crime (Home Office, 1998b).

The prospect of becoming a victim of crime probably prompts enduring fear in only a small proportion of the population; on the other hand, anxiety about being burgled, raped or robbed for example, is both commonplace and destructive in its consequences. While Garofalo (1981) argues that fear should be used to refer to only the emotional response of fearfulness, which accompanies the anticipation of physical harm, such pleas have been ignored and fear is now routinely used as an all-encompassing shorthand to refer to anxieties about crime. A further confusion lies in equating perceptions of the risk of crime with the fear of crime. Questions about perceived risks are obviously relevant to the explanation of fear but can hardly claim to measure either peoples' fearfulness in specific situations or their anxiety about unwanted events. There is a correlation between perceptions of risks and anxiety, and it is possible that not only perceptions of risk fuel worry, but also worry may amplify perceived risks. However, worry and perceptions of risk are conceptually distinct.

The problem of measurement and causality is compounded when one considers the influence the media may play in helping to shape the perception of fear of crime within individuals. Williams and Dickinson (1993) conclude that the reporting of crime by the British daily press, while varying enormously, has an influence upon individuals. Those papers that reported most crime (particularly crimes involving personal violence and in the most visual and stylistically fashion) were found to have readers who have the highest fear of crime levels. However, the causal link between fear of crime and newspaper readership is not clear and, of course, newspapers only represent one source of information people receive about crime. However, it is important to recognise that external factors can have a substantial impact upon survey results.

A separate area of concern when designing fear of crime surveys is to distinguish fear of crime from indifference concern about crime. People can regard crime as a very serious social issue without themselves having any concern about becoming a crime victim. In practice, one would expect a high degree of correlation between self-interested anxiety and concern for the state of the country.

Surveys are undeniably blunt instruments for assessing people's anxieties about crime. Worry can range from mild fretting to stomach-churning anxiety. Inevitably, people use different languages to describe similar levels of worry, and the same terms to refer to very different levels of worry. Some people are given to exaggeration, others to under-statement. Some such differences may vary systematically between social groups. Emotional under-statement or denial, for example, tends to vary between the sexes and is part of the cultural fabric of some social groups. The problems thus posed to survey research have to be recognised, even if they cannot be solved.

These issues were instrumental in helping to formulate the design of the questionnaire for the purposes of this research measuring perceptions of fear of crime, visibility of police presence and perceptions of crime and disorder within the community.

Once the concepts to be measured were formulated, it was necessary to operationalise them into such questions that would be understood by respondents. Questions were drafted first in a rough format with no real thought given to how they would require answering at this stage. All that was needed was an approximate wording that appeared to be easily understandable. For example, a question relating to contact with the police used in the questionnaire started off as, 'When did you last have contact with a police officer?' This is clearly a very imprecise question for three reasons. First, it assumes that the respondent has had contact with the police officer; second, it doesn't specify what contact means and third, it gives no timescale for the answer. However, by expanding upon this first rough draft question and resolving the problems inherent within it, the question evolved to become not only more precise and easier for the respondent to understand but also easier for me to measure. This process was repeated throughout the questionnaire until the first draft was completed.

Being careful at an early stage will surely pay off later, and after checking for omissions, mistakes or badly expressed questions, it was typed and checked thoroughly. Even after all the detailed preparation that had gone into the evolution of the questionnaire up to this stage, there were still some badly worded questions that had not been appreciated until they were seen in typed print. Included at this stage were the instructions for completion of the questionnaire. The most important instructions were those telling the respondent which questions to answer and those that said how the questions should be answered. Once this process was completed, an initial printing of ten copies was made and this initial questionnaire was then tested upon friends and acquaintances from within the immediate work environment as well as those who had no particular knowledge of the crime prevention initiative. Several of these individuals pointed out areas where improvements could be made, but in particular one area was singled out. This revolved around the question of the description of the respondent's household make-up. It was clear that while attempting to cover any combination of possible responses, several responses had been included such as single, single with children and so on. However, the category for a couple with non-dependent children had not been included. This was pointed out quite forcefully by some of the respondents who had tested the instrument and fell into that category and felt discriminated against! That was a lesson well learnt and a return to the questions and possible responses to them was undertaken.

Following these amendments to the instrument, it was felt to be necessary to test it again on a sample of individuals for accuracy, understanding and clarity. It was tested on a sample of 25 Criminal Justice degree students at the local university. The information gained by this exercise, which pointed out some typing errors, not only gave an idea as to how the instrument would be received but allowed the coding of the questionnaire responses for the purpose of analysis. As the results of the surveys were to be analysed using SPSS, this gave me an opportunity of creating a pilot analysis of the responses to ascertain if the coding of results worked and could be usefully analysed using this method. The coding of responses and the use of SPSS appeared to work quite satisfactorily and it was determined that the survey would progress using the finalised questionnaire.

Thus it was found that piloting in this manner not only assisted in the wording of the questionnaire, but also affected the style and type of question to enable the respondent to understand, complete and (hopefully) return the instrument. In order to ensure impartiality in the research and provide reassurance of confidentiality of the responses, an accompanying letter was designed for each questionnaire. This letter of introduction not only explained what the survey was about, but emphasised how important the respondent's views were. This, coupled with the inclusion of a pre-paid envelope, which, it was hoped, would enhance the return rate of the survey.

Having undertaken a long, and at times complex, process in designing and testing the questionnaire, the process of whom the questionnaires were to be sent to was addressed. This was achieved through the process of sampling.

2.12   The sampling procedure

Particular attention needs to be given to people sampling. There are some surveys where it is feasible to survey the whole of the population. A national census attempts to achieve this and there are occasions when the population of interest is manageably small, e.g. pupils in a school.

In principle, a representative sample of any population should be drawn so that every member of that population has a specified non-zero probability of being included in that sample. Usually this means that every member of the population has a statistically equal chance of being selected. The best way of ensuring this is by means of a completely random sampling method. Randomness in this case does not mean some arbitrary process. It is a statistically defined procedure that requires a table or set of random numbers, which can be generated by a computer or found in research textbooks.

For the purpose of this survey, the sample was chosen as follows. The area under consideration has a population of just over 4000 individuals of 18 years or over. Using the latest electoral role, a 10 percent sample was selected by use of a computer-generated random sampling list consisting of four numbers, and was seen as the most straightforward way of obtaining the sample. The percentages of the sample required were chosen having consideration to the amount of analysis that would need to be undertaken given a favourable return rate.

As Gilbert (1995) points out, the electoral register is the most widely used sampling frame of the adult population in Britain. However, use of the electoral register is not without some problems. It may not, for example, include all the people who live in the area for a variety of reasons including those who are under the age of 18 years, or those who have not returned completed census forms. At the same time, the very nature of its construction precludes those individuals who are under the age of 18 years. That said, the electoral register is particularly well suited to using systematic selection. Each elector has a unique identification number and is listed within their dwelling, dwellings listed in number order within each street, streets are listed alphabetically within each polling district and polling districts can easily be amalgamated to form wards and constituencies. It is therefore easy to work out a sampling interval for the systematic selection of a fixed number of individuals from a polling district or ward.

Having selected the individuals by this method, the questionnaires were posted to the randomly sampled population. Included in the envelope was a stamped addressed envelope, which it was hoped would assist in the return rate. Also included was an explanation letter, which outlined the purpose of the research and explained how useful the information provided could be for future policing in the area. To encourage the sense of independence in this study and to reinforce the issue of confidentiality, the letter was issued in official university notepaper. The data provide by the questionnaires were coded, made into a database and analysed using SPSS.

2.13   Reflection and conclusion

Any research process is fraught with difficulty and contains many areas of concern for the researcher. In particular, my location within an organisation that is very sensitive towards its public image yet agrees to be researched entails some very peculiar problems. This can be magnified somewhat by the limitations of evaluation research, where the sponsorship of the organisation requires a result based upon finding out what works in researching crime prevention methods. Validation research should not be dismissed out of hand, though, as it does provide useful results for policy-makers in certain circumstances. However, it is only right that powerful organisations that are responsible for social control activities, such as the police and other agencies involved in the partnership delivery of policing activity, are open to examination. If the future of policing lies in the multi-agency approach of partnerships with non-elective agencies and organisations, the question of accountability and power structures, coupled with the effectiveness of service delivery, needs to be researched. What has been achieved by employing these research methods, it is believed, is a picture of the interactions and results obtained in a partnership approach to community safety in an economically deprived area.

The methods chosen presented ethical problems for me, which had to be thought through very clearly if the research was to progress. Access, although not a problem in itself due to my position, brought its own problems concerning the choice of research methods. Ultimately, the choice of covert fieldwork as one method was decided upon, based on the fact that to do otherwise would have invited results that would not have been realistic. An intimate knowledge of the organisations and individuals involved within the crime prevention initiative was an obvious deciding factor here as was the collection of data from other methods and sources.

There were several areas that caused me some concern even though the methods used were thoroughly considered. Using the electoral register, for example, meant that not all the people on the receiving end of this initiative were consulted prior to and after it had finished. The youth of the area, who were in some respects regarded as the recipients of the so-called zero tolerance schemes, had no input into its design and implementation. Indeed, they were the marginalised individuals who should have been involved from the start, and this is one area that would need exploring should this type of research be undertaken again.

In terms of the questionnaire design and layout, much work went into providing the final instrument for measuring any perceived effects of the initiative and it is believed that it was due to this painstaking procedure that the postal returns for the questionnaire survey were reasonably good. In terms of reliability of the research, there is no doubt that this research using the methods employed could be replicated and produce valid results. However, it must be recognised that the wider social context within this type of research is placed, may have had an effect upon the issue of causality.

For me, the research process itself was a journey of discovery. It became necessary to know and respect many people who one would not have ordinarily met. Many of the people observed and spoken to were people who were involved in what was considered by many at the time as ground-breaking activities. Whether they achieved what they perceived to be justified will be examined in the findings of this work but this attitude was the driving force for some key players in the initiative.

What this research also revealed was the realisation that what was, in fact, being witnessed was not a 'snapshot' of partnership policing in action. Rather, as Whyte (1975) might have put it, this was the viewing of a 'video recording' or 'film' of the social interactions taking place around the research area. These interactions, steadily moving along with time, were affected by diverse happenings, constantly responding and reacting to changes. Here was a form of policing that was, in a sense, fragile and dependent upon a level of commitment not previously witnessed, showing individual preferences of agencies and a local political groundswell, which are usually outside the control of the police officer at ground level and the community involved.

Lessons learned from this research

1. Covert observational field work is difficult to justify and can produce major ethical problems for the researcher.
2. Maintaining objectivity in fieldwork is difficult, especially if an insider/insider researcher.
3. The use of criminal and other statistical information needs to be placed in context and their limitations understood and explored.
4. It is difficult for 'outsider' researchers to access organisations such as the police.
5. When dealing with community, it is difficult to obtain full representativeness of that community, e.g. young people's views.
6. Questionnaire design is complex and requires much thought regarding its design, use and the concepts it wishes to operationalise.

References

Bradley, R. (1998) *Public Expectations and Perception of Policing*, Policing and Reducing Crime Paper 96, London: Home Office.

Bulmer, M. (Ed.) (1982) *Social Research Ethics*, New York: Holmes and Meier.

Burgess, R. (1993) *In the Field, an Introduction to Field Research*, London: Routledge.

Fielding, N.G. (1995) 'Ethnography', in Gilbert, N. (Ed.) *Researching Social Life*, London: Sage, pp 154–171 (1st ed.).

Garofalo, J. (1981) 'The Fear of Crime; Causes and Consequences', *Journal of Criminal Law and Criminal Policy*, 72: 839–857.

Gilbert, N. (1995) *Researching Social Life*, London: Sage (1st ed.).

Glover, M. and Rushbrook, P. (1987) *Organisational Studies*, Brighton: Wheatsheaf.

Goffman, E. (1990) *The Presentation of Self in Everyday Life*, London: Penguin.

Hammersley, M. (1993) *Social Research, Philosophy, Politics and Practice*, London: Sage.

Hibberd, M. and Bennett, M. (1990) *Questionnaire and Interview Surveys, a Manual for Police Officers*, London: The Police Foundation.

Hobbes, D. (1992) *Doing the Business: Entrepreneurship, Detectives and the Working Class in the East End of London*, Oxford: Oxford University Press.

Holdaway, S. (1984) *Inside the British Police: A Force at Work*, London: Blackwell.

Home Office. (1998a) *Reducing Offending: An Assessment of Research Evidence on Ways with Dealing with Offending Behaviour*, Research Study 187, Research and Statistics Directorate, London: Home Office.

Home Office. (1998b) *Crime and Disorder Act 1998*, London: HMSO.

Humphreys, L. (1975) *Tea Room Trade: Impersonal Sex in Public Places*, Chicago: Chicago University Press.

Lee, R.M.C. (1995) *Doing Research on Sensitive Topics*, London: Sage.

Lewis, D.A. and Salem, G. (1986) *Fear of Crime, Incivility and the Production of a Social Problem*, New Brunswick and Oxford: Transaction Books.

McNeil, P. (1990) *Research Methods* (2nd ed.), London: Routledge.

Oppenheim, A.N. (1996) *Questionnaire Design, Interviewing and Attitude Measurement*, London and New York: Pinter Publishers.

Punch, M. (1985) *Conduct Unbecoming, The Social Construction of Police Deviance and Control*, London and New York: Tavistock.

Reiner, R. (1992) 'Police Research in the United Kingdom: A Critical Review', in Tonry, M. and Morris, N. (Eds) *Modern Policing, Crime and Justice Volume 15*, Chicago and London: University of Chicago Press, pp 435–508.

Reiner, R. (1994) 'A Truce in the War Between Police and Academe', *Policing Today*, 1, 1 October.

Reiner, R. (2000) *The Politics of the Police* (3rd ed.), London: Harvester Wheatsheaf.

Reynolds, P.D. (1982) 'Moral Judgements: Strategies for Analysis with Application to Covert Participant Observations', in Bulmer, M. (Ed.) *Social Research Ethics*, New York: Holmes and Meier, pp 185–213.

Rose, G. (1991) *Deciphering Sociological Research*, London: Macmillan.

Seiber, J.E. (1992) *Planning Ethically Responsible Research*, London: Sage.

Skogan, W.G. (1986) *Methodological Issues in the Study of Victimisation*, Bureau of Justice Statistics, U.S. Dept. of Justice, Washington DC: Govt. Printing Office.

Warwick, D.P. (1982) 'Tearoom Trade: Means and Ends in Social Research', in Bulmer, M. (Ed.) *Social Research Ethics*, New York: Holmes and Meier

Webb, E. J. (1966) *Unobtrusive Research in the Social Sciences*, Chicago: Rand McNally

Whyte, W. F. (1975) *Street Corner Society*, Chicago: University of Chicago Press.

Williams, K.S. (1994) *Textbook on Criminology* (2nd ed.), London: Blackstone Press.

Williams, P. and Dickinson, J. (1993) 'Fear of Crime: Read All About It? The Relationship Between Newspaper Crime Reporting and Fear of Crime', *British Journal of Criminology*, 33: 1.

3

Researching the Police: Personal Insights and Reflections

James Gravelle

Research methods involved

1. Quantitative

Questionnaire survey and data statistical analysis

2. Qualitative

Overt observational fieldwork, in-depth interviews and documentary and policy analysis

About the research

This research examines the change in police resource deployment through the introduction of a Demand Management and Tasking Unit (DMTU). It analyses the work carried out by the DMTU in its attempt to rationalise the delivery of policing services to the public. With increasing pressure being placed on already finite policing resources, it has become increasingly difficult for the police to attend each call by deploying a physical resource such as police officers or community support officers (CSOs). In the light of this need to change, some police services have developed DMTUs to investigate a specific and limited number of crimes by telephone, in the anticipation that they can reduce pressure on 'front line' police staff. The study assesses the impact of this change on policing services, police officers and the public.

As its primary objectives, the research is concerned with three principal goals:

1. Examining the impact on the delivery of policing services utilising the new knowledge management system, DMTU, along with associated integrated software.

2. Exploring the perceptions of police officers of the introduction of the new knowledge management system and examining the impact of these systems on their performance.
3. Exploring public perceptions of the new delivery and administration method of policing and examining their impact on the public.

This research was conducted between 2008 and 2011.

3.1   Introduction

Perhaps more than ever, the issue of police research is essential to the successful continuation of the police and policing in England and Wales. Further, the HMIC (2010) report, while concentrating upon achieving the three 'E's', namely effectiveness, efficiency and economy, adopts as its approach an encouragement of 'doing more for less'. Implicit in this keynote is finding new ways for the police service to carry out its day-to-day business. With policing being intrinsically linked with so many factors such as the criminal justice system, social changes, the forces of globalisation and advances in technology, the police service must therefore constantly adapt to reflect such changes, finding new ways to ensure it provides an effective, efficient and appropriate service. This research took into account these pressures and requirements, aiming to add knowledge and understanding while being grounded in established theory. The police service is under pressure from all quarters including the external recipients of services, internal users and government to increase the efficiency, effectiveness and economic viability of the service that is being provided.

3.2   Research methodology

> Methodology is the system of explicit rules and procedures upon which research is based and against which claims for knowledge are evaluated
>
> Nachmias and Nachmias (1996: 13)

A methodology is an integral part of any major analysis or research. Nachmias and Nachmias (1996) identify three practical reasons for this. Communication is the first as the aim of this research was to communicate findings from its conclusions and assist with policy recommendations. If successful, this should enable individuals to understand the complexities and technicalities of the study without having an in-depth knowledge of the underlying concepts. The public, academics and police practitioners and policy-makers can then draw meanings from the research. This research attempted to inform policy, improve delivery of service to the public and ultimately improve effectiveness, efficiency and economic viability for the organisation itself. Only through effective communication can 'gatekeepers' and other stakeholder groups have the ability to criticise, analyse and evaluate the findings, thereby implementing recommendations where required. Gatekeepers operate at mid-management level and can be obstructive towards research, feeling threatened as to the findings and consequences of research (Draper, 2001). Gatekeepers will often have a significant amount of authority and status within an organisation to influence subordinates and senior managers, misguiding and misusing the research findings and in some instances totally ignoring any recommendations if they are not viewed as being productive or positive to their personal set agenda. Second, a methodology should enable others to understand the policy, thus facilitating the way in which policy can be applied. From this, conclusions can be drawn from factual observations. Understanding the principles, procedures and other potent influences is integral to this and other research. Finally, inter-subjectivity or understanding will enable analysts from different specialist fields to critically evaluate each other's findings. This will underpin the independence, validity and objectivity of the research. Research should be easily understood and readily compatible with findings from other disciplines. Different styles of research are available such as ethnography, systematic reviews or randomised controlled trials. However, for the purposes of this study, the use of evaluation research techniques has been selected.

3.3 Characteristics of the research

Formulating elements of this evaluation research, each of the following frameworks was used to assess the impact of the knowledge management systems being introduced by the police with particular reference to the research aims listed above. The following analytical methods were employed to examine the programme processes, outputs, outcomes and feedback process. Sarantakos (2005) and Trochim (2010) refer to these as types of evaluations, explaining how each analysis can be utilised.

Process evaluation

This evaluation was employed to assess how the new knowledge management system was affecting the delivery of policing services and achieving its stated objectives, e.g. improving the quality of service to the public or enabling a bespoke response to meet the needs of the individual (Grey, 2009). This was linked to research objective 1, which aimed to evaluate the impact of the DMTU on the delivery of policing services to the public.

Needs analysis

This assessed the overall needs of the public within the police area, assessing specific requirements anticipated of the police, e.g. do the public expect a physical resource such as a police officer to respond to each non-emergency call? Public perceptions of the service provided were essential in order to ensure the service provided meets the specific expectations of the end-user, which was linked to research objective 2.

Outcome analysis

The results of the DMTU were examined to assess if the published objectives of the programme had been achieved with each goal being accomplished with references to the end user, e.g. reduced pressure on front-line services, improved priority response and improved quality of service delivered. In addition, this will helped to assess objectives 2 and 3 of the research programme.

Impact analysis

This considered how the DMTU has affected the community, assessing the implications of its application across a wider geographical area. This analysis further evaluated the impact of the new policing model, with an emphasis on whether or not a customer-focussed neighbourhood response was meeting the expectations and needs of the community.

Cost–benefit analysis

Additionally, the research examined the financial aspects of the initiative, evaluating costs of deploying a physical resource and prioritising responses against a different resolution procedure. The economic implications were assessed to determine if the unit was economically viable and sustainable (Grey, 2009). The cost–benefit analysis assisted in evaluating research objective 1.

3.4   Validity and reliability of data

Research relies on evidence to ensure that the conclusions and recommendations made carry authority and standing with others. Validity relates to

> The degree to which a measuring instrument measures what it is supposed to measure
>
> Nachmias and Nachmias (1996: 599)

For this reason the validity of data can only be as good as the measuring instruments employed. Validity is concerned with precision, accuracy and relevance of the instruments used throughout the research. Social science research can be uniquely subjective (Kirk and Miller, 1986), and it is at the discretion of the individual carrying out the research as to the behaviour, actions and commentary recorded in the field. In addition, the way in which such data is recorded and scrutinised can also be subjective. Individual cultural and behavioural norms, social and religious beliefs can influence objectivity. Sarantakos (2005) adds that validity will enable the researcher to produce findings that accurately reflect theoretical and conceptual values.

Internal validity

Internal validity is concerned with causality and examining the relationship between variables (Freund, 1974). In particular, internal validity considers two or more variables to establish if there are true associations or relationships. In some instances, it is possible to produce associations between variables that are spurious (Rowntree, 1981). For example, the sale of ice creams does share an association with the number of burglaries. Although statistically these two variables share a relationship, the sale of ice cream does not affect burglary rates. In this example, it is the weather that is associated with the two variables as the sale of ice creams and burglary rates are linked to good weather. As the weather improves, people leave windows open making it easier for criminals to carry out burglaries. In addition, weather also results in people buying more ice cream. It is important consequently to ensure that the research design addressed concerns surrounding internal validity.

As part of the design of this research, many steps were taken to improve internal validity. For example, the data collection tools were piloted. Best (2003) notes that testing instruments improves validity and this was undertaken as part of this research. Additionally, steps were taken to ensure that there was no bias in the sampling techniques used. If not carefully managed, this can also impact on the internal validity of the research. Finally, the Hawthorne effect can impact upon internal validity and mechanisms were in place to reduce its effect (Bryman, 2008).

External validity

External Validity is concerned with the issue surrounding generalisability (Bryman, 2008). This type of validity is concerned with having the ability to take research findings and apply them in a wider context (Moore, 1979). For example, could the findings of this study be applied across all of the police services? Although there was no systematic bias in the sampling frame used as part of this study, due to the limited number or respondents, it is unlikely that findings may be generalised and applied to all police services. However, it was not anticipated at the outset of the study to have generalisable results. It must be noted that this in no way detracted from the importance of this research. Instead, the aim of this study was to provide insights into some of the issues surrounding the rationalisation of services delivered by the police.

Reliability of research findings relates to

> The consistency of a measuring instrument, that is, the extent to which a measuring instrument contains variable errors
> Nachmias and Nachmias (1996: 597)

Instruments for this research included pre-prepared observational documents, questionnaires and interview schedules. Each of these measuring devices can generate erroneous data, which may affect the reliability of the findings. Reliability seeks to ensure that the instruments can produce the same findings and conclusions each time the research is carried out. Rigour is the primary objective for both validity and reliability, as often research can fundamentally influence the way in which processes are carried out. If the process is changed based on poor-quality research, the ensuing results could be catastrophic. It is for this reason that researchers spend an inordinate amount of time ensuring that data collection tools, theoretical viewpoints and epistemological positions have been thoughtfully and critically appraised. Many researchers avoid the concept of reliability, opting instead to use terms such as credibility, applicability, audit-ability, coherence, trustworthiness, transferability, dependability and conformity (Guba and Lincoln, 1989; Flick,

1998). The principles of validity and reliability can be reinforced by the principles of triangulation and these were examined and implemented as a central part of this research.

3.5 Triangulation

A solution to overcoming the problems associated with validity and reliability as part of this research was to employ a strategy commonly referred to as triangulation. Triangulation can be used in various ways, including adopting the strategy while deciding on the paradigm and sampling techniques to be used. Triangulation is most commonly used in research by using two or more different collection techniques to gather data. Denzin (1989) confirms that by using a number of different techniques such as interviews, questionnaires and observations increases the reliability and validity of the evidence gathered. Burgess (1984) describes the benefits of utilising a triangulation approach to research. Rigour, data enrichment, increased validity, credibility, less bias and more scientific objectivity are just some of the associated benefits of this technique. It is recognised, however, that some commentators such as Silverman (1985) note that triangulation does not necessarily guarantee that the data collected results in better quality research. In addition, Silverman (1985) argues that triangulation can work to legitimise personal views and that it is particularly difficult to replicate triangulated research. Having considered this, it was concluded that the benefits of using this approach throughout this research outweighed any disadvantages. Another major ethical concern to be considered was informed consent.

3.6 Ethical considerations

Informed consent

Informed consent is considered to be a prerequisite of any research being carried out involving members of the public (Dickson-Swift et al., 2008). Informed consent can be defined as

> The provision of information to participants, about the purpose of the research, its procedures, potential risks, benefits and alternatives so that the individual understands this information and can make a voluntary decision whether to enrol and continue to participate
> Emanuel et al. (2000: 2703)

Nachmias and Nachmias (1996) note that informed consent can have a bearing both legally and culturally. When conducting research within an organisation that operates under a hierarchical structure, consideration must be given to the level of consent required. It was believed that consent to research the police organisation would need to come from a senior officer. The police organisation operates under a relatively strict hierarchical structure, where rank confers seniority. Under such a rigid command structure, having the permission of a senior officer, usually beyond the rank of superintendent, ensures ready access will be granted by all departmental and divisional supervisors. In this study, consent to access was permitted by the most senior officer within the organisation, the Chief Constable. However, considerations must additionally be made to ensure an ethical standard is reached and maintained taking full account of each individual respondent within the organisation. Reynolds (1979) refers to four elements that should be measured when considering the level of consent needed. First, competence and the capability of being able to give consent, accompanied with the necessary understanding allowing the individual to fully appreciate complicated and high-risk factors associated with the research, must be measured. If any individual cannot for any reason meet these criteria, additional provisions must be put in place. Voluntarism where the individual is given a choice to partake in research must also be considered. If any pressure, demands or coercion are employed, then this will invalidate any consent made verbally or in writing. Disclosure about the intended research needs to be provided, as consent must be voluntary and informed. Failing to inform any individual through deception or omission may result in true consent not being obtained (Reynolds 1979). Only by adhering to and fully considering each of the above factors can true consent be obtained from any respondent. Covert researching under the premise of full true consent brings with it its own practical difficulties that must be carefully considered as discussed previously. The issues are compounded if the methodological design relies on a covert approach. This type of research is often controversial and has been used to research organisations such as the police in the past (Noaks and Wincup, 2004). Holdaway (1983) conducted early ethnographic research into the police and its organisational culture and his work is well documented as highlighting the issue of consent as a major methodological and ethical problem. Holdaway (1992) refers to the police as an impenetrable organisation and one for which a covert approach was necessary if research was to be effective, spending time embedded within the organisation conducting observational work and collecting qualitative data. In reality, there is often a trade-off and Jupp et al. (2000) explain that there will be a need to balance informed consent and the validity and accuracy of any findings. Fountain (1993) refers to this as ethical compromises, whereas Shaw (2003) supports this notion by alluding to the trade-offs as a balance of competing priorities. Weighing up public interest against the interests of those individuals involved is a difficult situation for any researcher and this study was no different. Many researchers who have employed a covert research technique often argue that it was necessary to ensure the validity of their findings, reasoning that individuals will react differently if they are aware that they are being observed or know the aims or objectives of the research. The technique, for all its advantages, was not employed to carry out this particular study for several reasons. It was felt that under these circumstances, such an option was not practicable. Consent given by the organisation was on the basis of an overt study and as I was of a non-police background, gaining access covertly would have been extremely difficult. In addition to this, observing individuals covertly brings with it its own ethical difficulties. The lack of informed consent is one example where the covert option highlights its inherent impracticalities. Throughout this research each respondent including the public and the police officers was issued with an information sheet and consent form. Prior to participating, each individual respondent received a statement describing in detail:

- *Respondent's rights* – the respondent may withdraw consent at any time and discontinue participation without penalty.
- *Benefits of the research* – the research aims to better inform policing and align the delivery of policing services closer to the public's needs.
- *Potential risks* – respondents should not be financially affected in any way. For this reason a pre-paid envelope was enclosed.
- *Confidentiality statement* – every effort was made to ensure confidentiality of any identifying information that is obtained in connection with this study. Following completion, the data was retained and stored securely and will not be made available to any other person or organisation. The data was kept for no longer than the length of the study, which was no more than 18 months. The data was kept electronically stored within the university premises on a secure password-protected computer in a locked office. As for hard data, this was also kept at the university premises in a secure locker.
- *Respondent withdrawal* – respondents could choose whether to be in this study or not. If initially deciding to volunteer for this study, the

respondents were clearly told that they could withdraw at any time without consequences of any kind. Additionally, respondents could exercise the option of removing their data from the study.

- *Research procedures* – each step of the process was included for each respondent to understand the procedure from data collection through analysis to publishing.

In addition to the above, each respondent was issued with contact details of the research faculty and me if they felt the need to discuss any additional concerns prior to giving consent. Privacy is another issue that was considered as part of the ethical considerations of the research.

Privacy

Privacy is related to the individual respondent and the right to which there is no requirement to partake in any research (Kimmel, 1988). Privacy can be defined as

> The claim of individuals, groups or institutions to determine for themselves when, how and to what extent information about them is communicated to others
>
> Westin (1968: 7)

Diener and Crandall (1978) identify three primary elements to privacy, which needed to be considered. While conducting any research, the 'sensitivity of information' must be evaluated as the research may intentionally or inadvertently expose sensitive and personal information. Information such as personal details, past criminal convictions and personal statements are held as extremely sensitive by most respondents. The researcher, where possible, abstained from gathering sensitive data such as income, religious beliefs, political views or sexual experiences, unless these had any significant bearing on the research (Bryman, 2008). Second, the 'settings being observed', which relates to the actual location in which the research will be conducted, must be carefully considered. By the nature of social science research, interaction and data gathering can be intrusive (Mcneill and Chapman, 2006). Through careful consideration of the environment where the research will be carried out, any unnecessary intrusions can be minimised. The police survey was deliberately distributed through the internal police mailing system. This provided the police staff involved in the research the opportunity to complete the questionnaire survey during work hours, thus minimising the intrusion on their private and personal lives. In addition to this measure, interviewing was conducted within the workplace and where possible made by an appointment system to suit the respondents, providing the minimum intrusion as the individuals could continue with ongoing work tasks. The added benefit of this was that it provided the opportunity to visualise and observe individuals as they interacted with the software and dealt with respondents in a natural work setting. 'Spamming' or sending documents in the form of letters or e-mails, followed by conducting telephone surveys at weekends and late evening, clearly impacts on privacy with scant regard to the setting being observed. The third and final aspect of privacy identified by Diener and Crandall (1978) relates to the 'dissemination of information'. Considerations must be made as to whether the published data will be robustly anonymous. This remains the obligation of the researcher and must be taken seriously. In some instances, however, Nachmias and Nachmias (1996) identify that the decision to keep the findings anonymous or confidential is no longer at the discretion of the individual researcher. For example, in a judicial hearing or in front of a committee where the research or its respondents can be identified (Babbie, 2004). Researchers are obligated to follow strict confidentiality guidelines through adopting official contracts and documents such as consent forms and protocols, which are discussed throughout this chapter. Specifically, each respondent received a consent form accompanied by an information sheet detailing respondent rights and research procedures. Additionally, full ethical approval was granted by the University Ethics Committee. Finally, the principles of the Data Protection Act were implemented robustly throughout the study including the storage, retentions and sharing of both hard and electronic data. During recent years, the focus on privacy and other human rights has undoubtedly changed across the world. The Human Rights Act (Home Office, 2000) formally includes the right to privacy under Article 8. This particular convention specifies that each person has a right to a private life, including privacy at home and of correspondence. Additionally, this article clearly states that there should be no interference with the exception of upholding the law. Kimmel (1988) argues that ethical codes such as the right to privacy are expressed in research professional practice doctrines across America and Europe. Under such standards, confidentiality and anonymity are guaranteed and constantly reviewed. Confidentiality and anonymity also needed to be considered as part of the ethical considerations of the research.

Confidentiality and anonymity

Confidentiality is concerned with the concealment and traceability of a respondent's identity via gathered data (Mcneill and Chapman, 2006).

> Information obtained about the research participant during the course of an investigation is confidential unless otherwise agreed upon in advance. When the possibility exists that others may obtain access to such information, this possibility, together with plans for protecting confidentiality, is explained to the participant as part of the procedure for obtaining informed consent
>
> American Psychological Association (1982: 7)

The primary difference between confidentiality and anonymity is that the former occurs only when the researcher knows the identity of the respondent, whereas the latter implies that the individual respondent cannot be identified by any person, including the researcher or any published research (Vaus, 2002). The issue of confidentiality and anonymity are usually referred to when obtaining informed consent where each respondent will be made aware of the research protocols. This will describe in detail what information, if any, will be disclosed – for example, names, addresses or any other distinguishable or identifiable information that will be obtained, stored or published. If any personal data is recorded, it will be for the researcher to inform the respondent of the strategies in place for ensuring confidentiality and anonymity. Such assurances of anonymity are particularly difficult when conducting qualitative research where at times there will be a need for direct contact between the researcher and the respondent through interview, focus group or respondent observation. While interviewing, anonymity could not be guaranteed by the reality of face-to-face interviewing, as in most cases I will come face to face with the respondent. Although anonymity could not be provided in this instance, confidentiality was assured by omitting to record any personal identifiable data. Vaus (2002) highlights the importance of setting out a clear and concise protocol for dealing with issues of confidentiality and anonymity. Adopting and relaying a clear strategy will improve the response rate from respondents as they will feel more comfortable and they are assured that, by participating, their identity will remain confidential or anonymous. In addition, it is likely that the respondent will be more frank as respondents feel comfortable expressing their true feelings, thus improving the quality of the data being generated. In addition to this, a clear protocol will improve representativeness as even marginalised opinions and views will be more likely to be openly expressed. Research conducted by Reaser et al. (1975) concluded that respondents were significantly more likely to respond to personal and difficult areas of research if a clear protocol dealing with confidentiality was in place. As part of the surveys to both the police and the public, confidentiality was assured by ensuring the security of hard and electronic data, making sure that the findings were non-identifiable and putting in place protocols for sharing data. This was conveyed to each respondent at a number of stages while obtaining their full informed consent. Respondents were repeatedly reminded not to include any personal data that could result in their identity being traced, e.g. names, addresses or numbers. Although confidentiality and anonymity can be essential to research, there will be instances where a breach of an established protocol must be considered. This may include instances that it is in the public's interest, where it is in the individual's best interest, for example, such as where there is danger to life. Such clauses should be considered prior to researching and clearly explained within the protocol and at the stage where informed consent is obtained. Issues of ownership of data can impact on confidentiality and anonymity agreements and should be considered at the design stage of the research. Often research can be conducted on behalf or in conjunction with an organisation. Under such circumstances, access to sensitive data should be discussed and agreed upon to ensure confidentiality can be maintained. In this research, the police were fully involved as they had provided access on the basis of receiving a copy of the report findings and the conclusions. It was identified early on in the research that ownership of the data was solely the property of the university. The police would only receive data in a generic format where no individual respondent could be identified. Vaus (2002) additionally refers to third-party data collections as a potential risk to confidentiality protocols. Senior officials or supervisors within an organisation will be responsible for collecting data such as questionnaires on behalf of the researcher. This should always be avoided as confidentiality agreements could be breached. In this instance, sergeants and inspectors would perhaps be more likely to fall into the category of third-party collectors. This was avoided by ensuring a pre-paid envelope was provided for the questionnaire to be returned directly.

Ensuring confidentiality and anonymity

By the very nature of social science research, personal data will need to be collected as the study of people, networks and society often relies on such data. For this study, previous crime experiences, feelings about new concepts and views on policing are just some of the issues on which respondents were asked to comment. As a result, it is important to ensure strategies were in place to reduce the likelihood of confidentiality or anonymity agreements being infringed or negated. These strategies include the following.

Third-party collectors

The use of individuals who could potentially have access to research data such as supervisors or managers was avoided. Providing a pre-paid envelope direct to the primary researcher eliminated or in part reduced the risk of any breach of confidentiality (Vaus, 2002). This strategy was employed throughout the study.

Specific personal data

Under no circumstances was specific personal data such as addresses or names stored unless absolutely essential to the research. All data was sanitised at source, therefore not infringing any part of Data Protection Act. I only collected necessary data, for example, address or employment details were not necessary and as a result such details were not included as part of the data collection procedure. Sensitive questioning was limited and only used if absolutely essential (Kimmel, 1988). An assessment of the data required was thoroughly reviewed at the design stage of this study.

Access to published data

Hard data was stored in a locked filing cabinet in a locked office. Access to the cabinet was restricted. Scripts, research notes and questionnaires did not contain any identifiable marks such as names, passport details, addresses or national insurance details. Omitting any identifiable information decreased the risk of a respondent's details being misused (Holmes, 2004)

Access to electronic data

Since the introduction of data storage devices such as hard drives and databases, legislation has been tightened concerning the use and dissemination of such material by the 'Data Protection Act' (Home Office, 1998). Briefly, this act sets out provisions for handing data, specifically in relation to storage, retrieval, disclosure and the sharing of personal data. For the purposes of this study, electronic data was stored on a secure server and was always password protected. In addition, encryption techniques were employed where possible. Similarly to hard data, electronic forms did not include any identifiable data such as names or addresses (Holmes, 2004)

Deduction

All possible procedures were employed to keep the data collected secure throughout this study. Through restrictions, the information was not made available on to any another institution or person. As a common practice, sanitisation of the data where possible was carried out to remove identifiable information (Picou, 1996). At the reporting and publishing stage of the research, broad categories, ID numbers and pseudonyms were used to ensure that no individual could be identifiable through deduction (Becker, 1998).

Researcher bias and objectivity

While conducting research, maintaining professional objectivity, distance and scientific clarity is essential (Reason and Bradbury, 2001). Although such notions are obvious and easy to write about, applying such concepts in practice is much more complex. As contact with individuals increases, the relationship between participant and researcher will undoubtedly develop and change. Perspectives can change, not only of individuals but also of departments, or even of the whole organisation. Punch (1985) in a study examining corruption and scandal within the Amsterdam police refers to 'going native', which relates to the ever-present danger of losing independence, objectivity and becoming part of the experiment rather than remaining a detached observer. With an organisation such as the police service, there is an organisational culture and individual culture that is naturally suspicious of all outsiders (Reiner, 2000). The fundamental challenge for any researcher is to

> Outwit the institutional obstacle-course to gain entry and... penetrate the mine-field of social defences to reach the inner reality of police work
>
> Punch (1979: 4)

In addition to entering and being accepted into the organisation, the additional challenge is to remain objective throughout the period of the research (Stoecker, 2005). The dilemma and paradox is that the process of becoming accepted into an organisation in order to gain access and trust is to gain good-quality data while maintaining the notion of researcher objectivity. Gaining trust often involves building relationships and getting to know individuals over a period of time. This ultimately results in researchers getting to know individuals intimately (Hammersley, 1993). The paradoxical element or opposing force is the necessity to remain detached, scientific and objective having been forced to build relationships often over considerable periods of time. While introducing new technological concepts into the police, many officers who were responsible for certain aspects of the projects would attempt to set out their position for additional resources, preference for support or access to increased budgets often looking to me for approval of their ideas, concepts and outlook. Remaining neutral by not siding with individuals and departments was difficult having spent hours with senior officers who would constantly seek me to take on such a role. Hobbs' (1988) advice when researching criminals was to 'keep your mouth shut' and further remarks that this principle should be strictly adopted when researching the police organisation. Where possible this approach was adopted in an attempt to limit any influence over individuals. Prolonged involvement with the same individuals almost certainly increased the risk of researcher bias, but being aware of such potential problems makes the implementation of provisions to negate the risks easier. Each visit to the police resulted in extensive field notes, which consequently resulted in me recording detailed personal feelings and experiences. In addition, each visit resulted in an informal debriefing by other research staff within the department. Talking over issues and points raised helped to reaffirm and refocus the researcher. Using a varied approach such as observational work and interviewing relying on triangulation of data collection methods additionally assisted in reducing bias, as the reliance on direct interactions with individuals was diluted. Observational data collection offered detachment from other individuals' summaries, thoughts, ideas and concepts. To have the ability to apply ethical principles, access to the organisation needed to be established, maintained and monitored throughout the period of research.

3.7 Access

Studying an organisation as large, complex and as compartmentalised as the police service brings with it unique difficulties. Additionally, the unique culture that exists within the organisation has been widely researched by other commentators (Ianni and Ianni, 1983; Reiner, 2000). Bell (1969) and Hammersley and Atkinson (1995) both make reference to the importance of access, while conducting social research. As previously briefly explored, research can be conducted both covertly and overtly. For the purposes of this research, all work was carried out overtly with informed consent and the full understanding of the senior police executive and also individual informed consent from all respondents. Punch (1985) refers to the barriers that exist within the police service to prevent outsiders from penetrating, exposing and prying into its inner mechanisms. By controlling access, the police service attempts to portray a favourable, positive and in some instances, a manufactured image of their world and its operating culture (Page, 2007). The challenge for any researcher is to overcome such difficulties. Unquestionably, the quality and representativeness of the data obtained through research will be highly dependent on the techniques employed to penetrate Reiner's (2010) protective shield in order to expose the authenticity of what is under observation. In addition to these techniques, any previous relationship between the organisation and the researcher will have repercussions. Brown (1996) refers to four possible permutations: insider's insiders, outsider's insiders, insider's outsiders and outsider's outsiders. Insider's insider refers to police officers or other staff that work within the organisation; this may include police officers or PCSOs. The advantages for the insiders are that access to data and individuals is already assured. Outsider's insiders refer to those individuals who have previously been a part of the organisation, but have subsequently left through transfer or retirement. Having left the service, such individuals no longer enjoy unprecedented access or cultural acceptability; however, it is likely that outsider's insiders will retain some influence and contacts within the service. Insider's outsiders are non-police officers but still have a role to perform within the justice or governance departments, e.g. Home Office, IPCC or HMIC. Access to such individuals needs to be formalised. However, in many instances it is unlikely that access will be denied as many locations will require unrestricted access for inspection purposes. Finally, there are 'outsider's outsiders'. This category is reserved for academics and researchers with no formal affiliation to the police service and it is to this category I was affiliated. This often is the most difficult category to gain formal access to the police service as the researcher is not employed or formally commissioned to conduct the research. Overcoming such difficulties is not impossible but agreeing to a memorandum of understanding between the researcher and the police organisation is essential. Having gained access, there were still other difficulties to overcome and circumnavigate. Having previously researched the police organisation, I was aware of some of the potential difficulties in building trust, forming relationships in order to gain a true representation of what was occurring. Lies, deceit and deception are just some of the techniques employed in attempts to hide the truth. The challenge for me was to penetrate this protective shield by interviewing staff and observing individuals while they were operating the various data systems. Deciphering behaviour through interviews and observations was an essential part of the data collection and analysis. Full access was granted by the Chief Constable to areas such as control rooms, call centres and service headquarters. In addition to this, full access to staff and senior officers was also sought and subsequently granted. Having access approved by the most senior police officer within the organisation was unquestionably the most valuable and useful asset throughout the entire study. On one occasion, there seemed some resistance to my presence within a department and only by informing gatekeepers that access was on the authority of the 'chief' that this attitude instantly changed, resulting in the individual becoming more helpful and cooperative. Having said this, this gatekeeper did not like the idea of me sitting with any officer and ensured that the visit was tightly restricted with me only observing a carefully selected number of respondents. It is important to state that only once was it necessary to inform respondents of this and much deliberation was given to whether or not to inform gatekeepers of the terms of access, given that it may affect how the respondent would respond if they were under the impression that I might report findings directly back to the Chief Constable. Managing my access on a daily basis was a police inspector whose primary function for the purposes of the research was that of a 'gatekeeper' (Saunders et al., 2009). Such individuals are 'powerful' within the police organisation with the ability, under certain circumstances, to withdraw access at any time. The success for any research is wholly dependent on the relationship and level of cooperation forged between gatekeeper and researcher. Interestingly, the terms of the access almost certainly changed during the period of the research. Initially, on visits to the police headquarters the research was closely monitored and regulated. Each visit had been pre-arranged via e-mail beforehand. On each occasion, a police officer having been summoned by the support worker at the main desk would come and an escort would be provided to the department that was to be visited. As time progressed and my presence became more familiar and regular, this whole ritual changed. No longer was I required to be escorted around the building, but I simply needed to sign in and be 'buzzed' through each of the security doors unescorted. This appears to be the physical manifestation of the police culture accepting my role no longer as a 'stranger' or 'visitor', but that of 'one of the chaps' (Hobbs, 1988: 6). By this time, staff knew me by my first name and would make casual conversation as progress was being made through the maze-like building. In addition to this change, no longer would the details of each visit need to be pre-arranged with the gatekeepers. Simply arriving, signing in, having a chat with the staff at the desk and being 'buzzed' through the many security doors and heading to the department that was under study. As the relationship developed further, upon arrival I would knock and enter the inspector's office and tea or coffee would be offered without delay. Having had a brief chat, remembering to implement the 'keep quiet' approach that resulted in the conversation becoming mostly one-sided, I could then sit anywhere, with any individual that needed to be observed or interviewed without being directed to an individual station or being monitored. Clearly, the terms of access had changed. No longer was I considered an outsider's outsider (Brown, 1996), but perhaps more fittingly would have been an 'insider outsider'. The ever-present danger, which really never left my thoughts, was the concept of 'GOING NATIVE'. Being so close to the culture could have easily resulted in bias or a loss of objectivity. Remaining conscious of this, accompanied by regular debriefs and informal chats with colleagues, helped me to constantly refocus and remain scientific. Having obtained access to the organisation and specific individuals within the police service, a range of data collection techniques was deployed.

3.8 Observational technique

Observational research can underpin a considerable part of a research programme and was invaluable in gaining first-hand experience and understanding of the systems and working practices of the police (Angrosion, 2007). In part, this is because of its 'directness' (Denzin, 1989). Direct observations enable researchers to observe working practices in a 'natural setting' (Nachmias and Nachmias, 1996). Direct observations limit contamination and subjectivity that could be present in an interview or focus group. Working norms and practices can be conveyed effectively to the researcher and this enables the capture of details that could be difficult to express verbally. Nachmias and Nachmias (1996) consider three areas while conducting observations. Behaviour can include both verbal and non-verbal forms of communication. Ekman (1957) suggests that non-verbal communication such as body language and facial expressions can transmit a great deal of information. Words, language, speech and gestures can all contribute as valuable data. Second, timing and recording need to be considered and where possible a time-scale should be pre-determined to minimise disruption to the individual's working practices. Records of all observations should also be made and stored. Records are important and will act as 'scientific proof' supporting any conclusions. Different apparatus such as video cameras and dictaphones can also be used to validate the data collected. In this instance using such devices would have been counterproductive as this research was conducted within a closed setting of a command and control room. Finally, the effect of inference must be acknowledged. This has a direct positive correlation with validity (Abrams, 2000). It must be ensured that observer inference is minimised to ensure maximum credibility, validity and reliability. There are three types of bias that are associated with the observational technique. Demand characteristics, referred to commonly as the Hawthorne effect, occurs when the respondent knows that they are being monitored and observed (Bailey, 2007). From this the respondent may react in a way in which he or she thinks the observer wants them to. There is little that can be done to negate or counteract this effect (Rosenthal and Rosnow, 1969). Revealing the research hypothesis can act to further multiply this effect. Second, experimenter bias occurs when the observer reveals his or her expectations to the respondent thus influencing the participant. Respondents can read the body language of the researcher and simple nodding can bias findings as participants react by answering as he or she expects the researcher may want them to. Rosenthal (1963) concluded following extensive research into observer bias that 8 of 12 observations were found to be biased. Finally, measurement artefacts originate in a set of parameters or scores. Respondents may give answers or perform in ways that are more 'favourable' to the observer if they are aware of the parameter based on which they are to be assessed (Nachmias and Nachmias, 1996).

> The ethnographer took for granted that the observations and records he made did not significantly disturb the behaviour of the people studied
>
> Filstead (1971: 237)

All researchers have a professional duty and a moral obligation to ensure that when conducting observational work, all of the above effects are minimised. This is done not only to maximise data validity but it also acts to ensure that the respondents are treated fairly. As previously mentioned, simply observing an individual may change their normal working habits. An observer will have no way of knowing whether they witness a true representation of the person under observation. This is similarly true in relation to interviews or questionnaires. There can often be discrepancies between a person's verbal expressions and their working behaviour (Nachmias and Nachmias, 1996). Having explored the associated positive and negative implications of utilising observational work within this study, ensuring use of varied techniques and adoption of the principles of triangulation was an essential methodological priority. To ensure that the data collected from observational work was verified, extensive field notes were also taken.

3.9 Field notes

Field notes are an essential instrument in conducting research, especially when engaged in observational research (Bailey, 1996). Research by its very nature can often be complex and from my experience, ideas and thoughts can frequently be stimulated while engaged in study. To effectively capture such thoughts, experiences and other data, field notes offer a sound option for researchers wishing to add depth to their findings. Attempting to remember details, however significant or insignificant, following a period of study can be problematic due to the frailties of the human mind. Attrition rates from memory to notes following research can be poor and consequently field notes offer the ability to ensure maximum contextual data is obtained and retained (Grey, 2009). Field notes throughout this study were particularly useful to summarise and to reflect on observations and interviews. Notes can be taken on any topic, including primary observations of people, behaviours, surroundings and conversations. Brief notes are also particularly useful for recording ideas and thoughts, and were used frequently to scribble flow charts of processes and system functions. Burgess (1984) highlights the importance of not limiting the scope of field notes referring to the importance of both primary observations and analytical and conceptual ideas. Field notes can encompass a wide range of collection techniques and are not restricted to paper notes. Sophisticated software, web-cams, audio devices and photographs can all be used to take notes in the field of research. Although field notes were used as part of the study, their use was limited. Notes in this sense were only used as an *aide mémoire*. While researching the police organisation, taking notes overtly within the natural setting can sometimes change the natural behaviour of respondents as they are conscious of the fact that they are being recorded in detail (McKernan, 1996). For this reason, brief notes were taken and, immediately following the study, more comprehensive notes were made on a word processor. Additionally, field notes can be distracting and time consuming to construct. Primarily, notes taken during the study were in the form of flow charts and key words representing themes where processes and ideas were formulated. While interviewing, I informed each respondent that notes may be taken and every effort was made not to hide the notebook. In my experience, this helped reassure respondents. In most cases and in particular in interviews, few notes were taken during the interviews. Immediately following its conclusion, extensive notes were drafted. In summary, clearly field notes have associated advantages and disadvantages that must be carefully evaluated. For this study, field notes complemented all the other data collection methods and acted to triangulate the process, increasing the validity and reliability of the findings by adding depth and contextualised meaning to the data. Another data collection technique used throughout this research was the questionnaire surveys.

3.10   Questionnaires

Questionnaires are a valuable method of data collection for this style of research (Scwab, 2005). They offer an 'impersonal' way of gathering bulk data to satisfy the quantitative demands of a study such as this. Achieving a high statistical significance by obtaining a relatively large number of completed surveys will make the research more robust and generalisable. However, there are some advantages and disadvantages to this approach that need to be carefully examined (Nachmias and Nachmias, 1996). Advantages to the use of questionnaires are considerable. Low cost must be a consideration for all research projects, especially small low budget projects where costs are paramount. Postal questionnaires are relatively easily constructed. Paper, printing, envelopes and postage are literally the only cost implications. Questionnaires can also reduce bias by eliminating error and offering a degree of respondent independence. Greater anonymity is another associated advantage, enabling the respondent to reply knowing their identity will remain secret. This is important when dealing with sensitive issues such as sexual offences, child issues and other similar crimes. This will enable all respondents to give considered answers following consultation if required, being especially useful in dealing with individuals when a specific answer is required, or when consultation and reflection is needed to fully answer the questions. The final advantage is accessibility. This enables researchers to contact any individual easily with relatively little cost. Questionnaires were used extensively within this research to provide a large body of qualitative and quantitative data. Large amounts of quantitative data can make the results more meaningful and more generalisable (Holloway, 1997). Specifically, both the public and police questionnaires were used to satisfy research objectives 1 and 2. Namely, the public survey was designed to ascertain the perceptions of the introduction of the knowledge management system (DMTU) including an examination of its impact on public perceptions and confidence. The police survey was similarly designed to ascertain individual police officers' opinions of the DMTU, thus examining any impact on the police organisation. Following the return of both the police and public surveys, SPSS or predictive analytics software was used to store and analyse the data. As with any data collection method, if there are advantages, inevitably there are also disadvantages to be considered (Foddy, 1993). Questionnaires will often limit the researcher to asking relatively straightforward questions. If the question being asked is too complicated, or cannot be answered without extensive consultation, then it is simply inappropriate for a questionnaire. In-depth probing questions in some cases may not be included for this reason. Similarly, questionnaires do not give the researcher a chance to probe, as there is often little scope for the researcher to pose follow-up questions following the initial response. Finally, it is not guaranteed that the questionnaire will be completed by the person to whom it is addressed. Controls over such factors are limited. Finally and inherently with questionnaires, the return rate is often low and there are many factors that can affect the response rate (Babbie, 2010). Chiu and Brennan (1990) suggest that a response rate between 10% and 30% is not uncommon. The factors affecting response rate are explored below in greater detail.

Factors affecting questionnaire response rate

It may be argued that the single greatest drawback to employing questionnaires is the respondents' failure to complete and return the form. Nachmias and Nachmias (1996) and Kirby et al. (2006) identify several factors that influence the return rate.

Sponsorship

Sponsorship can legitimise questionnaires. If the sponsor is respected and well known, it encourages respondents to complete and return the form. Fowler (1989) found that the US census on health reported a return rate of 95% primarily because it was government sponsored. Other postal questionnaires reported 5% return rates with no sponsorship. For this reason, a clear joint representation of both the university and the police service was included with the postal survey questionnaire.

Inducements to respond

Encouraging individuals to participate is another technique used by appealing for compliance and relying on goodwill (Bailey, 1989). The importance of the research was set out as part of an information sheet that was attached to the questionnaire. The information sheet included commentary on how important individual perceptions were on the delivery of policing services.

Format and mailing procedure

The overall image of the questionnaire is an important considera- tion. This will include letter type, spacing, paragraph, font, colour and other aesthetic considerations. Alreck and Settle (1985) note that using unusual colours and other techniques can have an impact on the response rate. All of the above were considered as part of the initial ques- tionnaire design. The design of the questionnaires was formatted to be legible, readable, concise and user-friendly.

Covering letter

An integral part of any survey. The covering letter should aim to briefly explain to the respondent the aims and objectives of the research. Bias or inducing the public into answering questions in a particular way should be avoided. The opportunity to thank, reassure and repeat the fact that data will remain confidential was also taken at this stage.

Type of mailing

The inclusion of a pre-addressed and pre-paid envelope will usually increase the return rate. Few respondents will readily pay for an enve- lope and stamp. All postal questionnaires sent out were accompanied by a pre-paid envelope to ensure a higher response rate and avoid the respondent having to incur any out-of-pocket expenses.

Timing of mailing

The time of the year is a crucial consideration. Holiday periods such as Christmas or Easter will clearly reduce the return rate. This is especially true for the internal police survey and consideration around timing was crucial. It appears that more staff take leave during school half-terms when child care is more problematic.

Total Design Method (TDM)

Both Rossi et al. (1983) and Nederhot (1988) conclude that there are two main issues for design: questionnaire construction and survey implementation. Additional considerations include following up through telephone calls or post cards. E-mail has partially revolutionised surveys, eliminating the cost of printing, ink and postage, with the additional advantage of making the follow-up process quicker, more economical and less intrusive.

Respondents

Selecting respondents to increase the return rate is difficult and often beyond the control of the researcher. If such respondent characteristics are available that may promote the return of the questionnaire, then that must be considered.

Questionnaire pilot and survey

A major part of the data collection for this study was assembled using a questionnaire survey. The introduction of the DMTU and its effects were primarily measured using this data collection technique. The police and the public were surveyed using a questionnaire designed to measure specific issues, such as the perceptions of a unit designed to conduct telephone investigations, assessments of the public confidence and satisfaction, through to a measures of police attitudes. Essential to the success of any questionnaire is its ability to be readily understood. Questionnaires take time to develop and there is certainly a science behind their construction (Brace, 2008). Clear objectives must be formalised prior to writing questions at the design stage and the questionnaire must reflect the data being sought for the research. Following this, the types of questions to be included were evaluated to ensure there was a balance between open-ended and closed questions in order to enable the respondent to give comprehensive and thoughtful responses. Measurement scales such as Likert were considered and used where appropriate. Branding to promote professionalism and authenticity was also considered, along with aesthetical considerations and overall layout. A time-consuming process following the design stage must also be factored in (Czaja and Blair, 2005). This included an assessment of how the questionnaire would be disseminated, collected and analysed using different software. Testing, amending and re-testing are required frequently at each stage of development. To do this, a pilot survey for the public survey was undertaken within the university department, utilising students who were undertaking a module on questionnaire design.

The students ($n = 61$) were asked at the end of the module to complete and appraise the actual questionnaire as to its layout, design, bias and overall user friendliness. From this, changes were made where appropriate and the survey was ultimately disseminated throughout the two basic command units within the police jurisdictions. Initially, it was felt that the initial information sheet was too long. Therefore, the main points were condensed to fill one page, thus ensuring each respondent could quickly and easily read and understand the basic information. To compensate for removing some information while condensing the documents, the information sheet highlighted my contact details so that any respondent wishing to receive additional information regarding specific issues could do so by e-mail or telephone. Interestingly, only one respondent felt the need to contact me during the data collection period. Following consultation, it was felt that a standard university faculty consent form should be used as it had been operationally utilised and tested. As a result, a consent form was obtained as a guide to follow and a form was designed using basic principles. As for the public questionnaire, one consideration proposed by the reviewers was to include a third gender field to cover those who chose not classify themselves as male or female. Having considered this point carefully, I decided on this occasion not to incorporate this into the design of the questionnaire. Additionally, feedback revealed that the reviewers felt that increasing the respondent's ability to include up to three previous experiences of crime would benefit the data. Although this had already been considered, I was not sure if this would over-complicate and therefore compromise the design of the questionnaire. Having received the feedback, the issue of three fields/boxes for respondents to include previous experiences of crime was implemented. This significantly increased the 'richness' of the data as a brief history of past experiences could be examined at the analysis stage of the study. Finally, the inclusion of the question used as part of assessing public opinion about the police and its statutory partners was included. Referred to as the Public Service Agreement 23 (PSA 23), this question has been robustly tested and widely utilised in surveys across England and Wales. Until abolished by the coalition government, this key performance indicator was used to determine police performance. For this reason, it was felt that its inclusion as part of this questionnaire would be beneficial as results from this survey could then be compared with a number of other similar data sets. The police questionnaire had been used previously as part of a small study into a different police organisation. Minor revisions were made to ensure that the questionnaire was 'area specific' and was piloted within the University by academic staff. Question 5 relating to length of service was amended to enable respondents who had less than one year's service to indicate this. The final question in this questionnaire was included intentionally to stimulate discussion and give the respondents a feeling of inclusion and consultation. Many respondents took the opportunity to give their perceptions, feelings and comments concerning the DMTU. The success of ensuring statistical significance and generalisability of any questionnaire survey underpins the integrity of the sampling strategy.

3.11 Sampling

A key element of any research entails using data collection techniques such as interviewing, observation, surveys or questionnaires. Sampling key police and civilian staff was essential to enable the aims and objectives of the research to be met. It would be unrealistic and illogical to consider researching all potential respondents. This would prove to be both time consuming and extremely expensive. Indeed, it is important to note that this is not always the case, as some research can include all eligible respondents into the study, for example micro-research on a small ward in a hospital. Throughout this research, this approach was not feasible. To overcome this problem, a wide range of different sampling techniques could be used to ensure a representative sample of the wider target population.

> looseness-1Sampling provides a means of gaining information about the population without the need to examine the population in its entirety
>
> Statistical and Technical Team (1992: 4)

My project focussed on two primary sets of respondents: the police and the public.

The police

It was necessary to construct a sampling frame, consisting of a number of police officers within the police; this is referred to as the total population. This sampling frame consisted of serving police officers within the police service researched, not including officers beyond the rank of inspector, special constables, PCSOs or other civilian support staff. The sample frame contained a list of some 753 eligible respondents within the police. Police officers were not included if they were on long-term sick leave, on attachment with other units/agencies or worked in back office functions. Primarily, this sampling frame consisted of front-line police officers, not senior officers or administrative officers working in business support, HR, procurement units or other similar functions. As the research consisted of both a qualitative and quantitative approach, it is recognised that there will be a need for a larger sample size for the quantitative element of the research to be robust. Sampling size is an important element in research and much thought was given to decide this crucial detail. The sampling units known as subsets needed to be as representative of the total population as possible (McBurney and White, 2009). The sample size therefore should be neither too large nor too small. Many researchers have attempted to apply a simple working percentage, such as 5%. However, Nachmias and Nachmias (1996) disagree, stating that sampling size should depend on the degree of accuracy required of the data. An estimated figure of 75–100 completed questionnaires for both the police and the public was sought to ensure that both statistical significance and relevance could be attained. With any postal survey, an average response rate of between 20% and 30% rate can usually be anticipated.

Sampling method

Stratifying the sample best fits this research for many reasons (Brown and Dowling, 1998). The sampling frame provided identification numbers, rank, sex and department of police staff eligible within the criteria specified. From this, a randomised stratified sample was taken. This enabled me to ensure that the sample was representative of the target population by rank. No names or personal addresses were needed for the purposes of this research, in accordance with the Data Protection Act. The advantage of this sampling method is that the sample is accurate, representative and error should be minimised. This approach does, however, have drawbacks. Problems arise when frames are incomplete or contain erroneous data. This can distort the representativeness of the sample (Nachmias and Nachmias, 1996). To ensure that the sample obtained is as accurate a representation as possible, the researcher needs to be aware of the population, the sampling design and the size of the sample (Selltiz, 1981). In addition, this method can require many complex calculations, needing cross-referencing and cross-tabulation of various factors, increasing the risk of computational error.

Table 3.1 illustrates the stratified sample frame utilised as part of the study.

Table 3.1 Stratified sample by rank of police officers

Rank	Number	Percentage of service	Number of officers surveyed
Patrol Officers	323	43	129
Patrol Sergeants	96	13	38
Neighbourhood Officers	69	9	27
Neighbourhood Sergeants	18	2	7
Inspectors	27	4	11
Detective Constables	166	22	66
Detective Sergeants	43	6	18
Detective Inspectors	11	1	4
Total	753	100	300

The public

Respondents for the public survey were selected by using a stratified random selection process according to the gender of respondents selected from two different Basic Command Units or BCUs within the police jurisdiction. The sampling used was the electoral register and a computer-generated random list of numbers made the selection process (Teddie and Tashakkori, 2009). There are some disadvantages to using the electoral register and it is important that these are considered. Often, young people, those who are poor, mobile, sick, mentally ill and homeless, are statistically less likely to be included in the register (Mann, 2003). Additionally, large data sets can contain erroneous data. Representativeness was also a major consideration throughout the entire sampling procedure and steps were taken to ensure this. Positively, the electoral register enabled me to have access to large stores of data containing auxiliary information such as gender, names and addresses that proved invaluable. This approach allowed me to obtain respondent data, which was relatively time and cost effective, enabling some 800 questionnaires to be distributed through the two BCUs. The first task prior to posting the surveys was to establish some additional demographic information regarding the whole area. Following the analysis of census data, the percentage of males and females was calculated; the findings are shown in Table 3.2.

The response rate

The response rates for both questionnaires were reasonably high, reaching the anticipated 20%–30% range. The police questionnaire provided a response rate of 30% ($n = 90$) and the public questionnaire recorded

Table 3.2 Demographic profile

Basic command unit names	Total population	Total males	Total females
Area 1	69,097	33,497	35,600
Area 2	172,398	84,360	88,038
Area 3	88,445	43,395	45,050
Area 4	140,714	68,474	72,240
Area 5	91,097	44,263	46,834
Area 6	561,751	273,989	287,762
	Percentage of total population	**48.77**	**51.23**

Stats Wales (2009).

a response rate of 22% ($n = 173$). As engagement and collaboration has been encouraged between both the police and public through initiatives such as PACT meetings, the public, or at least some members of the public were clearly interested in what the police are doing, thus sponsoring the high response rate. Similarly, the DMTU has unquestionably changed the ways in which the police conduct their daily activities; this could explain the reason why police officers were keen to engage with the postal questionnaire. In keeping with the principles of triangulation, qualitative interviewing was used as an integral part of the data collection techniques.

3.12 Interviewing

Qualitative interviewing

Interviewing was another approach used to obtain data for the study (Kvale, 1996). Within this data collection method, there are different forms of interview structures.

Structured interviewing

Structured interviewing, also known as schedule-structured interviewing, is the most rigid style of interviewing, which would require a pre-planned format (Wengraf, 2001). The questions asked must remain precisely the same for each respondent. This style allows no scope for expansion or deviation from the interview guide. This style is particularly useful to ensure consistency and equality by keeping each question identical. Richardson et al. (1965) note that changing vocabulary or intonation can distort meaning, thus influencing the response.

Semi-structured interviewing

A semi-structured approach is less structured than the previous style. It allows the researcher to ask a range of different questions related to a particular topic. These may be contained in an 'interview guide' (Bryman, 2004). In general, all questions asked should be contained within this guide. This allows the researcher a degree of flexibility as questions can be asked according to responses received. It is for this reason that an interview schedule was designed and it was decided that a semi-structured approach would best fit this research.

Flexible interviewing

Finally, flexible scheduling, also known as unstructured or non-directive interviewing, is the most flexible format of all interviewing types. The researcher may use an *'aide mémoire'* as a brief but other than this no more guidance would be needed (Bryman, 2004). This style encourages the respondent to give long and comprehensive answers with little or no prompting from the researcher. This style is often used to obtain opinions or feelings where the answers are subjective and individual.

Overall, Nachmias and Nachmias (1996) consider that there are several advantages and disadvantages to interviewing. Interviewing offers the researcher a degree of flexibility as the interviewer can decide on the style of interview to best extract the appropriate information from the respondent. This can offer the researcher control, steering the interview in a particular direction. In addition, this approach often ensures a far higher response rate than that can be obtained using a questionnaire. Accompanied by the fact that a higher response rate can be obtained, interviewing can offer the potential for obtaining greater amounts of detailed information and data. As previously noted, there are always disadvantages to consider. Cost is perhaps an issue for all researchers and interviewing can in certain circumstances have higher costs in comparison with a postal questionnaire. This is due in part to travelling expenses and other costs. Bias is another factor to be considered as the interviewer can influence responses. Finally offering any degree of anonymity is particularly difficult as the respondent in most circumstances will come face to face with the researcher. Due to the nature of the research, using any digital device to record interviews would, in my experience and judgement, have been counterproductive. Recording police officers through such devices would simply act to bias the findings as officers rarely speak frankly and candidly knowing they are being recorded. As a result, it was decided that a combination of brief paper notes and mental notes was the best way to capture data from interviews. Writing long abstracts as the respondent is talking is at best off-putting and can, in some instances, disrupt the flow of the interview. Short words and reminders seemed to reassure the respondent and also help to focus the interviews. In addition to short sentences, contextual information was also recorded, e.g. time, location and date, in order to add detail to the data collected. The flexibility and freedom offered by field notes complemented the semi-structured interview approach (Foster, 1996). Similar to interviewing, focus groups were also considered as part of the data collection techniques.

3.13   Focus groups

Despite consideration, this approach was not used as part of the study. In part, this method was not utilised as it offered me little, if any, control over the direction of the interaction, and that could potentially generate unfocussed discussion. Focus groups often encourage a small number of speakers, allowing the dominant members to control the discussions, leaving the other quieter individuals relatively mute and unrepresented (Morgan, 1997). This approach consists of a group of people discussing a wide range of pre-determined topics. Positively, however, focus groups are used often to survey organisations where the workforce is large (Hakim, 1987). This method is often relatively cheap and saves time (Bryman, 2004). By involving a group of people, individuals may be happier to discuss topics, feeling that there is safety in numbers. Groups on occasion can promote and encourage discussion. Although this method offered some real advantages, it was felt that interviewing, observational work and postal surveys offered a range of practical advantages to obtain the data required. Postal surveys in particular offered a way of obtaining large quantities of both qualitative and quantitative data. Reinforced by interviews and observational data, it was decided that focus groups in this study were not needed as one of the data collection instruments. Secondary data and official records can often play a vital role in research of this nature.

3.14   Secondary analysis and official archives

Secondary data, archives and official statistics are unquestionably an integral part of any police organisation and as a consequence should be analysed thoroughly. Types of secondary data may include previous research, internal or external reports, press statements, including government or Home Office publications. This literature is invaluable in as much as it allows the researcher to understand in detail the inner workings of an organisation, with an in-depth evaluation and knowledge of existing research. Analysis of secondary data can allow the researcher to identify unrepresented areas and any limitations within the specific field of research. Dale et al. (1988) record that there are several advantages to using secondary sources while conducting research. First, cost and time. At a fraction of the expense and time of conducting research, studies that have already been conducted and secondary analysis can be accessed. Data quality can be of a high standard, particularly if the research has been carried out by the government and is often accessible to the public. Finally, by utilising secondary data the researcher can have more time for data generation and analysis. This stage of the research is often condensed due to time constraints. Not dissimilar to every other research method evaluated so far, secondary data analysis also has disadvantages as identified by Bryman (2004). Lack of familiarity with data, especially complex data, is one difficulty faced by researchers. Both unfamiliar terminology and vast quantities of data relate to this. Another drawback is that the researcher has no control over either the data collection or content. There is often no way to validate the data and the methods used to collect it. The data may be flawed, containing problems such as bias or poor design. The final issue to be identified is access. Data may be difficult to locate, requiring the researcher to look through hundreds, sometimes thousands, of records to obtain relevant data and information. This approach may not prove economic, time effective, appropriate or straightforward.

Official records and statistics

Official records consist of government publications: judicial publications the Crime Survey for England and Wales and all of these are derived from public sources such as the police and the NHS. For this research, internal police documents, combined with Home Office publications, were analysed. Such documents offered me data otherwise unavailable and at a fraction of the cost and time. Time and money could be saved, while gaining a wealth of data in a relatively short amount of time. It must be remembered, however, that publications can often be biased. Objectivity of the findings must be considered before attaching weight to any reports (Bryman, 2004). In using crime statistics, Bryman (2004) notes that figures can be manipulated. The police and the government in publishing statistics can use the data to highlight or mask particular problems. This can be done by directing police officers to target a particular crime such as drug offences and not record others such as antisocial behaviour. In turn, this will produce data relating to drug offences, showing drug offences to be on the rise and incidents of antisocial behaviour to be in decline.

3.15   Reflection

Reflection on the journey of research is essential to reinforce and reaffirm experiences, beliefs and understandings encountered during the expedition of field research. From the initial proposal of this project through the completion and submission stages of the research, the journey had been difficult, challenging, rewarding, enjoyable and illuminating. This combination of feelings experienced over the years of research, unquestionably added to the excitement, creating a unique working experience. Building a working relationship with the police and getting to know key individuals was one of the most difficult aspects of this research. As explained previously, the unique working culture in which the police exist and operate created exceptional complications that needed to be overcome. Building networks and contacts within the organisation was initially painstakingly slow and required both patience and skill. Enabling police officers and other staff to feel comfortable with the research and my presence required an inordinate investment of time. The ever-present danger of losing scientific objectiveness and 'going native' was always a consideration. As to the question of 'did I go native?', then if feeling some empathy with individuals or understanding concerns would constitute 'going native', then the answer would be a tentative 'yes'. Having said this, gauging the extent of 'going native' is particularly complex. There were times when I would agree or disagree with certain statements and procedures. For this reason, it is my sense that judgements were always based on scientific facts. Bias and objectivity were always going to be major issues throughout this research. Remaining aware and conscious of the potential pitfalls and dangers of losing scientific objectivity almost certainly made evaluating and responding to situations much easier. In addition to building a network of contacts, the internal layout and dynamics of the police needed to be mapped. By this I mean the physical layout of the organisation including jurisdiction boundaries and buildings. A working knowledge of the organisation with a clear idea of how the organisation worked, key 'movers and shakers' who could get things done and some idea of internal political struggles undeniably assisted in ensuring that the research could progress expeditiously. Another obstacle that required some thought was 'informed consent'. Obtaining informed consent and balancing this against the need to assure a favourable response rate posed a difficult dilemma at the data collection stage of this study. Although having consulted the University's Ethics Committee, there was no actual requirement to ask respondents to complete a consent form as part of the questionnaire survey. Completion would have been sufficient as this would have demonstrated that respondents wished to participate in the research. Having considered this carefully, a decision was taken to include a consent form along with the questionnaire. This decision was taken primarily in the light of the sensitive nature of the questionnaire as respondents were asked about previous crime experiences. This decision was not taken lightly and, in truth, I changed position on this issue, opting to begin by excluding a consent form, but changing this prior to mailing. Having mailed the questionnaire survey to the police and the public, the time waiting for replies was the most anxious of the entire research process. It was at this stage that a range of emotions were felt, being almost halfway through the journey and success depended on the quality and quantity of the replies. Although a pilot questionnaire survey had been successful, in reality, this did little to alleviate the feeling of anxiety and worry. So much of this particular research work depended on the questionnaire. The successful end of the data collection stage offered relief and the response rate was more than adequate. Although the data collection stage had been competed relatively successfully, there still remained much work to be completed and a sense of success was short-lived and only temporary. In summary, the whole process of this research was both physically and mentally challenging. Having said this, the feelings of exhilaration, anticipation and elation certainly compensated for this and made the work worthwhile. The toxic mix of emotions encountered from beginning to end combined to make this an unforgettable and rich experience.

3.16 Conclusion

Research constantly generates an unlimited number of scenarios, issues and difficulties. Foremost for this research is the relationship between the police organisation and the academic world. This is, in part, built on fear and suspicion, as identified by Reiner (2000) when he makes reference to a cultural protective shield engulfing the entire police organisation, thus preventing any outsider from seeing the internal workings of the organisation. This research encountered some cultural resistance through direct observations and encounters. The somewhat nebulous subject of occupational culture at the 'coal face' accompanied by the physical manifestations of its existence was fascinating and enlightening. There appears to be almost a 'love/hate' relationship between some members of the two institutions. This relationship would, in my opinion, disintegrate and erode if interest and criticism from political parties, the public and the media were not so strong. Politically, the police and policing is now more than ever seen as a party political issue and frequently used as a 'political football' (BBC, 2010). The objective of this research was to inform policy at a local and national level, disseminate good practice and to ultimately ensure long-term sustainability through efficiency, effectiveness and inevitably economic viability.

Lessons learned from this research

1. Building a working relationship between the police organisation and the academic world was essential during this research. This will help with the cultural protective shield encompassing the entire police organisation, thus preventing any outsider from seeing the internal workings of the organisation.
2. Objectivity is difficult to maintain in fieldwork, even as an outsider/outsider.
3. Access and its associated difficulties relating to bias and objectivity will bring along its own complications and apprehensions.
4. When dealing with community, it is difficult to obtain full representativeness of that community, e.g. young people's views.
5. Going native and losing scientific objectivity is always a concern. Putting in place rituals and processes such as note taking and debriefing sessions all help to maintain a professional relationship.
6. The electoral register has been criticised for its lack of representativeness. This was a concern identified early on and was carefully balanced in terms of its advantages and associated disadvantages.
7. Getting to know officers and gatekeepers along with being granted full access to an organisation such as the police is essential to the success of any research.

References

Abrams, B. (2000) *The Observational Research Handbook: Understanding How Consumers Live with Your Project*, Chicago: NTC Business Books.

Alreck, P. and Settle, R. (1985) *The Survey Research Handbook*, Homewood: Irwin.

American Psychological Association. (1982) *Ethical Principles in the Conduct of Research with Human Participants*, Washington D.C.: American Psychological Association.

Angrosion, M. (2007) *Doing Ethnography and Observational Research*, London: Sage.

Babbie, E. (2004) *The Practice of Social Research* (10th ed.), Belmont, USA: Wadsworth Thomson Learning.

Babbie, E. (2010) *The Practice of Social Research* (12th ed.), Belmont: Wadsworth, Engage Learning.

Bailey, C. (1996) *A Guide to Field Research*, Thousand Oaks, CA: Pine Forge Press.

Bailey, K. (1989) *Methods of Social Research*, New York: Free Press.

Bailey, K. (2007) *Methods of Social Research* (4th ed.), New York: Simon and Schuster.

BBC. (2010) *Sir Ian Blair Outlines His Blueprint for Future Policing*. Available at: http://news.bbc.co.uk/1/hi/programmes/newsnight/8583713.stm [Accessed 20 January 2014].

Becker, P. (1998) 'Making Inclusive Communities: Congregations and the "Problem" of Race', *Social Problems*, 45(4): 451–472.

Bell, C. (1969) 'A Note on Participant Observations', *Sociology*, 3: 417–418.

Best, J. (2003) *Research in Higher Education*, Welwyn Garden City: Person Higher Education.

Brace, I. (2008) *Questionnaire Design: How to Plan, Structure and Write Survey Material for Efficient Market Research* (2nd ed.), London: Kogan Page Publishers.

Brown, J. (1996) 'Police Research: Some Critical Issues', in Leishman, B., Loverday, B. and Savage, S. (Eds) *Core Issues in Policing*, London: Longman, 179–190.

Brown, A. and Dowling, P. (1998) *Doing Research/Reading Research: A Mode of Interrogation for education*, London: Flamer Press.

Bryman, A. (2004) *Social Research Methods* (2nd ed.), Oxford: Oxford University Press.

Bryman, A. (2008) *Social Research Methods* (3rd ed.), Oxford: Oxford University Press.

Burgess, G. (1984) *In the Field: An Introduction to Filed Research*, London: Allen & Unwin.

Chiu, I. and Brennan, M. (1990) 'The Effectiveness of Some Techniques for Improving Mail Survey Response Rates: A Meta-analysis', *Marketing Bulletin*, 3(1): 13–18.

Czaja, R. and Blair, J. (2005) *Designing Surveys: A Guide to Decisions and Processes*, California: Sage.

Dale, A., Arbor, S. and Proctor, M. (1988) *Doing Secondary Analysis*, London: Urwin Hyman Ltd.

Denzin, N. (1989) *The Research Act: A Theoretical Introduction to Sociological Methods* (3rd ed.), Prentice Hall: Englewood Cliffs.

Dickson-Swift, V., James, E. and Liamputtong, P. (2008) *Undertaking Sensitive Research in the Health and Social Sciences*, New York: Cambridge University Press.

Diener, E. and Crandall, R. (1978) *Ethics in Social and Behavioural Research*, Chicago: University of Chicago Press.

Draper, G. (2001) 'Being Evaluated: A Practitioner's View', *Children and Society*, (15): 46–52.

Ekman, P. (1957) 'A Methodological Discussion on Non-Verbal Communication', *Journal of Psychology*, 43: 14.

Emanuel, E., Wendler, D. and Grady, C. (2000) 'What Makes Clinical Research Ethical?' *Journal of the American Medical Association*, 283(20): 2701–2711.

Filstead, W. (1971) *Qualitative Methodology*, Chicago: Markham Publishing Company.

Flick, U. (1998) *An Introduction to Qualitative Research*, London: Sage.

Foddy, W. (1993) *Constructing Questions for Interviews and Questionnaires: Theory and Practice in Social Research*, Cambridge: Cambridge University Press.

Foster, P. (1996) *Observing Schools: A Methodological Approach*, London: Paul Chapman Publishing Ltd.

Fountain, J. (1993) 'Dealing with Data, in Interpreting the Field: Accounts of Ethnography', *Oxford, Clarendon Press*, 45(5): 375–385.

Fowler, F. (1989) *Survey Research Methods*, Newbury Park, CA: Sage.

Freund, J. (1974) *Modern Elementary Statistics* (4th ed.), New Jersey: Prentice Hall International.

Grey, D. (2009) *Doing Research in the Real World* (2nd ed.), London: Sage.

Guba, E. and Lincoln, Y. (1989) *Fourth Generation Evaluation*, Newbury Park, CA: Sage.

Hakim, C. (1987) *Research Design: Strategies and Choices in the Design of Social Research*, London: Routledge.

Hammersley, M. (1993) *Social Research: Philosophy, Politics and Practice*, London: Sage.

Hammersley, M. and Atkinson, P. (1995) *Ethnography: Principles in Practice* (2nd ed.), London: Routledge.

Her Majesty's Inspectorate for the Constabulary. (2010) *HMIC Response to Consultation on Value for Money Profiles*. Available at: http://www.hmic.gov.uk/SiteCollectionDocuments/Consultations/CTN_VFM_20100307.pdf [Accessed 20 January 2014].

Hobbs, D. (1988) *Doing the Business: Entrepreneurship, Detectives and the Working Class in the East End of London*, New York: Oxford University Press.

Holdaway, S. (1983) *Inside the British Police: A Force at Work*, Oxford: Basil Blackwell Publisher Limited.

Holdaway, S. (1992) *Crime and Deviance*, Issues in Sociology, London: Nelson.

Holloway, I. (1997) *Basic Concepts for Qualitative Research*, Oxford: Blackwell Science Ltd.

Holmes, L. (2004) *Guidance for Ensuring Confidentiality and the Protection of Data, Understanding Research for Social Policy and Practice: Themes, Methods and Approaches*, Bristol, Policy Press.

Home Office. (1998) *Data Protection Act 1998*, London: Stationery Office.

Home Office. (2000) *The Human Rights Act 2000*, London: Stationery Office.

Ianni, E. and Ianni, F. (1983) *Two Cultures of Policing: Street Cop Management Cop*, United States: Transition Publishers.

Jupp, V., Davies, P. and Francis, P. (2000) *Doing Criminological Research*, London: Sage.

Kimmel, A. (1988) *Ethics and Values in Applied Social Research*, London: Sage.

Kirby, S., Greaves, L. and Reid, C. (2006) *Experience Research Social Change: Methods Beyond the Mainstream* (2nd ed.), Peterborough: Broadview Press.

Kirk, J. and Miller, L. (1986) *Reliability and Validity in Qualitative Research*, California: Sage.

Kvale, S. (1996) *Interviews: An Introduction to Qualitative Interviewing*, California: Sage.

Mann, C. (2003) 'Observational Research Methods, Research Design 11: Cohort, Cross sectional and Control Studies', *Emergency Medicine Journal*, 20: 54–60.

McBurney, D. and White, T. (2009) *Research Methods* (8th ed.), Belmont: Wadsworth.

McKernan, J. (1996) *Curriculum Action Research: A Handbook of Methods and Resources for the Reflective Practitioner* (2nd ed.), Oxford: Kogan Page Limited.

Mcneill, P. and Chapman, S. (2006) *Research Methods* (3rd ed.), Abingdon: Routledge.

Moore, D. (1979) *Statistics: Concepts and Controversies*, San Francisco, W.H. Freeman and Company

Morgan, D. (1997) *Focus Groups as Qualitative Research* (2nd ed.), California: Sage.

Nachmias, C. and Nachmias, D. (1996) *Research Methods in the Social Sciences* (5th ed.), London: St. Martin's Press, Inc.

Nederhot, A. (1988) 'Effects of Final Telephone Reminder and Questionnaire Cover Design in Mail Survey', *Social Sciences Research*, 17: 353–361.

Noaks, L. and Wincup, E. (2004) *Criminological Research, Understanding Qualitative Methods*, London: Sage.

Page, A. (2007) 'Behind the Blue Line: Investigating Police Officers Attitudes Toward Rape', *Journal of Police and Criminal Psychology*, 22(1): 22–32.

Picou, S. (1996) 'Sociology and Compelled Disclosure, Protecting Respondents Confidentiality', *Sociological Spectrum*, 16(3): 207–238.

Punch, M. (1979) *Policing the Inner City: A Study of Amsterdam's Warmoesstraat*, London: Macmillan, 1–18.

Punch, M. (1985) *Conduct Unbecoming: The Social Construction of Police Deviance and Control*, USA: Tavistock Publications Ltd.

Reaser, J., Hartsock, S. and Hoehn, A. (1975) 'A Test of the Forced Alternative Random Response Questionnaire Technique, Arlington,' *Human Resources Research Organization*: 75–9.

Reason, P. and Bradbury, H. (2001) *Handbook of Action Research: Participative Inquiry & Practice*, London: Sage.

Reiner, R. (2000) *The Politics of the Police* (3rd ed.), London: Oxford University Press.

Reiner, R. (2010) *The Politics of the Police*, (4th ed.), London, Oxford University Press

Reynolds, P. (1979) *Ethical Dilemmas and Social Science Research*, San-Francisco: Jossey-Bliss.

Richardson, S., Dohrenwend, B. and Klein, D. (1965) *Interviewing: It's Forms and Functions*, New York: Basic Books.

Rosenthal, R. and Rosnow, R. (1969) *Artefact in Behaviour Research*, Orlando, FL: Academic Press.

Rosenthal, R. (1963) 'The Effects of Early Data Returns on Data Subsequently Obtained by Outcome-Biases Experiments', *Sociometry*, 26 (4): 487–498.

Rossi, P., Wright, J. and Anderson, A. (1983) *Handbook of Survey Research*, Orlando, FL, Academic Press.

Rowntree, D. (1981) *Statistics without Tears: A Primer for Non-Mathematicians*, London: Penguin Books.

Sarantakos, S. (2005) *Social Research* (3rd ed.), Hampshire: Palgrave MacMillan.

Saunders, M., Lewis, P. and Thornhill, A. (2009) *Research Method for Business Students* (5th ed.), Harlow: Pearson Education Limited.

Scwab, D. (2005) *Research Methods for Organisational Studies* (2nd ed.), New Jersey: Lawrence Erlbaum Associates Inc Publishers.

Selltiz, C. (1981) *Research Methods in Social Relations* (4th ed.), New York: Reiner and Winston Holt.

Shaw, I. (2003) 'Ethics in Qualitative Research and Evaluation', *British Journal of Social Work*, 33: 107–120.

Silverman, D. (1985) *Qualitative Methodology and Sociology*, Aldershot: Gower.

Statistical and Technical Team. (1992) *A Practice Guide to Sampling*, London: National Audit Office.

Stats Wales. (2009) *Small Area Population and Local Authority Population Data*. Available at: http://www.statswales.wales.gov.uk/ReportFolders/reportFolders.aspx [Accessed 20 January 2014].

Stoecker, R. (2005) *Research Methods for Community Change: A Project Based Approach*, London: Sage.

Teddie, C. and Tashakkori, A. (2009) *Foundations of Mixed Methods Research, Integrating Quantitative and Qualitative Approaches in the Social and Behavioural Sciences*, California: Sage.

Trochim, W. (2010) *Evaluation Research*. Available at: http://www.socialresearch methods.net/kb/evaluation.php [Accessed 20 January 2014].

Vaus, D. (2002) *Surveys in Social Research* (5th ed.), Abingdon: Routledge.

Wengraf, T. (2001) *Qualitative Research Interviewing*, London: Sage.

Westin, A. (1968) *Privacy and Freedom*, New York: Atheneum.

4
Research Methodology, Methods and Design

Garry Thomas

Research methods involved

1. Quantitative

Self-completion questionnaire surveys and secondary data statistical analysis

2. Qualitative

Semi-structured interviews and unstructured covert participant observations

About this research

The main aim of this research is to explore and describe if community intelligence has an impact on local neighbourhood policing. The research questions the extent to which community intelligence impacts on local neighbourhood policing, within the context of the National Intelligence Model (NIM) and considers a number of other associated objectives, including:

1. What do the police consider to be local or neighbourhood policing?
2. How do the police engage with the diverse communities within their area?
3. What systems do the police have in place in relation to the processing of community intelligence?
4. What use is made of community intelligence, particularly in solving community problems?

5. Is community intelligence used to support or direct neighbourhood policing?
6. How can the use of community intelligence be improved to assist in the delivery of policing.

The unstructured covert participant observations component of this research was conducted between 2005 and 2010, while the self-completion questionnaire surveys, secondary data statistical analysis and semi-structured interviews elements of this research were conducted between 2011 and 2013.

4.1   Rationale for using a mixed methods research methodology

The mixed methods research methodology approach will adopt research methods from both the quantitative and qualitative methodologies, such as self-completion questionnaire surveys, semi-structured interviews, unstructured covert participant observations and secondary data analysis to address the research question, aim and objectives. The main rationale behind using a mixed methods research methodology is that of *Triangulation, Offset, Completeness* and *Enhancement*, but will also include elements of *Different research questions, Explanation, Credibility, Context, Illustration, Utility* and *Diversity of views* (Bryman, 2006: 105–107). As Webb et al. (1966: 3) suggest, 'Once a proposition has been confirmed by two or more independent measurement processes, the uncertainty of its interpretation is greatly reduced'. Citing the work of Webb et al. (1966), Denzin (2009: 26) concludes that 'no single method will ever permit an investigator to develop causal propositions free of rival interpretations'. Therefore, this research will use a mixed methods research methodology, which utilises a triangulation design incorporating a multilevel convergence model (Creswell and Plano Clark, 2007: 63–64).

The research methods used as part of this mixed methods research methodology will now be discussed in more detail below.

4.2   Research methods

With the limited resources available to me, I decided to focus on the four Basic Command Units (BCUs) within the police force area being studied, which will be referred to as 'A', 'B', 'C' and 'D' BCUs. However, due to logistical, time and financial constraints, it was impracticable to include the whole population of the police area in the sample for the collection of primary data. The main aim of this research is to explore and describe, if community intelligence has an impact on neighbourhood policing. Therefore, samples were drawn from police staff involved in local neighbourhood policing and the management of intelligence. A sample size of 414 local neighbourhood policing staff and a population of 60 intelligence managers were used in this research. Sampling methods and sizes will be discussed in more detail below.

Webb et al. (1966) argue that all research methods are subject to bias and weakness, and thus methods should be supplemented by other methods that test the same variables.

> No research method is without bias. Interviews and questionnaires must be supplemented by methods testing the same social science variables but having different methodological weaknesses.
>
> (Webb et al., 1966: 1)

By utilising a mixed methods approach, it is anticipated that any biases or weaknesses in individual quantitative and qualitative methods will be significantly reduced. Diesing (1971: 5) suggests that there is such a great variety of combinations of research methods in use that 'survey research and participant observation can now be seen as two ends of a continuum rather than as two distinct kinds of methods'. Grix (2002: 180), on the other hand, argues that 'Methods themselves should be seen as *free from ontological and epistemological assumptions,* and the choice of which to use should be guided by research questions'.

Having considered the aim and objectives of this research, how research on policing has previously been undertaken, research strategies, theoretical perspectives and research methodologies, a mixed methods research methodology, utilising a combination of quantitative and qualitative research methods, was used to investigate the research question. These methods included the use of primary data from postal survey self-completion questionnaires, semi-structured interviews and unstructured covert participant observations, and secondary data from archived research documents. It must also be noted that the choice of research methods was influenced by the fact that this research was undertaken by a single researcher, who was self-funded and thus subject to personal financial constraints.

Due to the large sample sizes in this research, a postal survey involving a self-completion questionnaire was considered to be the most appropriate research instrument for obtaining a large amount of data from the sample group across the four BCUs within a relatively short period of time (Neuman, 2000: 247; Mertens, 2005: 167). Other methods of surveying such as the online web-based survey questionnaires (Mertens, 2005: 205–206; Bryman, 2012: 216–217, 670–678), the telephone survey questionnaire (Newell, 1993: 97–98; Neuman, 2000: 272; Mertens, 2005: 198–199; Bryman, 2012: 214–215) and the interview schedule questionnaire (Neuman, 2000: 272–273; Bryman, 2012: 210) were not considered appropriate for this research, due to logistical, time and financial constraints (Neuman, 2000: 272–274). The quantitative and qualitative data obtained from this survey would also act to corroborate other qualitative data obtained from interviews and observational studies.

Semi-structured face-to-face interviews were considered to be the most appropriate means of interview for obtaining more detailed qualitative data from a smaller sample group of intelligence managers (Bryman, 2012: 470). Structured and unstructured face-to-face interviews were considered, but were found to be inappropriate for this research. Semi-structured telephone interviews were also considered, but were found to be impractical and raised ethical issues in relation to the tape recording of interviews over the telephone, without the use of specialist equipment.

Unstructured covert participant observation studies were made as part of my day-to-day duties in the management of community intelligence and local neighbourhood policing at local (force), regional and national levels between 2005 and 2010. Documentation from this period, including minutes of meetings and field notes, was also analysed since they served as a record of the observations made.

Secondary data from other research papers on intelligence and neighbourhood policing were studied and discussed as part of the literature review. Further secondary data from previous research undertaken in relation to community intelligence and local neighbourhood policing at the four police BCUs being studied was analysed and used as supporting evidence for the primary data obtained from the postal survey self-completion questionnaire, semi-structured interviews and unstructured covert participant observations.

4.3   The postal survey self-completion questionnaire

Denzin (1978: 158) defines a survey as 'a methodological technique that requires the systematic collection of data from populations or samples through the use of the interview or the self-administered questionnaire'. Neuman (2000: 247) also adds that 'Surveys are appropriate for research questions about self-reported beliefs or behaviors', which also includes attitudes, opinions, characteristics, expectations, self-classification and knowledge.

Local neighbourhood policing staff

A postal self-completion (or self-administered) questionnaire was believed to be the most efficient and cost-effective method of systematically collecting data from a large sample of 414 local neighbourhood policing staff, spread across the four geographical BCUs within the police area being studied (Bryman, 2012: 233). The self-completion questionnaire was designed and piloted with the respondent's perspective in mind, by providing an introduction and clear instructions, guaranteeing anonymity, ensuring that questions were phrased so as to be comprehensible, avoided jargon and confusion, and were in a logical sequence, and by allowing the respondents to complete the questionnaire at a time convenient to them (Newell, 1993: 96; Neuman, 2000: 251–255; Mertens, 2005: 179–182; Bryman, 2012: 237–239).

The self-completion questionnaire consisted of nine pages, which included an introductory first page. It incorporated closed and open questions, both of which have certain advantages and disadvantages. Closed questions are easier to complete and provide clarity for the respondent, and are generally easier to compare, code and process for the researcher. However, answers are more restrictive, not exhaustive, and can prove frustrating for the respondent if their choice of answer does not appear. Open questions allow respondents more freedom to provide a more detailed response and thus give an indication of their knowledge and understanding of a certain issue. However, they are more time-consuming and require a greater effort to be completed by respondents. This may also have an impact on response rates, particularly with self-completion questionnaires. The coding process of developing themes or key words from the written response is also more difficult and time-consuming for the researcher (Neuman, 2000: 260–264; Bryman, 2012: 246–252). Neuman (2000: 260) suggests that the disadvantages of closed and open questions can be reduced by 'mixing open-ended and closed-ended questions in a questionnaire'.

A pilot study of the self-completion questionnaire was undertaken prior to the full survey, to ascertain if the instructions for the completion of the questionnaire were clear, if the mix of closed and open questions was suitable and comprehendible, if the format was user friendly, if the length of the questionnaire was appropriate and if the questions were effective in answering the research question (Bogen, 1996: 1020–1025; Neuman, 2000: 264–265; Mertens, 2005: 182; Bryman, 2012: 263–264).

The postal survey self-completion questionnaire was initially piloted in the 'B' BCU, where I was employed at the time of the pilot. The small stratified random sample of participants for the pilot survey included police sergeants, police constables, Police Community Support Officers (PCSOs), special constables and police Front Line Support Officers (FLSOs) who were involved in local neighbourhood policing on a daily basis.

All participants were provided with an Information Sheet, which outlined the purpose of the research, why they had been chosen as a participant and explained issues such as confidentiality, participant's concerns and withdrawing from the research. The sheet also described what would happen to the findings of the research and provided my contact details and those of my Director of Studies for the research should the participant require any further information.

All participants were also provided with a Consent Form, which highlighted data protection issues, their right to withdraw from the research study, future research publication and analysis, and confirmation that they had read and understood the information provided on the Information Sheet, that they had been given sufficient time to consider the information and ask further questions, that their participation was voluntary and that they could withdraw at any time. Participants were then requested to sign the Consent Form agreeing to participate in the research study. The issues of ethics and informed consent will be discussed in more detail below.

A copy of the self-completion questionnaire, information sheet and consent form were sent to prospective participants via the police internal mail system. In addition, participants were also sent pre-addressed envelopes for the return of the questionnaire and consent form to me.

Of the self-completion questionnaires initially distributed as part of the pilot, a significant number were returned and subsequently analysed for their suitability and effectiveness in answering the research question. The analysis revealed that the pilot self-completion questionnaire appeared to be effective in its design.

The pilot study of the self-completion questionnaire provided a response rate of 38.81%. Although the pilot study only involved a small sample size, it was a useful indicator when considering anticipated response rates for the full survey. Bryman (2012: 199) describes the calculation of the response rate as: the number of usable questionnaires divided by the total sample minus the unsuitable or uncontactable

$$\frac{\text{Number of usable questionnaires}}{\text{Total sample} - \text{Unsuitable or uncontactable members of the sample}} \times 100$$

Figure 4.1 Response rate
Adapted from 'What Is a Response Rate?' (Bryman, 2012: 199).

members of the sample multiplied by 100, which he expressed as an equation (see Figure 4.1).

Neuman (2000: 268) suggests that 'A response rate of 10 to 50 percent is common for a mail survey'. Bryman (2012: 199) agrees and states that research studies suggest that response rates have declined over the last 40 years, with some response rates being as low as 10% and 15%. Bryman (2012: 235) argues that when considering response rates, the researcher should not despair if they achieve a low response rate: 'The key point is to recognize and acknowledge the implications of the possible limitations of a low response rate'. Implications for the research include the observation that the reduced number of respondents may not fully represent the sampled population, the increased possibility of bias and weakened validity.

Bogen (1996) conducted a review of the literature to determine the effect the length of a questionnaire had on response rates. The common perception held is that the shorter the questionnaire the higher the response rate (Neuman, 2000: 264–265; Bryman, 2012: 236). However, on completion of the review, Bogen (1996: 1020) admitted that 'The results are still confusing and contradictory, the conclusions are still not clear'. Thus, there is no empirical evidence to suggest that the response rate for a shorter questionnaire would be higher than that for a longer questionnaire. Bogen concludes that very little experimental work has been undertaken to assist researchers in making a practical decision about the length of a survey.

Bogen (1996) also suggests that basic follow-up procedures can negate any distinction between questionnaire length and response rate. Neuman (2000) and Bryman (2012) agree that two or three follow-up reminders can greatly increase response rates. Other factors that can increase response rates and were considered in this research include a letter of introduction or information sheet, clear instructions and pre-addressed envelopes for returns (Neuman, 2000; Mertens, 2005; Bryman, 2012).

Having considered the above and the results from the pilot study, the pilot self-completion questionnaire was utilised for the full survey with the remaining participants from the local neighbourhood policing staff sample. These participants also included police sergeants, police constables, Police Community Support Officers (PCSOs), special constables and police Front Line Support Officers (FLSOs) who were involved in local neighbourhood policing on a daily basis.

In a similar manner to that of the pilot study, the self-completion questionnaire, information sheet, consent form and pre-addressed envelopes were sent to all the remaining participants via the police internal mail system during the period April 2012 to September 2012. Initial response rates were monitored and follow-up reminders including copies of the self-completion questionnaire, information sheet and consent form were sent via e-mail to participants who had not yet replied. This process was repeated three times at intervals of approximately one month for those who had not replied. The overall response rate was 23.42% and all the data from the questionnaires was later analysed and the findings recorded.

Intelligence managers

A postal self-completion questionnaire was again believed to be the most efficient and cost-effective method of systematically collecting data from the population of 60 intelligence managers, who were also spread across the four geographical BCUs within the police area being studied.

A similar process was used in relation to the administration of the self-completion questionnaire for intelligence managers as for the local neighbourhood policing staff. The questionnaire was initially piloted and then the full survey undertaken concurrently with the local neighbourhood policing staff survey. An overall response rate of 33.33% was achieved and again the data from the questionnaires was later analysed and the findings recorded.

4.4   Semi-structured interviews

Mason (2004: 1020) suggests that 'The defining characteristic of semi-structured interviews is that they have a flexible and fluid structure, unlike structured interviews, which contain a structured sequence of questions to be asked in the same way of all interviewees'. Semi-structured interviews were chosen for this research because it provided a more flexible method of interviewing and collecting data from the population group of intelligence managers, which included Local Policing Inspectors, Detective Inspectors (Intelligence), Detective Sergeants

(Intelligence), Local Intelligence Officers (LIOs) and Field Intelligence Officers (FIOs). This population group had a variety of different roles and responsibilities in the management of intelligence, which made the use of structured interviews using an interview schedule impractical (Barriball and While, 1994: 330). Conversely, the use of unstructured interviews using at most an *aide memoire* to assist in a conversation with the interviewee lacked the structure required to discuss the research topics identified by this research (Bryman, 2012: 471).

The same population group of 60 intelligence managers who had been sent a self-completion questionnaire, information sheet and consent form were also invited at that time to participate in the semi-structured interviews. The same process used to monitor response rates and follow-up reminders for the self-completion questionnaires was also utilised for the semi-structured interviews.

The semi-structured interviews were arranged with all the participants at a time, date and location that were convenient to each individual interviewee. The interviews were generally held in an office within a police station at or near to the interviewee's normal place of work. Prior to the commencement of the interviews, the interviewees were again provided with an information sheet and reminded of the terms and conditions under which they had given their consent to be interviewed. Each interviewee was also given the option of whether their interview would be tape recorded or not. Participants were also informed that the tape-recorded interviews would be transcribed and they were offered a copy of the transcript of their interview. All interviewees declined this offer. Notes were made of the interviews where the participant did not wish the interview to be tape recorded (Bryman, 2012).

The semi-structured interviews lasted between 45 and 60 minutes and took place during the period December 2012 to July 2013. The interviews were conducted using an interview guide to allow as much freedom as possible when discussing the research topics, while providing sufficient structure to the interview process to be able to answer the research question (Bryman, 2012: 471). The interview guide included similar themes and questions to those used in the self-completion questionnaire for intelligence managers and afforded the opportunity to ask additional questions specifically aimed at the particular area of expertise of the interviewee (Mason, 2004: 1020).

Bryman (2012: 470) argues that structured interviews are quantitative, while semi-structured and unstructured interviews are qualitative. This view is also supported by Kvale (1996), Mason (2004) and Mertens (2005). Kvale (1996: 1) suggests that 'The qualitative research interview attempts to understand the world from the subjects' point of view, to unfold the meaning of peoples' experiences, to uncover their lived world prior to scientific explanations'. Thus, the intention of the qualitative semi-structured interviews in this research was to obtain an account of the interviewee's perceptions, views, experiences and understanding of the research topics, and to complete and enhance the data collected from the self-completion questionnaire survey with the intelligence managers (Mason, 2004).

4.5   Unstructured covert participant observation

Denzin (1978: 183) defines participant observation as 'a field strategy that simultaneously combines document analysis, interviewing of respondents and informants, direct participation and observation, and introspection'. Bryman (2012: 273) suggests that participant observation 'entails the relatively prolonged immersion of the observer in a social setting in which he or she seeks to observe the behavior of members of that setting (group, organisation, community, etc.) and to elicit the meanings they attribute to their environment and their behavior'. Bryman also suggests that most participant observation is 'unstructured observation', as generally an observation schedule is not used to record behaviour. Instead, as much detail as possible is recorded in order to develop a 'narrative account' of the behaviour of the participants (2012: 273).

Bulmer (1982) defines covert, secret or disguised participant observation as

> ... research situations where the real identity of the observer as a social researcher remains a secret and entirely unknown to those with whom he or she is in contact. The investigator purports to be a complete participant and is in fact something else.
>
> (Bulmer, 1982: 252)

Unstructured covert participant observations were undertaken over a five-year period between August 2005 and August 2010, while I was directly involved in the management of neighbourhood policing and community intelligence, locally with the police force being studied, regionally with the All Wales Neighbourhood Policing Development Group and nationally with the National Policing Improvement Agency (NPIA). Unstructured covert participant observation raises a number of ethical issues, particularly in relation to informed consent, as the participants are unable to give their consent as they have not been informed and are unaware of the observations. The issues of ethics and informed consent will be discussed in more detail below.

Observations within the police, locally, regionally and nationally

Observations within the police force being studied were undertaken between August 2005 and December 2008 when I was part of a small group of police staff responsible for the implementation of neighbourhood policing across the whole of the geographical area covered by this police force. This role involved providing expert advice on local neighbourhood policing and community intelligence to chief police officers, senior managers and BCU implementation teams within that police force. These key individuals were observed covertly within their working environment, either individually or as part of a small group. These observations also gave me the opportunity to visit and observe the working environment of these key individuals. The various groups were also observed in a more formal meeting environment, where minutes of the meetings were recorded and distributed.

Similarly, observations within the All Wales Neighbourhood Policing Development Group occurred between October 2005 and December 2008 and within the National Policing Improvement Agency (NPIA) between December 2008 and August 2010, when I was seconded to the Agency as a Local Policing and Confidence Unit Field Officer. These observations provided me with the opportunity to observe the management and development of neighbourhood policing and community intelligence at a local, regional and national level, and to gain a greater understanding of the interactions and dynamics between the groups at each level.

4.6 Secondary data analysis

Hakim (1982: 1) defines secondary data analysis as 'any further analysis of an existing dataset which presents interpretations, conclusions or knowledge additional to, or different from, those produced in the first report on the inquiry as a whole and its main results'. Bryman (2012: 312) suggests that 'Secondary analysis may entail the analysis of either quantitative data (Dale et al., 1988) or qualitative data (Corti et al., 1995)'. Heaton (2000: 4) agrees and further suggests that secondary data analysis may also involve the analysis of a mixture of both quantitative and qualitative data. Church (2001: 33) is more specific and suggests that secondary data analysis can be performed on statistical information, text, tables, graphs and appendices published in articles or upon the original primary data.

Heaton (2008: 35) also argues that there are three main modes of secondary data analysis, namely *formal data sharing* (where data is 'deposited in public or institutional archives' and accessed for secondary research); *informal data sharing* (which can involve the analysis of data by a 'mix of researchers who were and were not involved in the original research'); and *self-collected data* (where the researcher uses their own data to 'investigate new or additional questions to those explored in the primary research or, alternatively, to verify their previous findings'). Denzin (1978) and Webb et al. (1966) suggest that secondary data analysis using archived material may also be considered an unobtrusive measure of observational research.

Denzin (1978: 256) defines an unobtrusive measure of observation as 'any method of observation that directly removes the observer from the set of interactions or events being studied', which would include the analysis of archival documents. Webb et al. (1966: 3) outline three main types of unobtrusive methods or measures, namely 'physical traces, archives, [and] observations'. *Physical traces* refer to the physical evidence left behind by some process of erosion or accretion (deposit). *Archives* are the continuous or discontinuous records of society. *Observations* are further divided into 'simple observation', and 'contrived observation' (Webb et al., 1966: 112, 142). In the *simple observation* method the observer 'plays an unobserved, passive, and nonintrusive role in the research situation', whereas in the *contrived observation* method the observer plays 'an active role in structuring the situation, but in which he is still unobserved by the actors' (Webb et al., 1966: 112). Thus in the latter method the observer exhibits an element of control and can introduce hardware, such as video cameras to assist in the observation. Webb also suggests that unobtrusive measures are useful when it is believed that a participant's awareness that they are being investigated is likely to affect their response to the research.

Heaton (2008: 39) also identified five main types of secondary data analysis, namely 'supplementary analysis', 'supra analysis', 'reanalysis', 'amplified analysis' and 'assorted analysis'. *Supplementary analysis* involves 'a more in-depth analysis of an emergent issue or aspect of the data, that was not addressed or was only partially addressed in the primary study'. *Supra analysis* occurs when 'the aims and focus of the secondary study transcend those of the original research'. *Re-analysis* involves the re-examination of data 'in order to confirm and validate findings of a primary study'. *Amplified analysis* involves comparing or combining 'two or more existing qualitative datasets'. *Assorted analysis* involves the re-use of existing qualitative data 'alongside the collection and analysis of primary qualitative data for the same study'.

This research will adopt the formal data sharing mode and the assorted secondary data analysis type promulgated by Heaton (2008) utilising data from independent research previously deposited in the archives of the police force being studied. The archived material in relation to community intelligence was subject to secondary data analysis during the period of the primary data analysis in accordance with the chosen multilevel triangulation design methodology. The issues of ethics and informed consent will be discussed in more detail below.

4.7 Sampling

At the time of the sampling process for this research in March 2012, the police force being studied had an establishment of 2893 regular police officers, 306 Police Community Support Officers (PCSOs), 147 Special Constables and 1625 police support staff members (including 19 Front Line Support Officers (FLSOs), now known as Sector Support Officers) – a total of 4990 full- and part-time staff.

The number of full- and part-time staff (of all ranks/positions) directly involved in operational policing in each BCU (including FLSOs) was found to be as follows: 'A' BCU had 484 staff, 'B' BCU had 760 staff, 'C' BCU had 544 staff and 'D' BCU had 747 staff. A total of 2535 staff involved in operational policing across the four territorial BCUs. The above figures were derived from the unpublished establishment lists provided by the business managers from the four BCUs at my request, while I was still employed by the police and were also used to calculate the number of staff designated to local neighbourhood policing and the management of community intelligence in each BCU.

The number of staff designated to local neighbourhood policing in each of the BCUs including regular police officers (Neighbourhood Sergeants, Neighbourhood Beat Managers (NBMs) (Constables) and Police Schools Community Officers (PSCOs) (Constables)), PCSOs, Special Constables and FLSOs was as follows: 'A' BCU had 153 staff (31.61%), 'B' BCU had 177 staff (23.28%), 'C' BCU had 137 staff (25.18%) and 'D' BCU had 217 staff (29.04%). A total of 684 staff (26.98%) were designated to local neighbourhood policing across the four territorial BCUs. This equates to 20.32% of the police establishment of regular police officers, PCSOs, special constables and FLSOs at the time of the sampling process. Local Policing Inspectors were not included in the total of 684 staff as they formed part of the intelligence managers' population group for the purposes of this research.

The number of identifiable staff involved in the management of community intelligence in each of the four BCUs was as follows: 'A' BCU had nine staff, 'B' BCU had 16 staff, 'C' BCU had 13 staff and 'D' BCU had 22 staff. A total of 60 identifiable staff (including Local Policing Inspectors, Detective Inspectors, Detective Sergeants, Local Intelligence Officers (LIOs) and Field Intelligence Officers (FIOs)) were involved in the management of community intelligence across the four BCUs.

With the main aim of this research in mind, the population groups considered most suitable for the postal survey self-completion questionnaires, were the 684 designated local neighbourhood policing staff and the 60 intelligence managers involved in the management of community intelligence.

Similarly, the population group considered most suitable for the semi-structured interviews was the same 60 intelligence managers involved in the management of community intelligence.

The population groups considered most appropriate for the unstructured covert participant observations were as follows: (1) members and managers of the local Neighbourhood Policing Implementation Teams for the police force being studied; (2) members of the regional All Wales Neighbourhood Policing Development Group; and (3) neighbourhood policing managers from the NPIA.

In relation to the secondary data analysis, the most appropriate data for analysis was considered to be the data from the independent research by Rogers (2007), and Rogers and Gravelle (2008), which had previously been deposited in the archives of police force being studied.

Postal survey self-completion questionnaires samples

For the purpose of sampling, the unit of analysis for the postal survey self-completion questionnaire component of this research was each individual member of staff (or unit) designated to local neighbourhood policing from a population of 684 and each intelligence manager (or unit) involved in the management of community intelligence from a population of 60. Bryman (2012: 187) describes a population as 'the universe of units from which the sample is to be selected' and a sample as 'the segment of the population that is selected for investigation'.

Cognisance was taken of my experience as an 'inside-insider' (Brown, 1996: 180–181) within the police service, when determining the sample size for the postal survey self-completion questionnaires. A relatively

low, but not unusual, response rate (of approximately 25%) was anticipated, due to apathy or refusal to participate (Bryman, 2012: 235). Other
factors taken into consideration were spoilage rates whether intentional
or otherwise, the total population size, the resources available to me
(such as time and funding), the strength and depth of the participants'
views being measured and the overall extent of the analyses that would
need to be undertaken at the end of the data collection process (Bryman,
2012: 197–200). Therefore, in relation to the local neighbourhood policing staff population of 684 an estimated sample size of 410 (60%) was
considered to be appropriate. In practice the actual sample size was
414 (60.52%). I also decided that due to the relatively smaller number
of intelligence managers, this population group would not be sampled and the whole population of 60 (100%) would be used in this
research.

The establishment lists provided by each of the four BCUs were used
as the sampling frame for the local neighbourhood policing staff population in this part of the research. Bryman (2012: 187) describes a
sampling frame as 'the list of all units in the population from which
the sample will be selected'. The four establishment lists (although in
different formats) all contained details of the name, rank/position, role
and location of each member of staff employed in the BCUs and were
also used to identify the intelligence managers population group.

Non-probability and probability sampling were both considered as
sampling methods for this research. Bryman (2012: 187) describes a
non-probability sample as 'a sample that has not been selected using a
random selection method' and thus, 'some units in the population are
more likely to be selected than others'. By contrast, Bryman (2012: 187)
describes a *probability sample* as 'a sample that has been selected using
random selection so that each unit in the population has a known
chance of being selected', providing a more representative sample and
minimising sampling error (see also: Leming, 1997; Tashakkori and
Teddlie, 2003; Handwerker, 2005; Mertens, 2005; Teddlie and Yu, 2007).
In order to provide a more representative sample of the population being
studied and to minimise sampling error, probability sampling was used
in this research.

Mertens (2005: 314–316) suggests that once the sample size is estimated, there are five main types of probability sampling, namely 'simple
random sampling', 'systematic sampling', 'stratified sampling', 'cluster
sampling' and 'multi-stage sampling'. *Simple random sampling* means
that every unit of analysis is allocated a number, and the sample is
selected by the use of computer-generated random numbers (or through

the use of a table of random numbers) to produce the sample size required. Thus, each unit has an 'equal and independent chance of being selected' (Mertens, 2005: 314). *Systematic sampling* involves taking 'every *n*th name' from the sample frame to provide the sample and the sample size required (Mertens, 2005: 315). *Stratified sampling* is used when there are 'subgroups (or *strata*) of different sizes' that need to be investigated as part of the research study (Mertens, 2005: 315). For example, in this research, subgroups (or strata) within the local policing staff population would include Neighbourhood Sergeants, NBMs, PSCOs, PCSOs, Special Constables and FLSOs. Bryman (2012: 192–193) prefers the term 'stratified random sampling' and advises that this method should only be used when there are easily identifiable units of analysis that can be allocated to each strata. *Cluster sampling* is used where there are 'naturally occurring groups of individuals' at a particular location and when a sampling frame (or list of all the units in the population) is not available, but a list of clusters is available (Mertens, 2005: 316). *Multi-stage sampling* consists of a combining a number of sampling methods. For example, combining cluster sampling with simple random sampling (Mertens, 2005: 316). Bryman (2012: 193–195) reduces the number of main types of probability sampling from five to four, by combining cluster sampling and multi-stage sampling into 'multi-stage cluster sampling'. Bryman (2012: 194) argues that 'cluster sampling is always a multi-stage approach', because clusters are always sampled first, followed by further clusters or units in the population.

Stratified sampling and in particular 'stratified random sampling' (Bryman, 2012: 192–193) was considered the most appropriate sampling method for this research, to provide a random sample from each strata of Neighbourhood Sergeants, NBMs, PCSOs and Special Constables. However, because the population size of PSCOs and FLSOs was so small, 25 and 19, respectively, the whole of the population of these two strata was used in this research.

Having identified the strata for stratified random sampling as Neighbourhood Sergeants, NBMs, PCSOs and Special Constables, a sampling frame for each strata was produced and each unit of analysis within the strata was allocated a unique number. The sample from each strata was then selected by use of computer-generated random numbers to achieve the estimated sample size of 60%. The population of PSCOs (25) and FLSOs (19) was added to the stratified random sample to produce the overall sample of 414 units of analysis for this research.

Semi-structured interviews

For the purpose of the semi-structured interviews component of this research, the unit of analysis was specified as each individual intelligence manager involved in the management of community intelligence. Due to the relatively smaller number of intelligence managers (a population of 60), it was decided that this population group would not be sampled and the whole population would be used in this research.

Unstructured covert participant observations

In relation to the unstructured covert participant observations component of this research, the unit of analysis was also defined as each of the following three groups: (1) members and managers of the local Neighbourhood Policing Implementation Teams from the police force being studied; (2) the regional Neighbourhood Policing Development Group; and (3) the neighbourhood policing managers from the NPIA. Again, due to the relatively smaller number of members of these groups, (a population of 23, 12 and 18, respectively), I decided that this population group would not be sampled and the whole population would be used in this research.

Secondary data analysis

For the purpose of the secondary data analysis, the unit of analysis was determined to be the individual documents from the independent research conducted by Rogers (2007) and Rogers and Gravelle (2008).

Sampling error

Although probability sampling minimises sampling error, it may still occur through chance, random error, bias or even pure bad luck. Non-sampling errors may also occur through researcher error, such as data analysis error and participant error, such as the inability or unwillingness to participate, non-response, cheating and participant bias (Mertens, 2005; Bryman, 2012).

Data analysis

Data analysis was undertaken concurrently on the primary data collected from the postal survey self-completion questionnaires, semi-structured interviews and unstructured covert participant observations and on the secondary data collected from the independent research documents previously deposited in the archives of the police force being studied. Quantitative data was analysed using the International Business

Machines (IBM) Statistical Product and Service Solutions (formally Statistical Package for the Social Sciences) (SPSS) Version 20.0 for Microsoft Windows and qualitative data using thematic analysis. Bryman (2012: 717) describes thematic analysis as 'A term used in connection with the analysis of qualitative data to refer to the extraction of key themes in one's data'. A framework or matrix approach to thematic analysis was used in this research utilising Microsoft Excel.

4.8 Ethical considerations

Diener and Crandall (1978: 7) suggest that there are four main ethical principles that are generally considered in relation to the treatment of participants in social and behavioural research, namely 'harm to participants', 'informed consent', 'privacy' and 'deception'.

Harm to participants

Factors that may be considered harmful to individual participants are psychological harm, such as anxiety and stress, physical harm, the invasion of privacy, lack of anonymity, breaches of confidentiality, damage to reputation and the use of deception (Diener and Crandall, 1978; Punch, 1994; Hammersley and Atkinson, 1995). Physical harm was not considered to be a factor in this research. However, careful consideration was given to minimising other potentially harmful effects of this research on the participants.

The provision of information to prospective participants about the postal survey self-completion questionnaire and semi-structured interview components of this research was considered an essential part of the research design to enable participants to make informed decisions on whether they wished to consent to take part in this research. It was also used to minimise any unnecessary anxiety and stress by offering assurances that their privacy, anonymity, confidentiality and reputation would be maintained, and that they were not being deceived.

Harm to participants can also be minimised in relation to unstructured covert participant observations and secondary data analysis, even though the participants in the primary research in each case are not aware that they are participating in a research process. The same potentially harmful factors mentioned above can be minimised during and after the research process (Punch, 1994).

Other considerations when studying large public organisations such as the police include, for example, the damage to their reputation, which has to be balanced against the search for knowledge and truth. All these factors were considered in relation to this research and informed consent, privacy and deception are discussed in more detail below.

Informed consent

The Economic and Social Research Council (2010: 40) define informed consent as follows: 'Informed consent entails giving sufficient information about the research and ensuring that there is no explicit or implicit coercion so that prospective participants can make an informed and free decision on their possible involvement'. This view is supported by the Social Research Association (2003) and the British Sociological Association (2004: 3), both of which also advise that 'As far as possible participation in sociological research should be based on the freely given informed consent of those studied'. Sieber (1992: 26) suggests that in addition to being an agreement about the conditions of a participant's involvement in the research, voluntary informed consent is 'an ongoing two-way communication process between the subjects and the investigator'. Diener and Crandall (1978) argue that voluntary informed consent is based on Western cultural values and legal systems, which emphasise freedom of choice. Article 9 (Freedom of Thought, Conscience and Religion) and Article 10 (Freedom of Expression) of the Human Rights Act 1998 (Home Office, 1998b: 24–25) and the European Convention on Human Rights (Convention for the Protection of Human Rights and Fundamental Freedoms) (Council of Europe, 2010: 11–12) tend to support this argument.

Although accepted as a common strategy by researchers, the concept of voluntary informed consent is not as straightforward as it may first seem and is not a panacea for all ethical problems (Kimmel, 1988; Hammersley and Traianou, 2012). Concerns arise when determining how to fully inform prospective participants of the research and how much detail to communicate to them, as this could become a technically complicated, laborious and possibly unattainable task. Stanley et al. (1987: 736) advise that 'The comprehension of consent information is relatively poor' and the lengthier and more complex the information, the less it is understood. Therefore, the information should be presented in such a way that it is comprehensible to each individual prospective participant (Kimmel, 1988; Wiles et al., 2004). Freely given informed consent also poses other issues about how free the consent actually is. Hammersley and Traianou (2012) argue that prospective participants are not truly free and independent individuals, as they are influenced by certain social factors and relationships, which affect their decision-making. Particularly if those factors and relationships involve an organisation that has power or influence over them and they feel obliged to agree or disagree to consent due to the constraints, the organisation or individuals within the organisation place upon them. Hammersley and Traianou (2012) also argue that cultural issues within society and within organisations will also influence full and free informed consent. Although full and free informed consent may not always be possible in certain circumstances, it is still desirable. However, this may not be the case when considering covert research.

Spicker (2011: 119) defines covert research as follows: 'Covert research is research which is not disclosed to the subject – where the researcher does not reveal that research is taking place'. Covert research, particularly covert participant observation, is often seen as controversial and even unethical, mainly because the participants being observed are unable to give their voluntary informed consent and cannot refuse their involvement (Bulmer, 1982: 252; Lee, 1993: 143; Lugosi, 2006: 542–543). However, Lee (1993: 143–144) advises that social science researchers have taken three positions in relation to the ethics of covert research, namely 'absolutist', 'pragmatic' and 'sceptical'. The *absolutist* position is that ethically, covert methods of research cannot be used. The *pragmatic* position is that it wishes to protect the rights of participants and is obliged not to harm them, but will reluctantly use covert methods when there is no other way of obtaining the required data. The *sceptical* position is that there is positive justification for covert research methods. Although Lee's three ethical positions specifically relate to covert research, there are similarities to three of Bryman's (2012) five main stances on ethics. Comparisons may be seen between the *absolutist* position and *universalism,* the *pragmatic* position and *situation ethics,* and the *sceptical* position and the *anything goes (more or less)* stance (Bryman, 2012: 133–134).

Privacy

Privacy, confidentiality and anonymity are inextricably linked when discussing ethical issues in research, which is emphasised by the following paragraph from the British Sociological Association's Statement of Ethical Practice:

> The anonymity and privacy of those who participate in the research process should be respected. Personal information concerning research participants should be kept confidential. In some cases it

may be necessary to decide whether it is proper or appropriate even to record certain kinds of sensitive information.

(British Sociological Association, 2004: 5)

Diener and Crandall (1978: 55–57) identify three dimensions of privacy, which they describe as 'sensitivity of information', the 'setting being observed' and the 'dissemination of information'. The *sensitivity of information* relates to 'how personal or potentially threatening it is', as some information such as religious beliefs, sexual orientation, racial prejudices, personal finances and honesty are considered more sensitive than other information, such as a name (Diener and Crandall, 1978: 55). The greater the sensitivity of the information, the more safeguards have to be put in place to protect the privacy of the individual. *The setting being observed* considers the 'continuum from very private (e.g. your bathroom) to completely public (e.g. a downtown sidewalk)' (Diener and Crandall, 1978: 57). The more private the setting, the more precautions have to be taken to ensure privacy. Spicker (2011) argues that it is a difficult and often complex task to distinguish the boundaries between private and public settings. For example, if a group hires a normally public room in a public house for a meeting, does that room become a private setting for the purposes of ethical research? This is a very difficult question to answer, as each case would have to be examined on its own merits. *The dissemination of information* is concerned with the number of people that 'can connect personal information to the name of the person involved' (Diener and Crandall, 1978: 57). The greater the number of people with knowledge of the personal data of an identifiable individual, the more concern there must be for privacy. Thus, in all cases the researcher should assess the sensitivity of the information, the setting or location to be used for the research and how the resulting information will be disseminated to ensure that safeguards are put in place to protect the privacy of the individual.

Privacy is also linked to the provision of information to participants, so that they can determine what impact the research may have on their private lives prior to giving informed consent (Bryman, 2012). The British Sociological Association (2004: 5) suggests that 'covert methods violate the principles of informed consent and may invade the privacy of those being studied'. Thus, even a greater focus should be given to the three dimensions of privacy highlighted by Diener and Crandall (1978) when considering covert research.

However, Spicker (2011) argues that the actions of public agencies such as the police are still in the public domain even behind closed doors.

> Some actions are public in their very nature. The formal actions of governments and public agencies, even in closed rooms, are intrinsically public.
>
> (Spicker, 2011: 124)

The main way that researchers prevent accidental disclosure and protect research participants is through the use of anonymity. Mertens (2005: 333) suggests that 'Anonymity means that no uniquely identifying information is attached to the data, and thus no one, not even the researcher, can trace the data back to the individual providing them'. Complete anonymity, as suggested by Mertens above, is very difficult to achieve, particularly when the research methods include the researcher interviewing the participants. By the very nature of the interviewing process, it is generally undertaken face to face with a smaller population or sample group of participants. Even if the data is coded and anonymised to prevent identification of participants by a third party, the researcher will undoubtedly be able to identify a number of participants from the specific data they provided. However, this should not prevent the researcher from being able to ensure anonymity for the participants in respect of any third party.

For the purpose of this research, every effort was made to ensure the privacy, confidentiality and anonymity of participants in all aspects of the research, even though the participants may be regarded as officials in a public organisation (i.e. the police) (British Sociological Association, 2004).

Deception

Spicker (2011) argues that deception is often confused with covert research and many of the objections to covert research are actually objections to deception. In contrast to Spicker's definition of covert research above, Spicker (2011: 119) defines deception as follows: 'Deception, by contrast, occurs where the nature of a researcher's action is misrepresented to the research subject.'

I tend to agree with the definitions of covert research and deception offered by Spicker (2011) above. Although covert research in the form of unstructured participant observations was utilised in this research, I am of the opinion that no deception has taken place. I did not misrepresent my actions to the research subjects and merely fulfilled my normal role and responsibilities as a fully participating member of the groups being observed. I did not pretend to be someone or something I was not and there was no intent to deceive. No form of deception was used in any of the other components of this research.

Political considerations

Political considerations differ from the ethical considerations described above as they are concerned with the substance and use of the research rather than with the research methods used. Hammersley (1995: 103) suggests that there are two main ways in which research may be seen as political: first through the 'exercise of power' and second through the 'making of value judgements' and the action taken as a result of those judgements. Hammersley argues that the exercise of power can be seen from two opposing perspectives. The first perspective concerns researchers and research institutions maintaining their autonomy from external powers, such as the state and others in society with power and influence. The second perspective concerns the power exercised by researchers and research institutions themselves, where the research or knowledge itself is power. Hammersley (1995: 109) also argues that the making of value judgements also has a political aspect, as research cannot be totally value-free or neutral, as it is influenced by the quest for knowledge and the social, political and economic conditions, and intellectual presuppositions of the time.

Unlike ethical considerations, there is no professional code of conduct for political issues, but it is generally accepted that the researcher's political views should not be allowed to interfere with or influence the research. During the course of this research, I was aware of the political issues to be considered and made every effort to minimise their effect on this research.

Research can also be undertaken and used to advise central government on policy issues, which can ultimately lead to changes in legislation. Thus, in this respect political considerations may also be linked to legal considerations.

Legal considerations

In addition to the ethical and political considerations above, attention was also given to the legal considerations associated with consent, privacy, confidentiality and anonymity. Wiles et al. (2004: 8) argue that 'Article 8 of The Human Rights Act 1998 and the Data Protection Act 1998 have relevance to consent in relation to all research'.

Article 8 (Right to Respect for Private and Family Life) of the Human Rights Act 1998 (Home Office, 1998b: 24) and the European Convention on Human Rights (Convention for the Protection of Human Rights and Fundamental Freedoms) (Council of Europe, 2010: 10–11) states that 'Everyone has the right to respect for his private and family life, his home and his correspondence'. Thus, privacy is regarded as one of the most fundamental rights of an individual, which is protected by legislation.

The Data Protection Act 1998 (Home Office, 1998a: 47) also outlines eight statutory principles for the processing of personal data to ensure that it is processed for a lawful purpose, it is adequate, relevant, not excessive, accurate, timely and necessary, and that it is managed to prevent unauthorised or unlawful processing, accidental loss, destruction and damage. Therefore, these statutory principles serve not only to protect an individual's privacy, but also their confidentiality and anonymity.

In summary, having given careful thought to the ethical and legal considerations above, this research will adopt a pragmatic situational approach to ethics, while still taking into consideration the four main ethical principles of harm to participants, informed consent, privacy and deception (Diener and Crandall, 1978) and the main legal issues associated with freedom, privacy and confidentiality (Home Office, 1998a; 1998b). Concerted efforts were made during the course of this research to reduce the harm to participants, to gain informed consent where appropriate, to ensure the privacy, confidentiality and anonymity of participants and subjects, and to nullify all forms of deception, while operating within the associated human rights and data protection legislation.

However, there are other considerations that have to be taken into account such as the validity, reliability and objectivity of the research, which may also have ethical implications. Gorard (2010: 247) suggests that the 'quality of the research', the 'robustness of the findings' and the 'security of the conclusions drawn' are key ethical considerations for researchers, particularly for publicly funded research.

4.9   Validity, reliability and objectivity

The terms validity, reliability and objectivity are generally associated with the quantitative research methodology, and quantitative research methods and designs (Bryman, 2012). However, a number of researchers (e.g. Kirk and Miller, 1986; Mason, 2002) have applied these traditional criteria to the qualitative research methodology, while others (e.g. Lincoln and Guba, 1985) argue that because they are grounded in quantitative research, they are inappropriate for qualitative research and have proposed alternative criteria based on the concept of 'trustworthiness', which will be discussed in more detail below (Lincoln and Guba, 1985: 290). Golafshani (2003) suggests that if traditional criteria such as validity and reliability are to be applied to qualitative research then they need to be redefined. Morse et al. (2002) agree and argue that authors use different terminology for the same or similar criteria, which causes confusion and can undermine the issue of rigour in the research.

Validity

Bryman (2012: 47) suggests that 'Validity is concerned with the integrity of the conclusions that are generated from a piece of research'. He (also identifies four main types of validity, namely 'measurement validity', 'ecological validity', 'internal validity' and 'external validity'.

Measurement validity refers to whether an instrument devised to measure a concept actually does reflect the concept that it is measuring. Measurement validity is invariably linked to reliability as the measurement must also be stable and reliable for it to be valid (Campbell and Fiske, 1959; Neuman, 2000; Bryman, 2012) (see the section on *Reliability* below). The research instrument for the quantitative component of this research (the postal survey self-completion questionnaire) was piloted and a well-tested and widely used quantitative data analysis system, the IBM SPSS Version 20.0 for Microsoft Windows, was used to analyse the data to improve the measurement validity.

Ecological validity is concerned with whether the findings from social research are applicable to people's everyday lives in their natural social settings. The more the research interferes with those settings, the more unnatural they become (Bryman, 2012). The postal survey self-completion questionnaires in this research were completed by each of the participants in a social setting chosen by them, with no interference from the researcher.

Internal validity relates to the causality or causal relationship between two variables (the independent variable and the dependent variable) and whether the researcher is confident that any conclusion derived from this relationship is genuine (Bryman, 2012). Consideration was given to the Hawthorne Effect, where participants modify their behaviour when they are aware that they are the subjects of a research study (Bramel and Friend, 1981; Olson et al., 2004). This behavioural change can affect the causality between variables and adversely affected the internal validity of a study. This can also manifest itself in participants providing answers to a self-completion questionnaire that they think the researcher wants to see, rather than providing open and honest answers. Randomisation is one factor that can assist in increasing internal validity, but care must be taken not to introduce too many controls because the more controls put in place, the more contrived the research becomes. Therefore, internal validity has to be balanced with external validity, which requires generalisability (Jupp, 1989).

External validity is concerned with whether the results of specific research can be generalised in the wider context of further research. Sampling methods are important to external validity, as for the results to be generalised the sample must be representative of the population studied (Bryman, 2012). Stratified random sampling (Bryman, 2012: 192–193) was considered the most valid sampling method for the large population group of local neighbourhood policing staff and provided a representative random sample from each strata being studied. Triangulation can also increase the external validity of a research study by combining quantitative and qualitative research findings as a form of corroboration (Denzin, 1978) (see the section on *Sampling* above). However, generalisability cannot be guaranteed in this research, as it may be regarded as a snap shot of the relationship between local neighbourhood policing and community intelligence in the police force being studied at a single point in time. Priorities for this police force may change over time and other police forces may have different priorities with a greater or lesser emphasis on neighbourhood policing and community intelligence.

Reliability

Neuman (2000: 164) suggests that reliability 'means that the numerical results produced by an indicator do not vary because of characteristics of the measurement process or measurement instrument itself'. Thus, if the same measurement instrument and process are used again, the numerical results obtained should be the same (Campbell and Fiske, 1959). As mentioned above, reliability is linked to measurement validity and the same measures used to increase validity can be used to increase reliability. In order to increase reliability, the stability, representativeness and accuracy of the measurement was considered by piloting the postal survey self-completion questionnaires.

Objectivity

Payne and Payne (2004: 152) describe objectivity as follows: '...as far as possible, researchers should remain distanced from what they study so findings depend on the nature of what was studied rather than on the personality, beliefs and values of the researcher...'. Therefore, the researcher must try to remain objective and not allow personal biases to influence the research, while readers of the research must be confident that the researcher has constrained their personal prejudices (Payne and Payne, 2004: 153). However, opponents to this view suggest that complete objectivity is unattainable or inappropriate as researchers do not operate in isolation, but interact with and are influenced by others within the research setting (Scott and Marshall, 2009: 522). I was aware of my personal values and biases, and how they may affect my objectivity when dealing with the quantitative components of this research (see the section on *Reflexivity* below).

The concept of 'trustworthiness' was proposed by Lincoln and Guba (1985: 290) to answer the question 'How can an inquirer persuade his or her audiences (including self) that the findings of an inquiry are worth paying attention to, worth taking account of?' Lincoln and Guba (1985: 189) developed four aspects of trustworthiness for qualitative research, namely 'credibility', 'transferability', 'dependability' and 'confirmability' to parallel the four traditional quantitative research criteria of *internal validity*, *external validity*, *reliability* and *objectivity*, respectively.

Credibility

Credibility refers to the accuracy of the researcher's understanding and interpretation of an aspect of social reality and the acceptability of that account to others in that social setting (Lincoln and Guba, 1985; Bryman, 2012). Techniques for internally validating credibility include utilising well-established research methods, random sampling, reciprocity (a mutually cooperative interaction between participants and researcher), respondent validation (where respondents or participants involved in the research corroborate the researcher's account) and triangulation (Webb et al., 1966; Bloor, 1978; Denzin, 1978; Harrison et al., 2001; Shenton, 2004). In this research, well-established qualitative research methods such as semi-structured interviews and unstructured covert participant observations were utilised with the whole population groups of intelligence managers and local, regional and national neighbourhood policing managers, respectively. Care was taken to ensure that the semi-structured interviews were conducted at or near to the participants' normal place of work and the unstructured covert participant observations were undertaken in the natural setting of management meetings, which would normally be attended by the research subjects.

Transferability

Transferability relates to the depth of the qualitative research findings produced by the researcher, which allows others to make judgements as to whether the findings are transferable to other social settings (Lincoln and Guba, 1985; Bryman, 2012). Techniques for externally validating transferability include thick descriptions to allow others to have a proper understanding of the phenomenon being studied (Geertz, 1973; Denzin, 1989; Harrison et al., 2001). Rich thick descriptions were used in this research to enhance transferability.

Dependability

Dependability refers to the researcher's account of any changes that exist in the social setting being studied and responding to those changes in reality by modifying the research design. This involves the researcher keeping detailed records of every stage of the research process, including the formulation of the research question, the research methodology, methods and design, sampling procedures, transcripts of interviews, field notes, data analysis and the research findings (Lincoln and Guba, 1985; Bryman, 2012). Dependability is closely related to credibility, thus ensuring credibility significantly helps to ensure dependability (Lincoln and Guba, 1985). Techniques for ensuring the reliability and dependability of the research include peer reviews (where peers act as auditors during or at the end of the research to establish that all procedures have been followed correctly) and researcher reflexivity (Bryman, 2012). Detailed records of this research were maintained throughout the research process and this research will be subject to review as part of the PhD process. Reflexivity was also used as part of this research process (see the section on *Reflexivity* below).

Confirmability

Confirmability is concerned with ensuring that the researcher remains as objective as possible and has not allowed their personal beliefs, values or biases to influence the conduct of the research or its findings while recognising the subjective nature of qualitative research (Lincoln and Guba, 1985; Bryman, 2012). Techniques for ensuring confirmability can be linked to the peer review (audit process) for ensuring dependability and a triangulation research design such as the one mentioned above (Denzin, 1978; Lincoln and Guba, 1985). Triangulation was also used in this context to reduce the effect of my own values and biases, and to ensure the findings were the result of the participants' experiences and ideas, not my personal preferences (Shenton, 2004: 72).

Following on from trustworthiness, Guba and Lincoln (1989: 245–250) also introduced the concept of 'authenticity', which is concerned with the quality of qualitative research and the wider implications of research on politics, but this concept has not been widely influential and still remains quite controversial in some quarters (Morse et al., 2002; Bryman, 2012).

Bryman et al. (2008) conducted a study to establish which of the criteria mentioned above was deemed by social policy researchers to be most appropriate for quantitative, qualitative and mixed methods research. Bryman et al. (2008: 264–267) found that researchers believed that validity and reliability were the two most appropriate traditional criteria for both quantitative and qualitative research while credibility was found to be the most appropriate alternative criteria for qualitative research. The majority of researchers (82.1%) considered that a combination of traditional and alternative criteria should be utilised for mixed methods research and over three quarters (76.5%) of researchers favoured utilising different criteria (traditional and alternative) for the quantitative and qualitative components of mixed methods research, respectively (Bryman et al., 2008: 268–269).

For the purpose of this research, a combination of traditional (validity, reliability and objectivity) criteria and alternative (credibility, transferability, dependability and confirmability) criteria was used to ensure the quality and robustness of the quantitative and qualitative components, respectively.

Reflexivity

Guillemin and Gillam (2004: 274) describe reflexivity in research as 'a process of critical reflection both on the kind of knowledge produced from research and how that knowledge is generated'. Hammersley and Atkinson (2007: 15) emphasise that 'the production of knowledge by researchers has consequences' in that publication of research findings can influence political and practical decision-making, and may even 'change the character of the situations that were studied'. They also argue that the orientations of the researcher are shaped by their socio-historical locations and they are not insulated from wider society or from their own biography and therefore, reflexivity is a 'significant feature of social research' (Hammersley and Atkinson, 2007: 15). Reflexivity allows the researcher to acknowledge and describe their socio-historical assumptions, beliefs, prejudices and values, and, through this reflective self-awareness process, minimise identified biases as the research proceeds (Creswell and Miller, 2000: 127).

Pels (2000: 3) suggests that reflexivity adds another level or dimension of self-reference, which moves the research 'one step up'. Lynch (2000: 34–35) disagrees and suggests that the term reflexivity has many different meanings and is often claimed as a 'theoretical or methodological virtue', taking the intellectual high ground. However, Lynch (2000: 35) also argues that there is very little evidence to suggest that contemporary research, which includes reflexivity, is of any greater value or authority than previous research, which did not.

Finlay, (2002: 209) suggests that there are five variants of reflexivity: 'introspection', 'intersubjective reflection', 'mutual collaboration', 'social critique' and 'discursive deconstruction'. *Introspection* involves the use of the researcher's own reflections, intuitions, thinking and experience as primary evidence for the research. *Intersubjective reflection* is concerned with the meanings emerging from the complex relationship dynamics between researcher and participants, and is more than mere reflection. *Mutual collaboration* occurs when the researcher and participants collaborate, and the participants become co-researchers sharing a reflexive dialogue. *Social critique* reflects on the management of the power imbalance between the researcher and the participants, taking into account issues such as, class, gender and race. *Discursive deconstruction* reflects on the ambiguity in the meaning of the language used in the research and how this is interpreted.

Watt (2007: 82) suggests that the researcher is the primary instrument for data collection and analysis, and thus reflexivity is essential. Therefore, for the purpose of this research, a more introspective reflexivity was used to reflect on the research process as a whole.

There are problems that can confront researchers in relation to reflexivity, such as the use of rhetoric to support biases, the outpouring of personal emotions, a cycle of deconstruction and reconstruction of elements within the research process and endless self-criticism, which may lose all meaning to the reader (Finlay, 2002: 226). With this in mind, it may be prudent to reflect on the following poem:

Reflexivity, like hypnotherapy, has various levels. Some dabble near the surface, dipping into reflexive moments, flirting with the images evoked in the reflection, before returning to the safety of the mundane. Others attempt to confront the fear of the monster lurking in the abyss by descending into the deeper realms of reflexivity. It is those who confront the beast who will truly know what is there, in the dark beyond. Reflect on this as you spin down down deep within.

(MacMillan, 1996: 29)

Lessons learned from this research

1. Using a mixed methods methodology, including methods such as questionnaires, interviews, observations and data analysis, is very complex.
2. This is also reflected in the complexity of the chosen mixed methods triangulation research design, which incorporated convergence and multilevel models for collecting and analysing data, and comparing and contrasting results.
3. The use of unstructured covert participant observation always raises ethical concerns and is often seen as unethical and deceptive. However, this view has to be balanced against its use as a method of searching for knowledge and truth, while still taking all the ethical issues into consideration.
4. Access to individuals and data was far easier as an Inside-Insider (police employee) at the commencement of this research compared to that of being an Outside-Insider and verging on becoming an Inside-Outsider (on retirement) towards the conclusion of the research.

References

Barriball, K.L. and While, A. (1994) 'Collecting Data Using a Semi-Structured Interview: A Discussion Paper', *Journal of Advanced Nursing*, 19(2): 328–335.

Bloor, M. (1978) 'On the Analysis of Observational Data: A Discussion on the Worth and Uses of Inductive Techniques and Respondent Validation', *Sociology*, 12(3): 545–552.

Bogen, K. (1996) 'The Effect of Questionnaire Length on Response Rates: A Review of the Literature', *Proceedings of the Section on Survey Research Methods* (American Statistical Association): Volume 91, 1020–1025.

Bramel, D. and Friend, R. (1981) 'Hawthorne, the Myth of the Docile Worker, and Class Bias in Psychology', *American Psychologist*, 36(8): 867–878.

British Sociological Association. (2004) *Statement of Ethical Practice for the British Sociological Association*, Durham: British Sociological Association (BSA).

Brown, J. (1996) 'Police Research: Some Critical Issues', in Leishman, F., Loveday, B. and Savage, S. (Eds) *Core Issues in Policing*, New York, NY: Longman, 249–263.

Bryman, A. (2006) 'Integrating Quantitative and Qualitative Research: How Is It Done?' *Qualitative Research*, 6(1): 97–113.

Bryman, A. (2012) *Social Research Methods* (4th ed.), Oxford: Oxford University Press.

Bryman, A., Becker, S. and Sempik, J. (2008) 'Quality Criteria for Quantitative, Qualitative and Mixed Methods Research: A View from Social Policy', *International Journal of Social Research Methodology*, 11(4): 261–276.

Bulmer, M. (1982) 'When Is Disguise Justified? Alternatives to Covert Participant Observation', *Qualitative Sociology*, 5(4): 251–264.

Campbell, D.T. and Fiske, D.W. (1959) 'Convergent and Discriminant Validation by the Multitrait-Multimethod Matrix', *Psychological Bulletin*, 56(2): 81–105.

Church, R.M. (2001) 'The Effective Use of Secondary Data', *Learning and Motivation*, 33: 32–45.

Corti, L., Foster, J. and Thompson, P. (1995) 'Archiving Qualitative Research Data', *Social Research Update* (Autumn 1995), Issue 10. Available at: http://sru.soc.surrey.ac.uk/SRU10.html [Accessed: 12 June 2013].

Council of Europe. (2010) *The European Convention on Human Rights (Convention for the Protection of Human Rights and Fundamental Freedoms), as Amended by Protocols Numbers 11 and 14*, Strasbourg: Council of Europe Publishing.

Creswell, J.W. and Miller, D.L. (2000) 'Determining Validity in Qualitative Inquiry', *Theory into Practice*, 39(3): 124–131.

Creswell, J.W. and Plano Clark, V.L. (2007) *Designing and Conducting Mixed Methods Research*, Thousand Oaks, CA: Sage.

Dale, A., Arber, S. and Proctor, M. (1988) *Doing Secondary Analysis*, London: Unwin Hyman.

Denzin, N.K. (1989) *Interpretive Interactionism*, Newbury Park, CA: Sage.

Denzin, N.K. (1978) *The Research Act: A Theoretical Introduction to Sociological Methods*, New York, NY: Praeger.

Denzin, N.K. (2009) *The Research Act: A Theoretical Introduction to Sociological Methods* (Paperback), Piscataway, NJ: Transaction.

Diener, E. and Crandall, R. (1978) *Ethics in Social and Behavioral Research*, Chicago, IL: University of Chicago Press.

Diesing, P. (1971) *Patterns of Discovery in the Social Sciences*, Chicago, IL: Aldine-Atherton.

Economic and Social Research Council. (2010) *Framework for Research Ethics*, Swindon: Economic and Social Research Council (ESRC).

Finlay, L. (2002) 'Negotiating the Swamp: The Opportunity and Challenge of Reflexivity in Research Practice', *Qualitative Research*, 2(2): 209–230.

Geertz, C. (1973) *The Interpretation of Cultures: Selected Essays*, New York, NY: Basic Books.

Golafshani, N. (2003) 'Understanding Reliability and Validity in Qualitative Research', *The Qualitative Report*, 8(4): 597–607.

Gorard, S. (2010) 'Research Design, as Independent of Methods', in Tashakkori, A. and Teddlie, C. (Eds) *SAGE Handbook of Mixed Methods in Social and Behavioral Research* (2nd ed.), Thousand Oaks, CA: Sage.

Grix, J. (2002) 'Introducing Students to the Generic Terminology of Social Research', *Politics*, 22(3): 175–186.

Guba, E.G. and Lincoln, Y.S. (1989) *Fourth Generation Evaluation*, Newbury Park, CA: Sage.

Guillemin, M. and Gillam, L. (2004) 'Ethics, Reflexivity, and "Ethically Important Moments" in Research', *Qualitative Inquiry*, 10(2): 261–280.

Hakim, C. (1982) *Secondary Analysis in Social Research: A Guide to Data Sources and Methods with Examples*, London: Allen and Unwin.

Hammersley, M. (1995) *The Politics of Social Research*, London: Sage.

Hammersley, M. and Atkinson, P. (1995) *Ethnography: Principles in Practice* (2nd ed.), London: Routledge.

Hammersley, M. and Atkinson, P. (2007) *Ethnography: Principles in Practice* (3rd ed.), London: Routledge.

Hammersley, M. and Traianou, A. (2012) *Ethics and Educational Research*, London: British Educational Research Association.

Handwerker, W.P. (2005) 'Sample Design', *Encyclopedia of Social Measurement*, 3: 429–436.

Harrison, J., MacGibbon, L. and Morton, M. (2001) 'Regimes of Trustworthiness in Qualitative Research: The Rigors of Reciprocity', *Qualitative Inquiry*, 7(3): 323–345.

Heaton, J. (2000) *Secondary Analysis of Qualitative Data: A Review of the Literature*, York: Social Policy Research Unit (SPRU), University of York.

Heaton, J. (2008) 'Secondary Analysis of Qualitative Data: An Overview', *Historical Social Research*, 33(3): 33–45.

Home Office. (1998a) *Data Protection Act 1998*, London: The Stationery Office.

Home Office. (1998b) *Human Rights Act 1998*, London: The Stationery Office.

Jupp, V. (1989) *Methods of Criminological Research*, London: Routledge.

Kimmel, A.J. (1988) *Ethics and Values in Applied Social Research*, Newbury Park, CA: Sage.

Kirk, J. and Miller, M.L. (1986) *Reliability and Validity in Qualitative Research*, Newbury Park, CA: Sage.

Kvale, S. (1996) *Interviews: An Introduction to Qualitative Research Interviewing*, London: Sage.

Lee, R.M. (1993) *Doing Research on Sensitive Topics*, London: Sage.

Leming, M.R. (1997) *Research and Sampling Designs: Techniques for Evaluating Hypotheses*. Available at: http://www.stolaf.edu/people/leming/soc371res/research.html [Accessed: 19 July 2013].

Lincoln, Y.S. and Guba, E.G. (1985) *Naturalistic Inquiry*, Newbury Park, CA: Sage.

Lugosi, P. (2006) 'Between Overt and Covert Research: Concealment and Disclosure in an Ethnographic Study of Commercial Hospitality', *Qualitative Inquiry*, 12(3): 541–561.

Lynch, M. (2000) 'Against Reflexivity as an Academic Virtue and Source of Privileged Knowledge', *Theory, Culture and Society*, 17(3): 26–54.

MacMillan, K. (1996) *Trance-scripts: The Poetics of a Reflexive Guide to Hypnosis and Trance Talk* (Unpublished PhD Thesis), Loughborough: Loughborough University.

Mason, J. (2002) *Qualitative Researching* (2nd ed.), London: Sage.

Mason, J. (2004) 'Semistructured Interview', in Lewis-Beck, M., Bryman, A. and Futing Liao, T. (Eds) *The SAGE Encyclopaedia of Social Science Research Methods* (Volume 1), London: Sage.

Mertens, D.M. (2005) *Research and Evaluation in Education and Psychology: Integrating Diversity with Quantitative, Qualitative and Mixed Methods* (2nd ed.), Thousand Oaks, CA: Sage.

Morse, J.M., Barrett, M., Mayan, M., Olson, K. and Spiers, J. (2002) 'Verification Strategies for Establishing Reliability and Validity in Qualitative Research', *International Journal of Qualitative Methods*, 1(2): 13–22.

Neuman, W.L. (2000) *Social Research Methods: Qualitative and Quantitative Approaches* (4th ed.), Boston, MA: Allyn and Bacon.

Newell, R. (1993) 'Questionnaires', in Gilbert, N. (Ed.) (1993) *Researching Social Life*, London: Sage.

Olson, R., Verley, J., Santos, L. and Salas, C. (2004) 'What We Teach Students About the Hawthorne Studies: A Review of Content Within a Sample of

Introductory I-O and OB Textbooks', *The Industrial-Organizational Psychologist*, 41(3): 23–39.

Payne, G. and Payne, J. (2004) *Key Concepts in Social Research*, London: Sage.

Pels, D. (2000) 'Reflexivity: One Step Up', *Theory, Culture and Society*, 17(3): 1–25.

Punch, M. (1994) 'Politics and Ethics in Qualitative Research', in Denzin, N.K. and Lincoln, Y.S. (Eds) *Handbook of Qualitative Research*, Thousand Oaks, CA: Sage.

Rogers, C. (2007) *Community Intelligence Initiative in 'A' Division (BCU): An Independent Evaluation*, Pontypridd: University of Glamorgan.

Rogers, C. and Gravelle, J. (2008) *Use of the Community Intelligence Diary (CID) System: An Independent Evaluation*, Pontypridd: University of Glamorgan.

Scott, J. and Marshall, G. (Eds) (2009) *Oxford Dictionary of Sociology* (3rd ed. Revised), Oxford: Oxford University Press.

Shenton, A.K. (2004) 'Strategies for Ensuring Trustworthiness in Qualitative Research Projects', *Education for Information*, 22: 63–75.

Sieber, J.E. (1992) *Planning Ethically Responsible Research*, London: Sage.

Social Research Association. (2003) *Ethical Guidelines*, London: Social Research Association.

Spicker, P. (2011) 'Ethical Covert Research', *Sociology*, 45(1): 118–133.

Stanley, B., Sieber, J.E. and Melton, G.B. (1987) 'Empirical Studies of Ethical Issues in Research: A Research Agenda', *American Psychologist*, 42(7): 735–741.

Tashakkori, A. and Teddlie, C. (2003) *Handbook of Mixed Methods in Social and Behavioral Research*, Thousand Oaks, CA: Sage.

Teddlie, C. and Yu, F. (2007) 'Mixed Methods Sampling: A Typology with Examples', *Journal of Mixed Methods Research*, 1(1): 77–100.

Watt, D. (2007) 'On Becoming a Qualitative Researcher: The Value of Reflexivity', *The Qualitative Report*, 12(1): 82–101.

Webb, E.J., Campbell, D.T., Schwartz, R.D. and Sechrest, L. (1966) *Unobtrusive Measures: Nonreactive Research in the Social Sciences*, Chicago, IL: Rand McNally.

Wiles, R., Heath, S., Crow, G. and Charles, V. (2004) *Informed Consent in Social Research: A Literature Review*, Southampton: Economic and Social Research Council (ESRC), National Centre for Research Methods.

5
Collaboration in Crime Prevention Partnerships: Research with a Multilevel Mixed Design

Bernhard Frevel

Research methods involved

1. Quantitative

Self-completion Questionnaire survey, quantitative network analysis and data statistical analysis

2. Qualitative

Problem-centred interviews, analysis of documents, participatory observation

About this research

The complex research project 'Cooperative Security Policy in the City' was designed as a project based on comparative case studies with intra- and inter-comparison of four fields of action using a multilevel mixed methods concurrent complementary and embedded design. The research aims were as follows:

- What is the definition and estimation of security problems?
- How is the need for action defined? By whom?
- How does the need for action lead to action?
- Is this action delivered in collaboration and cooperation?
- How is this cooperation organised?
- Which forms (communication, coordination and cooperation) of collaboration are implemented?
- Are measures evaluated and which criteria are used therefore?

This research was conducted between 2010 and 2012.

5.1 Methodological summary

The research project 'Cooperative Security Policy in the City' was designed as a study based on comparative case studies with intra- and inter-comparison of four fields of action. The research methods involved were of a mixed approach and comprised of the following:

- problem-centred interviews;
- analysis of documents;
- statistics (socio-demography, socioeconomy, crime data);
- quantitative network analysis;
- participatory observation;
- standardised survey.

5.2 Aims of research

The research project 'Cooperative Security Policy in the City' took place in the context of the German national funding programme 'Research for Civil Security', which is overseen by the Federal Ministry of Education and Research. This programme was first applied in 2007 and is now running in the second framework for another five years (BMBF, 2012). The ministry characterises the concept of security research:

> This security research programme is not purely technological. Numerous projects deal with realistic scenarios, such as football matches or concerts. This research concentrates on damage prevention as well as measures to deal with crises. In order to improve the security of visitors at such large events, new organizational concepts and strategies of action are being developed. Researchers in the fields of natural, technical, and social sciences, as well as in the humanities, are working closely with end-users and industry from the beginning onwards. Only in this way can security solutions be adjusted to meet practical needs.

Since 2007, in the average 50 m EUR per year are spent on research projects. Every year there are about three calls for proposals to different main topics, e.g.

- Societal aspects of civil security research;
- Urban security;
- Security of infrastructure and business;

- Protection and rescue solutions;
- Protection from hazardous substances, epidemics and pandemics.

Scientists from universities, institutes and R&D departments of companies are invited to come forward with proposals, which should be with an interdisciplinary approach and to be planned by an association of different partners. The research project 'cooperative security policy in the city' was carried out between May 2010 and September 2012 by University of Münster – Institute for Political Science (WWU), European Centre for Crime Prevention (EZK), University of Greifswald (EMAU), University of Applied Science for Public Administration of North Rhine-Westphalia (FHöV) and the Hessian University of Applied Science for Police and Public Administration (HfPV). At the University of Münster, two junior researchers were employed, and they were supported by two PhD students (responsible for the studies in two fields of action) and several student assistants (who were involved in the transcription of interviews, data entry, helping at conferences, etc.). The EZK employed one researcher and gave a special assignment for a theoretical study to a part-time researcher. The University of Greifswald and the Hessian University employed one research assistant each, while the FHöV was involved with a graduate assistant and the exemption of the KoSiPol-project coordinator from lecture tasks. All researchers were supervised by local professors or senior researchers.

Many problems of security and public order, crime and fear of crime are to be seen in the local area. In the villages, cities and neighbourhoods, different problems can be seen. Their cause lay in the social proximity and they often offend people. Up to the late 1980s, dealing with these problems was mainly separated by different responsibilities of police and Local authorities. However, in the 1990s, a fundamental shift could be seen in Germany. The collaboration of different stakeholders was developed and later also demanded by the government. Inspired by examples in the United Kingdom and Scandinavian countries, different networks such as Crime Prevention Councils and Public Order Partnerships, Round Tables, etc. were established.

For the purposes of this work, we decided to work with case studies. Having four fields of action, each was analysed in four cities. This made it possible to compare in and between the different fields and to find out about similarities and differences in the set of stakeholders, the policies and measures. The analysis followed sociological, criminological and political perspectives.

Trying to put the observable collaborative security policy in relation to the safety feelings and security estimation of citizens, a standardised survey was added.

Besides the more academic results, e.g. on safety and security governance or the changes in policing, it was an aim of the project to develop concepts for better networking and manuals for education and training to improve the collaboration in crime prevention. The concept of KoSiPol can be depicted as follows (Figure 5.1):

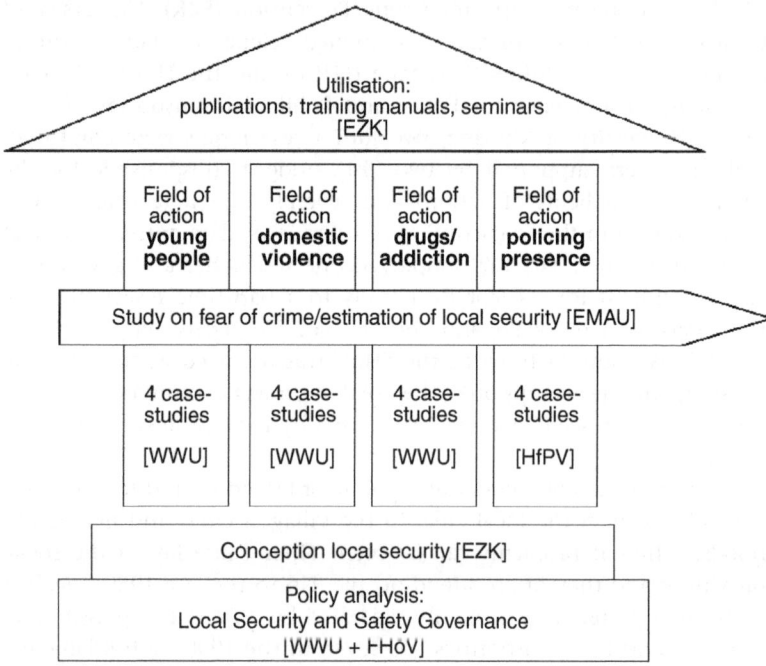

Figure 5.1   KoSiPol work packages and responsible institutes

Research questions

Compared to partnerships in England and Wales, there are no statutory requirements about the participants, organisational patterns or the aims of partnerships in Germany. Each city, police force and the other stakeholders are free to set an agenda, to decide about the approach and to admit or refuse membership. This offers the possibility for a wide range of concepts and measures. So we wanted to find out about the initiation of collaboration and the way to results, following the questions listed below:

- What is the definition and estimation of security problems?
- How is the need for action defined? By whom?
- How does the need for action lead to action?
- Is this action delivered in collaboration and cooperation?
- How is this cooperation organised?
- Which forms (communication, coordination and cooperation) of collaboration are implemented?
- Are measures evaluated and which criteria are used?

To answer these questions the researchers differentiated four main areas with several different topics, which were analysed with the instruments explained in the following sections.

(1) Organisation

- Involved stakeholders and disregarded players
- Organisational and operational structure
- Organisational development
- Qualification and position of representatives

(2) Agenda-setting and decision-making

- Definition and estimation of problems – evidence-based?
- Discussion and forming of the will
- Decision criteria
- Decision-making
- Implementation and evaluation

(3) Power structure and bargaining

- Resources of power and influence
- Barter items, e.g. information, knowledge, access to target groups, financial resources, infrastructure
- Role of police and local authorities

(4) Measures and activities

- Target course
- Focus on community, victims, offenders, situational context or institutions and service
- Knowledge-based methods

We had some fundamental questions on the methodology to answer when the project was introduced and the grant proposal had to be written.

- Do we want a representative result or would it be 'enough' to gain qualified insight in the collaboration and the committees?
- Do we want to explore a broad field of topics or would it be better to concentrate on a well-grounded selection?
- If we concentrate on this selection: Which criteria should be developed to justify the choice?
- How do we guarantee an acceptable variance of case studies?
- Which design of methods should be applied?

These and some more questions were discussed until we submitted the proposal. In the core, we decided to concentrate on four fields of action in which each four case studies should be analysed. The four fields were those who had in the studies of Kant/Pütter/Hohmeier (2006), Schreiber (2007) and the Landespräventionsrat NRW (2011) been characterised as the most often picked topics in local crime prevention activities and varied in the direction of impact. While the field of work 'juvenile delinquency' mainly focusses on the offenders, the committees on 'domestic violence' concentrate on the situation of the victims. In the field 'drugs and addiction', we witness the interdependency and interaction of criminal, social and health policies. The fourth field 'policing presence' shows a variance in the different setting of stakeholders like police, local authority, private security companies and police volunteers.

Case studies

As it was more important to learn about the internal structures of crime prevention councils and public order partnerships than to get an overview of those committees, the decision towards case studies and the comparative approach was soon made. In case studies, different cases are compared; the comparison allows us to explore the regularities, differences and similarities. Having more than one case makes the study more valid and reliable, but practical reasons of research limit the number of cases to about ten (Borchardt/Göthlich, 2007: 36–37). Another advantage of case studies is that they are not connected to a certain research methodology but allow a creative and pragmatic choice of instruments, quite often with a qualitative bias (Lamnek, 2005: 301). The combination of instruments and methods avoids the distortion of results based on single method approaches (Kromrey, 2006: 535). The analysis and

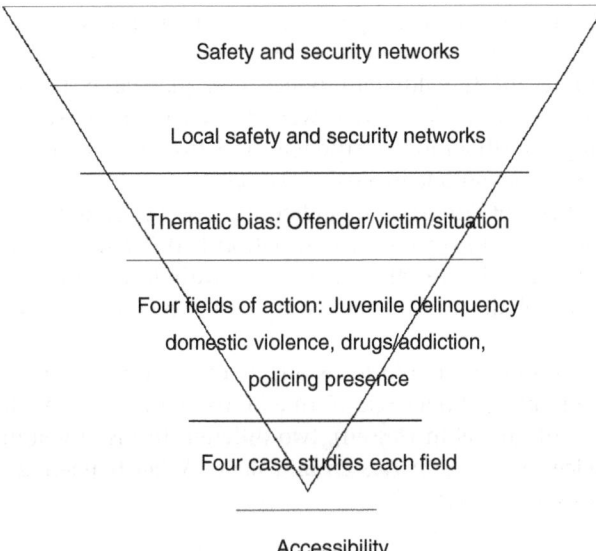

Safety and security networks

Local safety and security networks

Thematic bias: Offender/victim/situation

Four fields of action: Juvenile delinquency
domestic violence, drugs/addiction,
policing presence

Four case studies each field

Accessibility

Figure 5.2   Funnel of containment

description should regard many aspects, but 'it is not the aim to include dimensions and variables as many as possible, but it is crucial not to reduce the subject of investigation to just a few variables' (Lamnek, 2005: 299).

As the frame conditions are different in the four KoSiPol fields of action, the ways of selection had to be considered. The common core of all cases was the participation of police and municipality in the committee.

The planning followed the model of a funnel (Figure 5.2).

The criteria for the selection of the case studies varied between the fields of action:

- In the field 'domestic violence', we decided that the four studies should be in one member state of Germany, namely North Rhine-Westphalia, because it seemed important to have one judicial setting and organisational framing for the action of police and municipalities. Two cases should be in bigger cities (about 300,000 inhabitants) and two cases in counties, following the thesis that the social nearness and social control influence this form of violence and also the ways of handling the problems.

- In the field 'juvenile delinquency', it was more important to orientate on the situational context of bigger cities (>250,000 inhabitants) than to regard the different police and judicial systems of several member states. Two cities were chosen in the western part of Germany (North Rhine-Westphalia) and two in Eastern Germany, one in Saxony and one in Saxony-Anhalt.
- In the field of 'drugs and addiction', we believed that in bigger cities with universities, the situation is different from counties in rural parts. So we chose two cities with universities in North Rhine-Westphalia and Lower-Saxony and two counties in the same states.
- 'Policing presence' should focus on the collaboration of police with a sort of municipal police (uniformed force of the cities' public order department, model in Hessen), two different forms of volunteers in the police force like in Hessen and Baden-Wuerttemberg and with private security firms.

Having decided about the selection criteria, eligible committees were screened in an Internet research and database research. Committees were contacted by telephone and asked whether they work in the fields of action, and interested in being analysed by scientists and would support the studies. After this 'door-opening' contact, the networks were informed in a formal 'snail-mail' letter and – if wished – in a visit of a meeting. After we received the formal letter of agreement of the networks, all the ministries of interior, which are responsible for police and municipalities, were informed about the project and asked for permission to do research in the police forces.

The exploration of the field and the efforts to gain field access is a sensitive, strenuous and time-consuming task, which needs not only knowledge and information but also some sort of reputation of the enquirer – if you do not want to be 'expelled' too early. So the letters of intent were written on official note paper of the universities and signed by a professor.

Having decided about the field and identified the cases, the concrete methodology had to be developed and we chose a mixed methods design.

Mixed methods design

Intermixtures of different quantitative and qualitative methods, techniques and data are found in social science research since the 1960s

(Johnson/Onwuegbuzie/Turner, 2007: 113 pp.). But the discussion about mixed methods design only really took place in about the last 20 years. Tashakkori/Teddlie (2007a: 711) understand mixed methods as

> a type of research design in which qualitative and quantitative approaches are used in types of questions, research methods, data collection and analysis procedures and/or inferences.

KoSiPol follows a pragmatic conception, which is described by Tashakkori/Teddlie (2007a: 713) as

> a deconstructive paradigm that debunks concepts such as 'truth' and 'reality' and focusses instead on 'what works' as the truth regarding the research questions under investigation. Pragmatism rejects the either/or choice associated with the paradigm wars, advocates for the use of mixed methods in research and acknowledges that the values of the researcher play a large role in interpretation of results.

KoSiPol states a *multilevel mixed methods concurrent complementary and embedded design* (see Cresswell/Plano Clark, 2007: 62; Tashakkori/Teddlie. 2007b: 688). It is a multilevel model, because different methods of documentary analysis, written and oral questionings were used so as to encompass the different levels in local networks and to merge them in a comprehensive interpretation of findings (Cresswell/Plano Clark, 2007: 65). The core lies in the concurrent complementary design, in which parallel/concurrent quantitative data gathered in the written questionnaire and qualitative data from documentary analysis and interviews are collected and analysed.

With the combination of qualitative and quantitative data, the specific advantages and disadvantages of the different methods can be balanced and a broad picture of the local crime preventions partnerships can be drawn. To save the different strength of qualitative and quantitative data, these are collected independently and not merged until the interpretation phase. The results of the written and oral interviews, documentary analysis and other ways of data acquisition can be interpreted together. This has to be done in awareness of the overcoming of old paradigm wars and the comprehension that all research designs can be seen in a continuum of quantitative and qualitative aspects (Teddlie/Tashakkori, 2009: 93pp.).

The KoSiPol research was underpinned by documentary analysis and interviews as qualitative approaches but embedded was a quantitative study on the sense of security.

> The Embedded Design is a mixed methods design in which one data set provides a supportive, secondary role in a study based primarily on the other data type.
>
> (Cresswell/Plano Clark, 2007: 67)

The results of this study on fear of crime should answer questions about risk assessments of citizens, trust in security stakeholders, estimate of their coping competence and the knowledge and perception of local crime prevention networks. The integration of data widens the findings about the estimation of safety and security and allows a multidimensional perspective on local security on 'objective' and 'subjective' level. The data of this survey are not needed in the sense of triangulation to validate other findings but can be analysed independently (Figure 5.3).

As shown above, KoSiPol used a broad set of methods, which are now described to justify the approach.

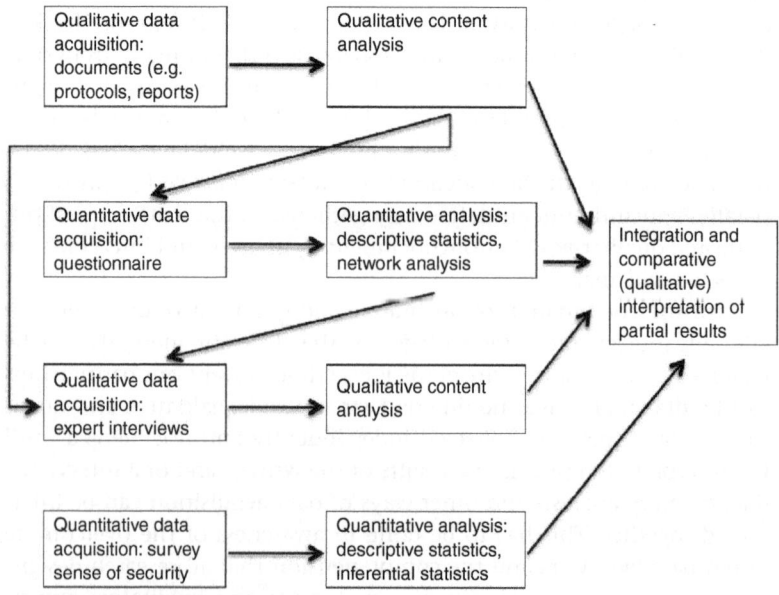

Figure 5.3   KoSiPol research design
Source: Adapted from Voelzke (2011: 13).

5.3 Analysis of documents

The analysis of documents was the starting point of the research. The most important documents were formal agreements about the networks, concepts, mission statements, protocols of meetings, brochures, activity reports and media reports. These documents gave insight into the structure of committees, approaches and measures, important persons, developments and critical incidents.

On the basis of these documents, several steps of analysis were taken:

(1) A characterisation of each committee could be written, which described the genesis of the network, the main aims, token measures and the set of stakeholders.
(2) The protocols were especially important to draw an organigram of each network, which showed the involved organisations and persons, the hierarchical structure, the division of labour and the communication between steering committees and work groups, etc. On this basis, a typology of networks could be developed.
(3) Important persons could be identified, who would be interviewed in the following steps of research.

The analysis of documents gave quite interesting information, that the continuity of work depends on a small circle of actors, that the discussion and decision about the aims of the networks and the understanding of 'prevention' is often avoided, that the mixture of stakeholders is not really based on strategic considerations but on personal acquaintance, sympathy and supposed qualification. The initial actor of the network has a special role, as he/she seeks his/her partners and recruits them by co-optation.

5.4 Questionnaire and quantitative network analysis

After gaining an overview over the networks, which expanded from small steering committees with a handful of members to large nets with more than 50 institutions and organisations, we had the aim to learn more about internal processes of the networks, the expectations and experiences of participants, the estimation of failures and success of previous work, e.g. in the aspects of efficiency, continuity and collaboration. Another aim was to detect the persons or organisations of influence and power and to find out, which resources found power and influence.

A standardised questionnaire seemed the best method for this research interest. With this instrument, it was possible to access the more than 300 participating persons in the 12 networks. A high grade of standardisation allows quantitative analysis with descriptive statistics. The instrument is 'faster' than face-to-face interviews and it was cheaper as the managers of the committees took the task of distribution of the papers. Another expected advantage of a questionnaire is the fact that they are completed anonymously, which allows for criticism better and easier than face-to-face interviews (Schnell/Hill/Esser, 2011: 315pp.; Atteslander, 2008: 121pp.).

The questionnaire contained open and scaled questions, e.g. about

- personal and the institutional reasons to participate in the committees;
- the invested time, money, manpower and other resources and competences;
- the estimation of adequate financial resources, agreement of common aims, the number and qualification of participants, competence of agenda setting, decision and implementation of measures;
- the assessment of function and role of the committees, the link to the institutions participating in the networks and the acceptance of the work done in the meetings;
- the rating of the most important successes and the three aims that have not been achieved.

In a second part of the questionnaire, the quantitative network analysis was placed. As we always talk about 'crime prevention networks', the network analysis seemed a 'born' method.

> The subject matter of network analysis is the inspection of the structure of social relations between actors. The relation of actors to each other and their particular position in a network of social relations are regarded as the crucial explicatory variable in a multitude of social phenomena.
>
> (Beckert, 2005: 286, translation bf)

The network analysis we implemented was not oriented to 'ego-networks', which try to find out which analysed person (ego) stays in contact to other persons (alter) and how different networks are connected and to examine the size, composition and density or interconnectedness of the resultant personal or ego networks. Instead, we wanted to describe the structure in the defined nets. Who stays in contact with whom? Are there gatekeepers in the committees? Who shares which resources with whom? Which person is regarded as important and powerful? (Jansen, 2006)

The questionnaire was a very important tool for the research project. It showed that the analysed committees were mainly led and structured by the representatives of the police and the municipalities. Welfare organisations were in nearly all networks involved, but only got in leadership position in the field 'drugs and addiction'. The answers made clear that the synergetic implementation of measures is not the main task. More important is the communication of stakeholders, the meeting of other persons in charge, the finding of shortcuts to the official chains of command. The valuable barter items in the networks are information, access to target groups and the integration of knowledge of different professions. The working of several professions in the committees bridged the gap between police, public administration and social work, and improved the acceptance and appreciation of the partners.

The quantitative network analysis was not as meaningful as the questionnaire. The analysis of different networks, such as reputation, several resources (such as finances, manpower, information), power, etc., was very complex and laborious. The visualisation in different graphs – constructed with the network analysis software UCINET – was not as informative as expected. The constrained evidence was due to the smallness of some committees and – in some cases – unsatisfactory return rate. The information we gathered could somehow validate the results of other methods, especially of the interviews and the questionnaire, but could not offer significant new insights and interesting perspectives. The cost–benefit ratio of this instrument was not satisfying.

5.5 Problem-centred interviews

The core task of the KoSiPol project was to learn about the networks, their participants, the agenda-setting and decision-making, the bargaining and barter goods in the collaboration, the self-set or given aims, the understanding of prevention and measures, the arrangements of influence and power, etc. The interview of participants of committees and also representatives of involved organisations and institutions was the selected method to gain information about these matters.

In social science, there are some different approaches for interviews such as

- narrative interview,
- episodic interview,
- problem-centred interview/expert interview,
- ethnographic dialogue,

which differ, e.g. in the grade of structure, the bias on monologue or dialogue and the role of the interviewer (Hirschmann/Kaup, 2011: 59).

The problem-centred interview, which is similar to expert interviews and guided semi-structured interviews,

> is a theory-generating method that tries to neutralize the alleged contradiction between being directed by theory or being open-minded so that the interplay of inductive and deductive thinking contributes to increasing the user's knowledge. The appropriate communication strategies aim firstly at the representation of the subjective approach to the problem, secondly the stimulated narratives are enriched by dialogues employing imaginative and semi-structured prompts. Theoretical knowledge develops by using elastic concepts that are further developed during the analysis by employing empirical analysis and which will be refined by 'testing' empirically grounded 'hypotheses' with the data.
>
> (Witzel, 2000)

The guided interview is principally a not-standardised method of collecting data, but gains its structure and steering through a prepared list of widely open formulated questions. This opens the chance for the interviewee to answer extensively and in his own tempo to the several aspects. This sort of interview is different from everyday communication because of the accepted asymmetrical role of the constellation of interviewer and interviewee and the predefinition of topics. But on the other hand, this interview is open for extra information, additional questions and the changing of interview sequences as it fits to the conversation. This is a main difference to oral structured interviews.

The ways to find the experts who were to be interviewed were (a) the definition of the 'fields', like regarded institutions (police, municipality, social service) and the hierarchical positions (chiefs, middle management, operative personnel); (b) the analysis of the protocols; (c) the questioning of 'gatekeepers' who know about the internal structure of the committees and the important persons.

The interview guide contained different questions about experience, knowledge, attitudes, position in the organisation (hierarchical position, belonging to departments) and the committees (leader, management board, member) and personal aspects (age, qualification).

After a short introduction by the interviewer about the research project and its aims, a description of the interview, the analysis and the promise of anonymity, the interview started with the chapter about the network and the participants. The interviewees were asked to describe the task of the network, the function of the organisation/institution the person represents, and the own way into the network (delegated, invited, self-application). The second block was about the collaboration. How do you typically collaborate? How do you deal with conflicts and differences? Who are the persons you work closely with? Which other persons, working in this field of action but outside your organisation and outside the network, are important for you? Who is missing from the committee?

The third part of the interview was about the interchange, the importance of the committee collaboration for the own institution, the relation of costs and benefits, the own input and the expected output, the estimation whether some stakeholders give in less than others and what this means for the communication. The fourth interview section was about the fields of action: estimation of the problem, measures taken and planned, etc. The fifth was about the personal positions. Do the persons like to work in the committee, do they think it is an important task, how do they rate their own importance and the own inputs? Are they satisfied with the cooperation? The last question was about the expectation for the further collaboration and the ideas for improvement.

More than 100 persons were interviewed mainly in face-to-face interaction of interviewer and interviewee, sometimes two researchers were involved in an interview and sometimes two interviewees were questioned. In some cases, the interview was held through telephone.

All interviews were transcribed and made anonymous. Therefore, a code was developed:

- the cities/counties were termed alphabetically, from A to P;
- the institutional belonging was abbreviated: P – police, K – Kommune (municipality), S – social work, J – justice...;
- the interviews were numbered consecutively.

The code 'AP2' would stand for the second interview held with a member of the police in city A.

A content analysis of the copied interviews followed a prescribed categorisation of elements, but these categories were evaluated during the analysis, so some categories were added, some other were combined, which allowed a dynamic gathering of data and comprehension of information.

The problem-centred interviews were the most valuable source of information and the most important method in this project. They provided information, which could not be found in written material (protocols, reports, etc.), which were necessary for the interpretation of the questionnaires. With the interviews, the similarities and differences between (a) the fields of action, (b) the cases, (c) the involved institutions and (d) the position of interviewees could be extracted and shown. Some core problems were mentioned in several interviews and pointed to fundamental difficulties of collaboration, of crime prevention and the need for improvement.

5.6   Statistics on socio-demography, socioeconomic, and crime data)

The case studies took place in very different cities and counties spread all over Germany. Some were located in poorer parts and some in wealthy regions; the smallest city had about 13,000 and the largest some million inhabitants. The case studies were done in the northern, western, eastern and southern member states of the federal republic. It is a basic criminological belief that the size of cities influences the crime level and that also the socioeconomic situation not only of individuals but also of communities has an effect on crime rates, incivilities and disorder. Therefore, it seemed necessary to look at some descriptive statistics of the cities and counties.

To achieve an overview of the cities, some core data were collected. These are, e.g.

- socio-demographic structure: total of inhabitants, age, sex, ethnic minorities
- socioeconomic structure: important sectors of economy (which sort of industry, service sector), employment, unemployment rate
- crime data: total offenses and cases, suspects (age, sex, nationality), clearance rate, number of suspects per 100,000 inhabitants, offense rate, selected offences in the sectors street crime, violent crime, drug offenses

Most of the data were online accessible on the Internet sites of the cities and counties, the local chambers of commerce and the job centres. The crime statistics in Germany are published by the Federal Criminal Police Office and the similar police authorities of the member states, but the data are highly aggregated and not differentiated for single cities. But the state offices for criminal investigation in the different states were able to provide the project with special statistical evaluations for the 16 cities and counties.

The data showed the expected similarities and differences and gave insight into the societal framing of the committees. They gave some explanations and were needed for illustration, but they were not really important for the analysis of the collaboration.

5.7   Participatory observation

If one wants to learn about the collaboration of persons and institutions, it is not enough to concentrate on written material and to believe the answers given in interviews. It is also worthwhile to observe the social processes, the atmosphere of meetings, the ways of decision-making, the art of discussion, the behaviour of important persons, the presentation of influence and power.

The arsenal of social scientific methods offers some different approaches for this sort of study. It is to differ between some modes (Table 5.1).

The only realistic way of observing the meetings and the arrangement of collaboration was the open and participatory observation. But the setting of the participation of the researchers in meetings was always different to the 'normal' setting. As soon as the researchers took part, the discussion was about the research project and the regular topics were postponed. The researchers had no chance of observing longer parts of the meetings and during the sessions they were themselves objects of interest. Only on a few occasions were some chances to learn about and feel the climate of the collaboration, but the validity of the observation was always unsatisfactory. So we could get some impression of the working atmosphere and of the behaviour of some people, but this never reached the level of reliable data and could not be considered as research in the narrower sense.

5.8   Standardised survey

Do the crime prevention networks deal with the real and – from the citizens' viewpoint – important problems? Do these networks influence the sense of safety and the estimation of security? What do the people

Table 5.1 Positive and negative aspects of observation

	Description	Positive	Negative
Systematic obs.	The observer is advised to look out for defined events and topics	Appropriate for quantitative analysis, distinct comparability (if the frame conditions are similar)	Some undefined events and topics are ignored even if they were important for the behaviour
Non-systematic obs.	The observer has not received any advice	In a complex situation, the (from the perspective of the observer) relevant aspects can be captured	Restrained comparability as different observers probably rate the events different
Participatory obs.	The observer is part of the social situation and embedded in the social interaction	As social reality only emerges in collective action, she can only be understood by participation	The behaviour of the observer influences the situation; risk of too much role identification and losing the scientific distance
Non-participatory obs.	Observer stands outside the situation	Especially unobservable in experimental settings; no influence of the observer on the situation	Nearly only unobservable in experiments in which the observer is outside the room and observes through a window or with video-technique
Open obs.	The observed people know about the observation	Easier execution, more honest to the observed people	The knowledge about the observation can influence the behaviour of the observed because they want to act 'correct'
Hidden obs.	The observed people do not know about the observation	Insight into an unadulterated situation	Juridical and ethical problematic

Source: Frevel (1999: 22–23).

fear and are they afraid to become a victim – and if so, which offence do they expect to happen? Do the men and women carry weapons (pepper spray, knives) to improve their ability of self-defence? Have the people experienced some sort of victimisation? Do the people trust the police? And what should the police and other actors do to improve the safety in the city?

As the other methods concentrated on the networks and the mainly professional participants in the committees, it was important to contrast their professional view with the citizens' estimation and expectations. Therefore, we decided to integrate a crime survey into the KoSiPol-methodology. In all 16 cities and counties, in which the case studies were conducted, the survey should be implemented. Two colleagues from the Department of Psychology at the Ernst-Moritz-Arndt-University Greifswald were assigned to develop the method and to lead the study.

The tradition of standardised surveys on fear of crime is quite young in Germany and started in the mid-1990s, nearly parallel with the 'boom' of crime prevention councils (Frevel, 1998). Following the fundamental study of Boers (1991), the methodological instrument was developed and in some parts standardised. The attitudes towards crime, incivilities and disorder, their cognitive, affective and cognitive dimensions, the context of fear of crime and other aspects were analysed in several surveys and 'best practice' items were developed. The Greifswald colleagues, Anne Köhn and Manfred Bornewasser, decided to orientate the study on these previous studies, their questions and scales, and they designed a questionnaire based on proved instruments. The objects of investigation were socio-demographic variables, the standard indicator for fear of crime (fear of the darkness in the neighbourhood), attitudes to crime, media consumption, social disintegration, variance of fear and optimism, direct and indirect victimisation, and vulnerability and social cohesion (Bornewasser/Köhn, 2012: 196–197). Also, they developed a special questionnaire, which should concentrate on questions specific to the four fields of action.

The distribution of the questionnaire was organised in three different ways:

(1) printed questionnaires were laid out in town halls, open libraries and other frequently used places, where they could be taken and given back; also, it was possible to send them back by mail;

(2) in the local press, the survey was announced and the motivated people could use an Internet link to the online survey;

(3) in some cities/regions, where the return rate was miserable, student research assistants led the standardised interviews face to face.

Nearly 4000 questionnaires could be utilised and at least 200 could be assigned to each case study. With this rate, it was still not possible to claim representativeness, but a well-founded trend could be drawn.

Most of the 'traditional' findings were proved in this study again. Women are more frightened than men, elderly people do not feel as safe as young people, the feeling of insecurity raises with the size of the city. Burglary, vandalism, theft and robbery are the most feared offences, while rape and sexual assaults are seldom mentioned. People who were already victimised felt more insecure than men and women without this experience.

More interesting were the findings that the crime prevention councils, round tables and other networks were unknown to often more than two-thirds, up to 80%, of the interviewees. This shows that the networks not only often work unrecognised and unnoticed, but with this they also fail in their – often manifested – aim to influence the citizens' estimation of safety and security. Also, they are not able to address people to contact them and discuss matters of crime prevention with them. This shows that most of the networks are established to improve the collaboration of professionals and do not have the character of community partnerships.

5.9   Ethical considerations

Empirical social science always concerns and affects people, influences their life and being, eventually shakes people and/or their situation up. Therefore, the scientists have to be aware of the risks they might trigger with their research.

All the universities in Germany have to develop a 'code of good scientific practice' and also the scientific associations, such as the 'German Association for Political Science', provide the researchers with an ethical codex. Putting aside the chapters about the rule to work *lege artis*, to aspire objectivity and integrity, to regard the rights of employed scientists and involved students, the very important part of the codex regards the situation of researched persons.

In brief, the research has to respect

- the voluntariness of participation and the always given right to break off being researched,

- the agreement of participation based on information about the aims of research and the usage of results,
- the right of not being damaged and harmed by the research,
- the personal rights.

Furthermore, the scientists have to be aware that the research can damage the field, hinder field access for other researchers and badly influence the reputation of scientists, science and research.

Ethical aspects have to be considered in building up a research design, of which all people involved in the research programme (researchers, research and student assistants, secretaries, administrative staff) must be aware.

In KoSiPol, the ethical risks were to some degree limited, as we didn't deal with vulnerable people and kept distance to intimate privacy matters. All interviewees were informed about the research idea, the aspired aims and the utilisation of insights in scientific reports and manuals for education and training. The anonymity was guaranteed and – by the techniques described above – applied.

All people involved in the KoSiPol research were issued with the codex. The implications were discussed in meetings and reflected during the empirical phases of research. Also, in the phase of writing the reports, we checked our structure and the conclusions under the aspects of ethical consideration.

5.10 Reflection

Including the time for the development of the research idea and the writing of the proposal for the funding, the preparation of the research, the implementation and analysis, the writing of reports and the subsequent workload (presentations, conferences and seminars), the project KoSiPol lasted about 3½ years – interesting, inspiring and laborious. The reflection of the lessons learned has to look at different aspects. On the one hand, we have to consider the findings. Which research questions could be answered and what did we discover and mirror to our analysed networks, the crime prevention 'scene'? On the other hand, we have to answer self-critically whether our research design was sufficient for the analysis. Let us start with the content and afterwards evaluate the methodology. Overall, the team and I were very satisfied with the decision to use a pragmatic way of research, avoiding the controversy of the fundamentalists in the hostile camps of QUALs and QUANs. In our opinion, the method must be metered at the levelling board of achieved finding and conclusions – and not at the paradigm of purist schools of methodology.

The use of a multilevel mixed design opened various insights, provided a system of 'checks and balances' and helped us to fit the jigsaw of social relations in crime prevention networks.

Lessons learned from this research

1. Most valuable and indispensable were the content analysis of documents, especially of protocols, agreements and reports. They provided (more or less) objective information about the history, the involved institutions and persons, the decisions and the measures.
2. At least of the same, if not higher, importance were the problem-centred interviews. They gave deep insights, offered ways of interpretation, showed the subtext of collaboration, shed light on attitudes and expectations, hidden conflicts and often not discussed problems and deficits.
3. The third essential method was the questionnaire in which the stakeholders and participants could answer the standardised questions about the structure, the barter items, the agenda and the invested resources.
4. The analysis of descriptive statistics about the socio-demography, socioeconomy and the crime level was quite interesting, was needed to picture the cities, counties and the networks. But the analytical output was quite poor and could only illustrate and validate the findings by other methods.
5. The network analysis was very laborious and expensive but gained only little information. The gathered information about the relationship between participants could be represented by numbers and presented as funny figures, but the needed knowledge for the interpretation of these data was gathered in interviews. The cost–benefit relation was poor and the instrument could fall away.
6. The idea of gaining better insights through participatory observations failed in the implementation. It was simply impossible to observe the measures and meetings without being involved and as soon as observers entered a situation, they were objects of observation themselves. So it was nice to see some meetings and get a feeling of the atmosphere, but this could not be considered as proper implementation of a method to gaining valid data.
7. The standardised survey on the fear of crime and the estimation of safety and security was nice to have, but brought no essential

knowledge. The 'traditional' findings of such surveys about the higher rates of perception of fear of crime among women and elderly people, the difference between cities of different size, etc. were confirmed. Most important was the realisation that the crime prevention networks were seldom known from the citizens.

8. The decision for the setting with case studies in four fields on action, the idea of comparison in and between the fields, still seems to us a good decision. We achieved an interesting variety of structures and sets of stakeholders; we found some fundamental patterns but also the proof that the idea of 'one size fits all' would not work. With the comparison, we were able to identify conditions of success and also risk factors. Four fields of action with each four case studies offered enough differences but were still a manageable amount of cases.

References

Atteslander, Peter. (2008) Methoden der empirischen Sozialforschung. Berlin.

Beckert, Jens. (2005) 'Soziologische Netzwerkanalyse', in Kaesler, Dirk (Hg.) *Aktuelle Theorien der Soziologie. Von Smuhl N. Eisenstadt bis zur Postmoderne* 286–312,: München.

BMBF – Bundesministerium für Bildung and Forschung. (2012) Research for Civil Security. Framework programme of the Federal Government 2012–2017. Available at: http://www.bmbf.de/pub/BMBF_rahmenprogramm_ sicherheitsforschung_2012_2017_engl.pdf [Accessed 11 December 2012].

Boers, Klaus. (1991) *Kriminalitätsfurcht. Über den Entstehungszusammenhang and die Folgen eines sozialen Problems.* Pfaffenweiler.

Borchardt, Andreas and Göthlich, Stephan E. (2007) 'Erkenntnisgewinnung durch Fallstudien', in Albers, Sönke, Klapper, Daniel, Konradt, Udo, Walter, Achim and Wolf, Joachim (Hg.) *Methodik der empirischen Forschung*: Wiesbaden. S 33–48.

Bornewasser, Manfred and Anne Köhn (2012) 'Subjektives Sicherheitsempfinden', in Frevel, Bernhard (Hg.) Handlungsfelder lokaler Sicherheitspolitik. Netzwerke, Politikgestaltung and Perspektiven. Frankfurt am Main. S. 190–225.

Cresswell, John and Plano Clark, Vicki L. (2007) *Designing and Conducting Mixed Methods Research*: Thousand Oaks.

Frevel, Bernhard. (1998) Wer hat Angst vor'm bösen Mann? Ein Studienbuch über Sicherheit and Sicherheitsempfinden. Baden-Baden.

Frevel, Bernhard. (1999) Grundzüge der empirischen Sozialforschung. Eine praxisorientierte Einführung für Studierende der Polizei- and Verwaltungsfachhochschulen: Greven.

Hirschmann, Nathalie and Claudia Kaup. (2011) Qualitative Interviewforschung. Zum leitfadengestützten Interview im Forschungsprojekt „Kooperative Sicherheitspolitik in der Stadt", in Frevel, Bernhard (Hg.) Forschungsmethoden. Überlegungen zum Projekt KoSiPol. Working Paper Nr. 3. Münster.

Jansen, Dorothea (2006) Einführung in die Netzwerkanalyse. Grundlagen, Methoden, Forschungsbeispiele. Wiesbaden.

Johnson, R. Burke, Onwuegbuzie, Anthony J. and Turner, Lisa A. (2007) 'Toward a Definition of Mixed Methods Research', *Journal of Mixed Methods Research*, 1: 112–133.

Kant, Martina, Norbert Pütter and Christine Hohmeyer (2000) 'Kommunale Kriminalprävention in Deutschland. Eine quantitative Annäherung', in Liebl, Karlhans and Ohlemacher, Thomas (Hrsg.) Empirische Polizeiforschung. Interdisziplinäre Perspektiven in einem sich entwickelnden Forschungsfeld. Herbolzheim, S. 201–219.

Kromrey, Helmut (2006) Empirische Sozialforschung. Modelle and Methoden der standardisierten Datenerhebung and Datenauswertung. Stuttgart.

Lamnek, Siegfried (2005) Qualitative Sozialforschung. Lehrbuch. Weinheim.

Landespräventionsrat NRW (Hg.) (2011) Kriminalpräventive Gremien in NRW. Düsseldorf.

Pütter, Norbert (2006) Polizei and kommunale Kriminalprävention. Formen and Folgen polizeilicher Präventionsarbeit in den Gemeinden. Frankfurt am Main.

Schnell, Rainer, Hill, Paul B. and Esser, Elke (2011) Methoden der empirischen Sozialforschung. München.

Schreiber, Verena (2007) Lokale Präventionsgremien in Deutschland. Frankfurt am Main, Göttingen.

Tashakkori, Abbas and Teddlie, Charles. (Eds.) (2007a) *Handbook of Mixed Methods in Social and Behavioral Research*: Thousand Oaks.

Tashakkori, Abbas and Teddlie, Charles. (Eds.) (2007b) 'The Past and Future of Mixed Methods Research. From Data Triangulation to Mixed Model Designs', in Tashakkori, Abbas and Teddlie, Charles (Eds.) *Handbook of Mixed Methods in Social and Behavioral Research*: Thousand Oaks.

Teddlie, Charles and Tashakkori, Abbas. (2009) *Foundations of Mixed Methods Research. Integrating Quantitative and Qualitative Approaches in the Social and Behavioural Sciences*: Los Angeles.

Witzel, Andreas. (2000) The Problem-Centered Interview [26 paragraphs]. Forum Qualitative Sozialforschung/Forum: Qualitative Social Research, 1(1), Art. 22, Available at: http://nbn-resolving.de/urn:nbn:de:0114-fqs0001228 [Accessed 05 October 2013].

6
Researching across Nations: The Anglo-American Experience

John Foust

Research methods involved

1. Quantitative

Questionnaire survey and data statistical analysis

2. Qualitative

Questionnaire survey and data statistical analysis

About this research

This research project provided an in-depth analysis of the history, development and current status of police labour in the United States, England and Wales. As policing developed in each geographic area, it was important to first obtain the historical perspective. Then, this research compared and contrasted the police systems as used in the identified countries, which included an examination of police unions and associations along with their relationships to police management. The main research aims were as follows:

1. What is the impact of police unions and staff associations on management decisions in England, Wales and the United States?
2. What are the specific roles and responsibilities of police unions or associations in England, Wales and the United States?
3. What is the current nature and extent of police unions and associations in England, Wales and the United States?
4. How does the existence of police unions and associations affect management decisions in England, Wales and the United States?

This research was conducted between 2012 and 2013.

142 *The Anglo-American Experience*

6.1 Research questions for this study

This research project provided an in-depth analysis of the history, development and current status of police labour in the United States, England and Wales. As policing developed in each geographic area, it was important to first obtain the historical perspective. Then, this research compared and contrasted the police systems as used in the identified countries, which included an examination of police unions and associations along with their relationships to police management. This research was designed to answer one primary question: What is the impact of police unions and staff associations on management decisions in England, Wales and the United States?

6.2 Discussion of research techniques and methods

This section provides a review of concepts relevant to research design, along with a review of possible research methods. This section is not meant to describe all possible methods of data collection, but rather to provide a brief overview of possible methods that were considered. Some of these methods fall into the quantitative category, while others are purely qualitative. Further, it was possible that some methods could be applied both quantitatively and qualitatively; for example, when combined for a mixed approach.

Quantitative/qualitative domains

The great assortment of data gathering methods available to researchers can often be placed in one of two categories: quantitative or qualitative. Bachman and Schutt (2008: 16) provided the following succinct distinctions:

Quantitative methods – Methods such as surveys and experiments that record variation in social life in terms of categories that vary in amount. Data that are treated as quantitative are either numbers or attributes that can be ordered in terms of magnitude.

Qualitative methods – Methods such as participant observation, intense interviewing, and focus groups that are designed to capture social life as participants experience it, rather than in categories predetermined by the research. Data that are treated as qualitative are mostly written or spoken words, or observations, that do not have a direct numerical interpretation.

Bailey (1987: 60) also provided a distinction between quantitative and qualitative. He reported, 'any attribute that we measure in numbers we will call a quantitative attribute or variable'. Although numbers may be obtained in qualitative data, the key is that they do not function as numbers. In other words, they are not treated as numbers and they cannot be added, subtracted, multiplied or divided. However, it is possible to calculate the frequency of qualitative variables, especially as a percentage in each category. For example, in a study it is feasible to calculate the percentage of police officers who hold advanced academic degrees, a qualitative category. Myers (2013) explained that qualitative research is useful for answering several types of questions, specifically those with the words what, why, how and when. For example, 'What is happening here? Why is it happening? How has it come to happen this way? When did it happen?'. Boeije (2010) also provided definitions of quantitative and qualitative. Quantitative research was defined as that which is used to deduce hypotheses. Through the use of adequate sample, quantitative research involves the testing of hypotheses and the examination of variables to determine relationships. 'Results are reached by working with numbers, and statistical criteria are used to determine whether the results offered support for the hypotheses or not' (Boeije, 2010: 5). Qualitative research was defined as methods that 'produce rich, descriptive data that need to be interpreted through the identification and coding of themes and categories leading to finding that can contribute to theoretical knowledge and practical use' (Boeije, 2010: 11). Additionally, Boeije (2010) explained that qualitative research seeks to discover participants' points of view or their social realities. Participants 'express their opinions on what they think is happening, they share experiences, show what they feel, demonstrate what they do' (Boeije, 2010: 13).

Political affiliation and religious affiliation fall into qualitative categories and, relative to this research, police union and association affiliation fell into categories as well. In working with qualitative categories, Bailey (1987: 60) offered the following advice: 'Some observers attempt to quantify their observational data, most researchers simply arrange their data into qualitative categories and give each category a name to distinguish it from other categories'. Given that this was a descriptive and exploratory study, the use of both quantitative and qualitative approaches was necessary. The choice of a qualitative approach was well suited for the research questions, including the possible additional question (on policy or change). Boeije (2010) explained that a qualitative design can be used for fundamental research that generates new knowledge or applied research that is designed to create change or improve situations. Also, based on the above distinctions, it was evident that this research was well suited for a qualitative approach as the research sought to obtain the social realities from police managers, which was in line with Boeije's description of qualitative research. Further, Bachman and Schutt (2008: 17) specifically reported that, 'Exploration is the most common motive for using qualitative methods' (17).

Quantitative research is closely associated with deductive reasoning, whereas qualitative research is associated with inductive reasoning. In other words, theory is often the starting point for deductive reasoning with the use of quantitative research while exploration of social phenomenon is the starting point of inductive reasoning with the use of qualitative research. Although, as Boeije (2010: 5) explained, 'In practice, however, it is never this black and white'. Boeije's observation was quite accurate for this research, especially as the descriptive component was largely quantitative but it did not start with theory. Table 6.1 helps us to illustrate and define key differences between qualitative and quantitative research.

Possible research methods

At various times, experimental methods have been used in the police sciences for particular research projects. Experiments generally have three elements: independent and dependent variables, pre-testing and post-testing, and experimental and control groups (Babbie, 2008). The experimental group receives the treatment while the control group does

Table 6.1   Basic differences between qualitative and quantitative methods

Qualitative research	Quantitative research
Inductive	Deductive
Subjective	Objective
Impressionistic	Conclusive
Holistic, independent system	Independent and dependent variables
Purposeful, key informants	Random, probabilistic sample
Not focussed on generalisation	Focussed on generalisation
Aims at understanding, new perspectives	Aims at truth, scientific acceptance
Cases studies, content and pattern analysis	Statistical analysis
Focus on words	Focus on numbers
Probing	Counting

Adapted from Patton (1990).

not receive the treatment. The goal is to measure any change that occurs. In other words, what was the change in the variable being measured after the treatment as compared to before treatment? Presumably, there will be no change in the control group; however, any change that is detected must be noted and further investigated. In the United States, the Kansas City Preventive Patrol Study is a classic example of the use of the experimental method in police research. Police beats in Kansas City were randomly varied in the early 1970s in an effort to evaluate the effectiveness of routine patrol. One group received no routine patrol and police responded only when called. A second group had no change (the control group) and they received the normal level of patrol. A third group was established and they had two to three times the number of patrols. The experiment was conducted to determine what effect police patrol had on crime, arrests, traffic accidents and other factors (Swanson et al., 2012). After having examined the purposes of this research and the requirements for an experimental method, it was determined that this research was not conducive to an experiment. For example, it is not possible to assign officers to unions as they are mostly already union members often as a condition of their employment and or the law. Also, although there are two groups of officers, those who are union members and those who are not, they are not randomly assigned to these groups, so again the use of the absolute experimental method is not a possibility. Finally, experiments are concerned with cause and effect or explanatory research. This research was concerned with description and exploration, not causation.

Participant observation was briefly looked at as a possible research method. This method involves 'developing a sustained relationship with people while they go about their normal activities' (Bachman and Schutt, 2008: 15). Data is gathered during this long-term observation as the researcher immerses himself in the setting that is under observation; this can be accomplished either overtly or covertly. Participant observation is commonly utilised by social scientists in an effort to study people. A classic example of participant observation is the 1963 covert study conducted by Erving Goffman. He worked as an Assistant Athletic Director in an asylum for the mentally ill in order to study mental hospitals to learn the reality of life in a mental institution. He sought to learn the patient's point of view, rather than the psychological diagnosis. Although a goal of this research project was to seek the police manager's point of view, the participant observation approach was not feasible. The US police forces are fragmented and numerous. This was further complicated by the fact that there are right-to-work states and states with no such laws. Further, this was an international study, which included an examination of 43 police forces in England and Wales. Although it would have been interesting to develop a relationship with a chief and observe the chief's activities over an extended period of time, the benefit would have been at best minimal. In other words, observing the daily activities of a chief would have produced little information because a chief's overall duties and attention is diverse, with only a small fraction of the time devoted to my particular research area.

A content analysis is a study of 'representations of the research topic in such media forms as news articles, TV shows, and radio talk shows' (Bachman and Schutt, 2008: 16). Historical documents, legal opinions, government records and other documents may be practical for a content analysis. Although this research studied many of the mentioned documents, this has taken place for the purpose of the literature review. After a careful consideration, it was determined that it was not practical to make use of a content analysis research method for this project for the reasons explained in the participant observation method. That is, the number of police unions is too large and the geography covers too much area, including different countries. Another consideration was secondary data analysis, which is the reanalysis of data that already exists. This data may come from multiple sources, some of which includes government documents (Bachman and Schutt, 2008). For example, in the United States, criminologists find the Department of Justice helpful as they publish annual crime reports. City planners may obtain necessary information from the US Department of Transportation as they publish annual reports on traffic accidents. Sociologists find the Centre for Disease Control helpful as they publish annual reports on causes of deaths. Similar government offices and reports are available in England and Wales. For this research project, the US Department of Labour was considered as a possible source for secondary data. However, upon examination of their reports it was discovered that they did not contain the details that are necessary. At best they provide a historical overview of the growth or demise of labour unions in the United States. The same is true for England and Wales. That is, there is no comprehensive source of secondary data that could be used to complete this research.

Having reviewed the above methods, along with other possibilities it was determined that survey research was a viable option for gathering data. As described by Babbie (2008: 304), survey research involves three actions: 'questionnaire construction, sample selection and data collection'. The process involves questions being asked of participants, they reply with answers, which are then recorded and analysed by the researcher. Answers that are provided by participants may be facts as they know them, feelings or opinions. For example, a factual response should be generated from this question: Do officers in your police department belong to a union or association? A feeling may be generated from this question: What have your experiences been with unions? An opinion may be generated from the question: Are police unions necessary? Survey research is used widely in a variety of diverse fields, some of which include criminology, sociology, medicine, political science and psychology. Relative to police science, Hagan (2010: 144) explained, 'Survey research, an area that is emerging as a strength in criminal justice research, is an excellent tool for primary data gathering'. A variety of survey methods may be used for data gathering, some of which include structured questionnaires, interviews and telephone surveys.

Mailed questionnaires have been used for decades and they have been one of the cheapest and most efficient methods of distribution of questionnaires. The use of mailed questionnaires eliminates any possible interviewer bias and the method allows for respondent's privacy, which can lead to more meaningful or personal answers being provided. However, mailed questionnaires do not allow for the respondent to ask questions or seek clarification. Further, some respondents may have difficulty reading, there is a certain amount of researcher control that is lost and some respondents may ignore the questionnaire and would not reply. Hagan (1989) reported that in the mid-1960s, researchers could expect a 75% response rate; however, that number had dropped to 60%–65% by the mid-1970s. It was believed that potential respondents were becoming overburdened and it was becoming more difficult to gain the interest of respondents: 'The chief problem with many mail surveys is non-response' (Hagan, 1989: 94). Miller (as cited in Hagan, 1989) reported that many inexperienced researchers, who are without sponsorship, obtain only a 20% return on surveys without follow-up.

In-person or personal interviews offer great flexibility, but they do have shortcomings. In-person interviews can be expensive and time-consuming for both the researcher and the interviewee. Also, as the meeting is face to face and interactive, there is the possibility of researcher bias. With a lengthy interview that is not recorded, it is possible that the researcher will not take complete or accurate notes and thus lead to inaccurate conclusions. On the positive side, in-person interviews allow for extended questioning and the ability to probe for additional information. Researchers are in control and they can focus on what is important and meaningful to the project. This could be especially important for gathering qualitative data.

Telephone interviews provide another means of interviewing participants. This technique may be more efficient than in-person interviews as larger numbers of participants can be reached. Also, it is useful for large geographic areas as participants who are located at great distances from the researcher can be contacted and interviewed. Drawbacks of this technique may be with research in an area of the world where telephone service is not readily available. A sample that is based on telephone numbers may present a sampling problem as many people today have multiple telephone numbers, along with unlisted numbers. Finally, it is slightly more difficult for participants to concentrate in telephone interviews as opposed to in-person interviews; there may be the tendency to become distracted. Also, telephone interviews do not appear to be as relaxed or sociable, as compared to in-person interviews.

Questionnaires distributed via the Internet have become increasingly popular in recent years.

Evans and Mathur (2005: 195) reported, 'Over the last 25 years in particular, technology has revolutionized the way in which surveys are administered – with the advent of the first e-mail surveys in the 1980s and the initial web-based surveys in the 1990s'. Evans and Mathur (2005) presented several advantages and disadvantages of online surveys as follows.

Major strengths

Global reach: – The internet will then be an even more valued tool to obtain information from respondents living in different parts of a country or around the world, simply and at a low cost.

Speed and timeliness: – Questionnaires can be both delivered and administered in a timely manner.

Technological innovations: – The researcher has multiple options that range from e-mail surveys to web-based surveys where respondents are provided a URL.

Convenience: – Questionnaires can be completed at a convenient time for the respondent, often with the ability to start it, save it and then return to it for completion.

Ease of data entry and analysis: – Electronic data is available immediately and responses can be tabulated and analysed easily, especially if imported directly.

Question diversity: – Questions can be dichotomous, multiple-choice, scaled, single-response, multiple-response, open-ended, or with a multimedia format.

Control of answer order: – Online questionnaires can require that respondents answer certain questions before they go to the next, allowing the researcher to maintain control of the desired order.

Required completion of answers: – Questionnaires can be constructed to require that certain questions are answered, thus eliminating non-responses.

Go to capabilities: (skip) – Questionnaires can allow for respondents to answer questions that are specific to them.

Low administration cost: – Costs can be reduced in both preparation and administration.

Ease of follow-up: – Reminders can be sent as needed, in a timely manner and around the world.

Controlled sampling: – Questionnaires can be distributed to those who they are intended for.

Major weaknesses

Perception as junk mail: – Online messages or questionnaires could be perceived as junk mail or Spam.

Questions about sample selection (representativeness) and implementation: – Applicable to web surveys, rather than targeted individuals, there is the possibility that improper sampling methods were used.

Respondent lack of online experience/expertise: – This population group is diminishing, but it is possible that the respondent is not proficient with computers.

Technological variations: – Completion of online questionnaires could be affected by the respondent's web browser and the internet connection.

Unclear answering instructions: – Like mailed questionnaires these are self-administered, so instructions must be clear.

Impersonal: – Again, like mailed questionnaires, these are impersonal as there is no face-to-face contact.

Privacy and security issues: – Research here seems to have been focussed on concerns about participant confidentiality in regard to commercial research and the fear private information would be sold. Relative to security, participants worry about receiving a virus with attachments sent via e-mail.

Low response rate: – There seems to be a need for additional research in this area, as in 2005 there was little evidence that that online questionnaires obtained higher response rates than other methods.

An issue not addressed by Evans and Mathur is the potential problem of someone other than the intended recipient completing the questionnaire. However, that issue exists with mailed questionnaires as well. In summary, as Madge and O'Connor (2004: 10) reported, 'It is unlikely that online research is going to replace onsite research but rather it is another option in the researchers' methodological "toolkit" '. They also reported that the advantages and disadvantages, relative to the specific topic, should be considered when deciding to use online research methods.

Research sampling

Whether data is gathered through surveys or other methods, the matter of research sampling is significant. As explained by Bachman and Schutt (2014: 87), a sample is a 'subset of elements from the larger population' while the population is defined as 'the entire set of elements.' They further explained that at times information cannot be obtained directly from the elements, and it may be necessary to use sampling units. Sampling units are those that actually provide information about the elements. For example, a researcher may wish to study the size of police facilities (the elements) across the country. However, in order to gather the data, it will be necessary to contact facility managers (sampling units) as they hold the information. This study did not require the use of sampling units. An alternative, though slightly different, definition is provided by Trochim and Donnery (2008: 35): 'The group you wish to generalize to is often called the population in your study. This is the group you would like to sample from because this is the group you are interested in generalizing to.' However, as explained by Boeije (2010), qualitative research samples are different from common sampling methods, especially such as those used for quantitative research. With quantitative studies, the primary focus is on statistical representation; however, that is not necessarily so with qualitative studies. Finally, it is important to note that with any of the definitions provided, the term sample does not necessarily mean the group of elements or people who completed the study. It is quite possible that I may have difficulty contacting some people, some may be non-responsive, or some may drop out of the study (Trochim and Donnery, 2008).

Just as the two categories, quantitative and qualitative, exist, two categories of sampling methods also exist: probability sampling and non-probability sampling. Bachman and Schutt (2014) explained that these categories provide the greatest distinction about samples. Probability sampling is based on a random selection of elements from the population, so that each has an equal chance of being selected. An example of probability sampling is the selection of winning numbers

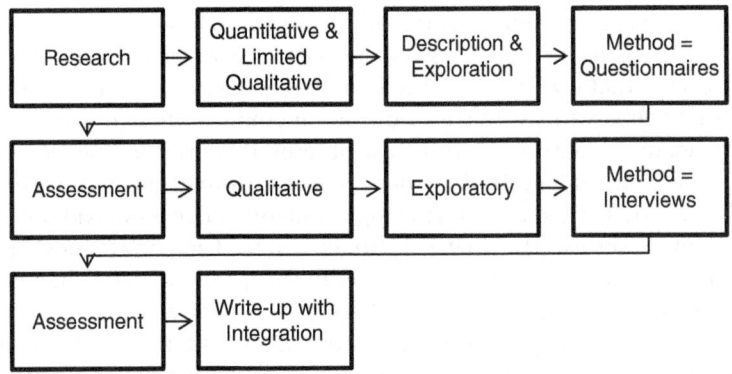

Figure 6.1 An illustration of the data gathering approach in phase I and phase II

in a state or national lottery. The winning numbers are selected randomly, with each having an equal chance, out of a population of numbers. Non-probability sampling includes those methods where the chance of selection is not known in advance.

Selected approach for this study

Having thoroughly reviewed strategies and possible methods to be used for this research project, it was determined that survey research was the most appropriate strategy, in both quantitative and qualitative manners that included a combination of questionnaires and interviews. While accepting that other methods may provide some value, they did not meet the needs for this research. As such, this means that a mixed methods approach was used, as illustrated in the chart below. The research was divided into two phases. Phase I consisted of descriptive and exploratory research with data collected through questionnaires. Phase II consisted of exploratory research with data collected through interviews (Figure 6.1).

6.3 Mixed methods approach

Punch (2009: 288) described mixed methods research as 'empirical research that involves the collection and analysis of both qualitative and quantitative data. In mixed methods research, qualitative and quantitative methods, and data are mixed, or combined in some way.' This straightforward definition can be appreciated as the topic has sometimes been less than specific throughout the years. For example, in name alone it has been called multi-method, blended, integrated and combined research. In 2006, Creswell and Plano Clark (as cited in Punch) advocated that regular use of the term 'mixed methods' would encourage researchers to see this as a distinct method. Although there now appears to be consistency in the use of term, there is still disagreement on what constitutes mixed methods research. Conrad and Serlin (2011: 151) reported, 'Despite their growing popularity, there is not widespread agreement on exactly what constitutes a mixed methods study'. For example, some argue that the gathering of qualitative and quantitative data is sufficient, whereas others believe that a mixed methods approach must include both qualitative and quantitative analyses. Still others believe the moment of mixing is what defines mixed methods. All things considered, this was a mixed methods approach. As described above and as illustrated in the above figure, this research clearly met the definition provided by Punch. A mixed methods approach was selected not only because of the need for gathering different types of data, but also to enhance the overall validity and quality of the research.

Myers (2013: 8) acknowledged that 'both quantitative and qualitative research approaches are useful and necessary in researching business organizations'. Police forces are business organisations of a sort and Myers explained that quantitative research is best used with large samples, when you want to gather data from many people in many organisations. Alternatively, qualitative research is best used when the researcher wants to gather in-depth data on a specific topic from only a small number of organisations. Both of these descriptions provided by Myers were goals of this research. This research sought to gather a large amount of data from many police chiefs and to gather in-depth data from selected individuals; therefore, such a mixed approach was necessary.

6.4   Phase I – questionnaire

Phase I consisted of a questionnaire that was distributed police chiefs in the United States, England and Wales. Selecting one approach over another was not a straightforward task, and it required much thought. As the purposes of this research involved description and exploration, it was first necessary to determine if those goals still existed. Brown et al. (2012), when looking at descriptive research, explained that it is designed to accomplish four functions: to describe the characteristics of certain groups; to determine the proportion of people who behave in a certain way; to determine relationships between variables;

and to make predictions. That said, these functions fit well with the desired outcomes. The use of descriptive research helped us to identify characteristics of police chiefs. In part, this included the number of years of service, educational backgrounds, along with other demographic information. More directly related to the research questions, descriptive research provided the opportunity to identify the proportion of police chiefs who felt that their decision-making ability (behaviour) was affected by police unions or associations. Also, descriptive research allowed for conclusions to be made regarding the connection between police chiefs, decision-making relative to the existence of police unions and associations. Lastly, descriptive research allowed for predictions to be made regarding the future of decision-making abilities as affected by the existence of police unions and associations. In looking at descriptive research methods, there are several possibilities: observation, case studies, secondary data analysis, content analysis and survey research. All of these possibilities were considered; however, with the exception of survey research, each method presented problems for this study. For example, secondary data analysis was briefly considered, but recall there has been little written on this topic and there has been no work completed that addresses the research questions in this study. For these same reasons, a content analysis was not practical. Survey research, specifically questionnaires, provided the most meaningful responses with rich information. Also, given that this was a cross-national study, survey research allowed for information gathering over great distances and in a timely manner. Also, as descriptive research takes place before explanatory research, this was a logical step. For example, an experimental method was determined to be ineffective as this was a descriptive and exploratory research study with largely inductive reasoning and no hypothesis had been formed. Further, as previously discussed, it is impossible to develop control and experimental groups for this research.

Data gathering – questionnaire sample

Once the decision was made to use a survey research method, specifically a questionnaire, a decision needed to be made to determine whether this would be a cross-sectional study with one-time data gathering or a longitudinal study with data gathered over time. It was decided that the cross-sectional approach was better for two reasons. First, cross-sectional studies are used more often in descriptive and exploratory research, so this was the most appropriate method. Although a longitudinal study could provide insight into trends and past practices, that is not necessarily a goal of this research. Second, given the time constraints, the data needed to be gathered so that this research could stay within its time frame.

The questionnaire was distributed to chief officers from the United States, England and Wales. It was sent to the entire population of chiefs in the 43 police forces in England and Wales. The questionnaire that was sent to chiefs in the United States required additional thought and planning. Policing in the United States is fragmented with nearly 18,000 police agencies that exist at the local, county, state and federal levels. Upon examination of the sizes of these police forces, it was seen that the vast majority were extremely small, with only a few officers in each police force. As compared to England and Wales, the police forces are large and they ranged in size from 809 to 31,435 officers. As the small sizes of US district police forces would prove useless for comparative purposes, further inquiry was needed. Upon examination of the 62 larger police agencies that belonged to the Major City Chiefs Association, it was discovered that they have many of the same characteristics of the 43 UK forces. That is, they are larger with sizes that ranged from 558 to 34,542 officers, they served larger populations and they were geographically spread across the country. Bachman and Schutt (2014: 90) advised, 'We need to determine the scope of the generalization we will seek to make from our sample'. With that in mind, along with extraordinary number of police forces in the United States, no attempt was made in this research to generalise the hundreds of small police forces in the United States. Rather, census research was used to reach the police forces. The 62 US police forces were spread across the country, which enabled the gathering of information from forces operating under differing state laws and labour agreements. Again, recall that politics and decisions in the United States are driven more by local and state levels of government rather than the federal government, as in the United Kingdom. There is no equivalent to the Home Office in the United States (Figure 6.2).

Questionnaire development

Questionnaires are popular among social science researchers and they provide (Table 6.2) great versatility as previously discussed. They can be administered with respondents answering the questions directly as in an electronically delivered survey or they can be administered during an interview. The main pitfall to questionnaires is that 'survey questions can result in misleading or inappropriate answers' (Bachman and Schutt, 2008: 15). That said, a close examination of the research on questionnaire development was necessary. The primary purpose of the questionnaire in this research was to gather descriptive data. However,

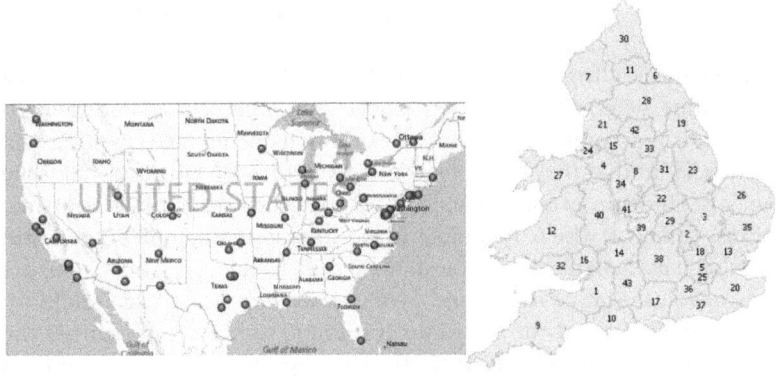

Figure 6.2 Locations where questionnaires were distributed. Left: 62 US police forces. Right: 43 England and Wales police forces

Table 6.2 Comparison of police forces selected for the research

	England and Wales	United States
Number of police chiefs questionnaire distributed to	43	62
Total numbers of officers working in the police forces	131,837	153,334
Range in size of police forces	809–31,435	558–34,542
Average number of officers per force	3066	2473

as questionnaires are used to gather data that helps us to measure variables that can include facts, attitudes and beliefs, it also proved useful for gathering exploratory data. This questionnaire fell primarily within the category of quantitative (descriptive) research, but there was a qualitative (exploratory) component. For the quantitative aspect, the questionnaire was designed with closed-ended questions. For the qualitative aspect, the questionnaire was designed with open-ended questions. Regarding the closed-ended questions, Babbie (2008: 273) advised that there are two fundamental requirements. 'First, response categories should be exhaustive.' In other words, researchers must ensure that answers' choices are available for all respondents, even if it includes the addition of an 'other' category. 'Second, the answer categories must be mutually exclusive'. For example, answer categories such as 1–5 years and 5–10 years would be unacceptable as the '5' is not mutually exclusive. Hagan (1989) suggested that questionnaires be written for the target population and that questions be clearly written. Biased and leading questions are to be avoided. Also, researchers must determine whether to ask open-ended questions, closed-ended questions or some combination thereof. Although open-ended questions are beneficial in that they allow respondents to provide greater detail, they may be difficult to code. Babbie (2008) provided similar recommendations, some of which included: make questions unambiguous, avoid double-barrelled questions, questions should be relevant, short items are best, avoid negative items, and avoid biased items or terms. Additionally, organisation of the questions was found to be as important as the questions themselves. Hagan (2010: 104) reported that it is a common mistake to begin surveys with demographic questions, such as age, sex and race. 'A questionnaire is best begun with items that arouse interest and gain the respondent's attention'. Babbie (2008) confirmed that the most interesting questions should go at the front of the questionnaire, so as to gain the interest of the respondent, while the more boring and demographic questions should go at the end.

Pre-test and procedures

The questionnaire was pre-tested prior to distribution to the chiefs. As Hagan (1989) explained, this was necessary as it allowed for suggestions and the clarification of any confusion items. Babbie (2008) advised that the pre-test individuals do not need to come from the sample or population but that the questionnaire should have some relevance to them. This meant that the individuals who participated in the pre-test of this questionnaire needed to be current or former police officers with supervisory experience. Therefore, the questionnaire was distributed to a group of five individuals in the United States who were known to the researcher and met these criteria. As this research involved more than the United States, it was necessary to pre-test the document in the United Kingdom. As Smith (2004: 431) explained, 'The basic goal of cross-national survey research is to construct questionnaires that are functionally equivalent across populations. Questions need not only be valid, but must have comparable validity across nations'. For that reason, an equivalent group of five experienced officers pre-tested the survey in the United Kingdom, as facilitated through the University. Suggestions were reviewed and incorporated where necessary and errors that were discovered were corrected. The questionnaire was developed for electronic completion through the use of Survey Monkey®. A link (URL) was obtained, so that respondents could go to the link and open the document. After pre-testing, the questionnaire was distributed to the chiefs, with an informed consent letter that preceded the actual questionnaire. The Major City Chiefs Association, the Association of Chief Officers and the University assisted with this electronic distribution, with an introductory e-mail message to the chiefs. The electronic format was selected for four reasons: First, an electronic format allowed for the simultaneous distribution of the questionnaire to multiple chiefs, spread across vast geographic regions. Second, given the international nature, the electronic format eliminated possible problems or delays with traditional mail delivery. Also, as chiefs have hectic schedules, often having to deal with crisis situations daily, an electronic format eased the process and encouraged participation. Lastly, the electronic format allowed for the questionnaire to be distributed through the chiefs' associations, which added legitimacy. As data was collected electronically, completion rates were monitored weekly. Reminder notices were sent through the respective associations to encourage completion. As Hagan (1989) advised, good timing is essential for completion, meaning that holiday and vacation periods should be avoided for distribution of questionnaires. This was taken into consideration during the distribution.

6.5   Phase II – interviews

Phase II consisted of four interviews, two participants were from the United States and two were from England/Wales. As this research sought to explore and gather qualitative data, Phase II was necessary. As quantitative approaches have different methods for gathering data, so do qualitative approaches. For example, Brown et al. (2012) mentioned focus groups as one such method. Focus groups are conducted by bringing together small groups of individuals to discuss the research topic. The number of participants may vary, but 8–12 is a common number. The group is led by a moderator who guides the discussions. Although rich information can be obtained from focus groups and they are useful for many projects, focus groups were not selected here for two primary reasons. First, it would be impossible to coordinate two times (one for a US group and one for a UK group) to bring 8–12 chiefs together to discuss this research. Second, focus groups were not practical given the vast geographic areas in this study. For example, the distance between New York, NY, and Seattle, WA, is over 2000 miles. Another possible method involves the literature search. While the literature search was an essential component of the research process, it did not provide answers to the research questions here. Although many news accounts have provided insight into current events, they cannot replace original research. A case analyses approach is yet another method that involves a concentrated examination of specific cases that serve as examples of the research topic. In part, this approach may involve interviews, observations and examination of records. Although this method of data gathering was considered, it too was dismissed (Brown et al., 2012). Similar to the focus groups, a problem with the method is related to the vast geographic areas. Also, many documents that would need to be examined in a case analysis may be classified or restricted, as they involve personnel matters. Interviews on the other hand allowed for rich information to be gathered and they proved to be the most effective method for acquiring the exploratory data needed for this research. The addition of the qualitative component was not seen as an academic concern as Boeije (2010: 7) explained, 'Qualitative research is blossoming at many universities and institutions'. As seen from the mixed methods discussion above, the combination of approaches offered numerous benefits. Also, as Myers (2013: 5) stated, 'Qualitative researchers contend that it is virtually impossible to understand why someone did something or why something happened in an organization without talking to people about it'. That said, interviews were necessary and once the decision was made to conduct interviews, it was necessary to determine the sample and structure.

Data gathering – interview sample

Four interviews were conducted: two in the United States and two in England and Wales. A purposive sampling technique was determined to be the most effective technique for the identification of this sample. This research called for the study of a certain domain with experts knowledgeable in the topic. One police chief was selected from the United States and one from the United Kingdom. Selections were made based on recommendations from the chiefs' associations, along with a willingness to participate as acknowledged in the questionnaires, and an assessment of diversity of the chief's background. The other two interviews were conducted with police union or association representatives, who were selected based on their experience and willingness to participate. These two interviews were conducted to provide for a balanced and fair assessment of the issues. Four interviews were deemed sufficient for this research, as the participants came from both the United States and the United Kingdom. Further, both sides (management and labour) were represented. Baker and Edwards (2012: 10) note: 'the number of people required to make an adequate sample for a qualitative project can vary from one to a hundred or more'. At the low end, there are many studies, especially in the field of policing, that have involved one subject. For example, Sutherland gained invaluable information from one participant in his 1937 study titled *The Professional Thief.* From this one individual, Sutherland accurately concluded that not everyone in society can become a professional thief. Carl Klockar's (1974) *The Professional Fence* is yet another classic study that focussed on one individual. Through the contact with that one person, Klockar accurately learned how stolen goods were trafficked. Also, Baker and Edwards (2012: 8) explained,

> Quantitative researchers capture a shallow band of information from a wide swath of people and seek to objectively use their correlations to understand, predict, or influence what people do. Qualitative researchers generally study many fewer people, but delve more deeply into those individuals, settings, subcultures, and scenes, hoping to generate a subjective understanding of how and why people perceive, reflect, role-take, interpret, and interact.

Interview question development

Interview questions were guided, in part, by responses obtained from the questionnaires administered in Phase I. Particular themes or unanswered questions were incorporated into the interview questions. As Berg (1989) explained, there are three possible types of interviews: the standardised interview, which contains formally structured questions; the unstandardised interview, with no predetermined questions where the interviewer creates questions during the interview; and the semi-structured interview, which lies between the two extremes and contains some predetermined questions, but allows sufficient freedom to deviate. A semi-structured format was used so as to gather the greatest amount of information, while at the same time ensuring that questions that were deemed vital were answered. The interview format used for this research closely resembled what Bachman and Schutt (2014) referred to as intensive interviewing. Intensive interviewing makes use of open-ended questions in order to learn about the respondent's feelings, experiences and perceptions. These interviews last longer than other interviews and may require follow-up conversations. Also, consistent with this research design is that 'Random selection is rarely used to select respondent.' (Bachman and Schutt 2014: 238). Probes were used during the interviews to solicit information and obtain complete accounts from participants. Berg (1989) reported that probes provide a means to have participants elaborate on what has been said. Common probes include phrases such as 'tell me more', 'what happened then?', and 'why is that?' The use of probes was appropriate for intensive interviewing as Bachman and Schutt (2014: 238) explained, 'Intensive interviews actively try to probe understandings and engage interviewees in a dialogue about the intended meaning of their comments'.

Pre-test and procedures

Just as the questionnaire was pre-tested, so were the interview questions, during mock interviews. However, rather than having a large number of individuals involved, one person from the United States and one person from the university served as interviewees. This number proved effective, especially as the questions were primarily open-ended. Suggestions that were made during the pre-test were incorporated into the interview. Once the interviewees were identified, they were sent an e-mail message asking for their participation. Once they agreed, interview dates were set. The two US interviews took place at locations as designated by the interviewees. The other two interviews were conducted via telephone. Before interviews began, the interviewees were provided with an informed consent document. This was done in person for the US interviews and it was delivered via e-mail to the overseas interviewees. The document was discussed and signed in person with the US interviewees. The document was discussed via telephone with the overseas interviewees and they provided an e-mail message with their consent. The informed consent document included the authorisation to use a recording device, which was activated only after consent was obtained. Notes were taken during the course of the interviews, which allowed for the notation of highlights and the identification of areas that needed additional clarification or explanation.

6.6   Triangulation

In the mid-1960s, Weber et al. (as cited in Bryman and Teevan, 2005) originally developed the idea of triangulation by expanding one method so as to develop additional measures in quantitative research. The purpose in using multiple measures was to gain confidence in findings in single studies. A few years later, Denzin (as cited in Bryman and Teevan, 2005) expanded that concept to include four possible ways to triangulate: use of multiple observers, use of multiple theoretical perspectives, use of multiple sources of data and use of multiple methodologies. The

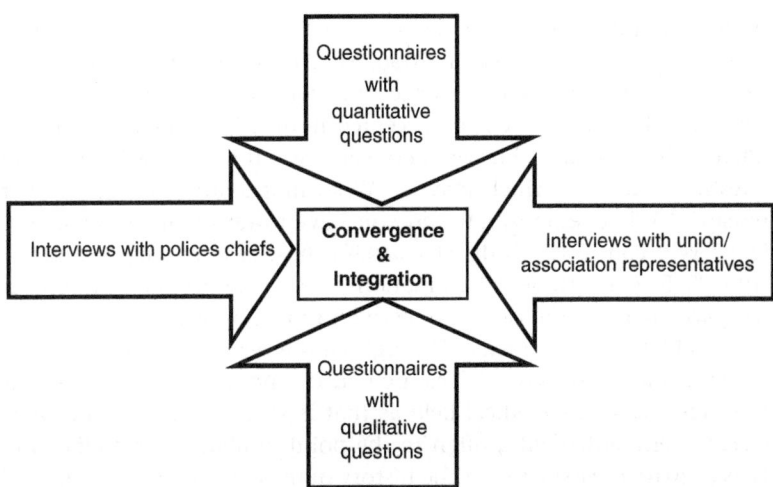

Figure 6.3 A visual representation of triangulation used in this research

emphasis seemed to have been on multiple methods and sources of data. That seems to be the most common today, as triangulation refers to a design where the researcher uses more than one technique to gather data or when a technique that is used that allows for the combination of qualitative and quantitative methods in the one study (Myers, 2013). Perone and Tucker (2003: 2) provided a historical perspective on the term and explained that triangulation is a surveying term that meant surveyors used two visible points to plot a third point: 'In research, triangulation refers to the combination of two or more theories, data sources, methods, or investigators in one study of a single phenomenon to converge on a single construct'. The convergence allows the methods or techniques to complement each other, draw upon their strengths and ultimately produce findings that are more reliable and valid. This research made use of multiple methods and sources of data to allow for this strength and to provide valid and reliable findings. Figure 6.3 provides an illustration of this research triangulation.

6.7 Ethical considerations

Generally speaking, ethics involves morality and making the right decisions. However, this seemingly simple concept is complicated as what is morally acceptable to one person may not be acceptable to another person. In research, the idea of ethics involves 'a complex set of values, standards and institutional schemes that help constitute and regulate scientific activity' (NESH, 2006: 5). That is, guidance is provided from multiple sources to manage and control research activities so that they do not deviate from accepted norms. Hesse-Biber and Leavy (2010) advised that to engage in ethical research requires asking several questions, some of which may be 'What moral principles guide your research? What responsibility do you have toward your research subjects? Will your research directly benefit those who participated in the study?'. To make these determinations, it may be necessary to look at the particular point in time and, perhaps more importantly, to examine what guidelines or laws exist. Throughout the years, attempts have been made to address the issue of research ethics and most early discussions were related to the medical field as that is where human participants were experimented with, often to the point of abuse. Hesse-Biber and Leavy (2010: 60) explained, 'The history of the development of the field of ethics in research, unfortunately, has largely been built on egregious and disastrous breaches of humane ethical values'. Because of abuses and maltreatment, numerous codes and ethical philosophies have come into existence. For example, over 60 years ago the *Nuremburg Code* was created to provide formal ethical guidelines, but only after the exposure of appalling medical experiments conducted by Nazi doctors and others was discovered (Bachman and Schutt, 2014: 55). The *Nuremburg Code* is considered to be the first modern documents that provided guidelines for experimentation with humans and by some accounts it is the 'most important document in the history of the ethics of medical research' (Shuster, 1997). American judges formulated the Code in 1947 in Nuremberg, Germany, while judging Nazi doctors who were accused of conducting experiments on humans that resulted in murder or torture (Shuster, 1997). The Code 'served as a blueprint' for today's principles that ensure the rights of participants in medical research (Shuster, 1997: 1436). Ten elements make up the Code, which includes such things as voluntary consent, the avoidance of physical and mental suffering, risk assessment, protection of participants and the right of participants to stop the experiment (Shuster, 1997). Although focussed on medical research, elements of the Code have carried over to social research as discussed later in this section.

Some years later, in 1964, the World Medical Association (WMA) adopted the *Declaration of Helsinki, Ethical Principles for Medical Research involving Human Subjects*. With 35 points, it provides guidelines for research with human participants and is an expansion and reinterpretation of the *Nuremburg Code*. The document set the groundwork for the establishment of a review process, or the Institutional Review Board (IRB), as it is commonly called today. For example, as stated in Section 15,

> The research protocol must be submitted for consideration, comment, guidance and approval to a research ethics committee before the study begins. This committee must be independent of the researcher, the sponsor and any other undue influence. It must take into consideration the laws and regulations of the country or countries in which the research is to be performed as well as applicable international norms and standards but these must not be allowed to reduce or eliminate any of the protections for research participants set forth in this Declaration. The committee must have the right to monitor ongoing studies. The researcher must provide monitoring information to the committee, especially information about any serious adverse events. No change to the protocol may be made without consideration and approval by the committee.

Unfortunately, despite the existence of codes and guidelines, some researchers continued to practise unethically. Nearly 50 years ago, Beecher discussed ethical considerations when he wrote his prominent article in the *New England Journal of Medicine* (1966). In that article he discussed ethical issues and, more importantly, he discussed how experienced researchers sometimes conducted questionable practices. He described 22 cases where ethics were either questionable or controversial. Although Beecher's cases were related to medicine and experiments, his concern for ethical standards can be applied universally. For example, he found cases that involved deception, putting participants at risk, coercion, withholding information and the lack of informed consent. Specific to experiments and the medical field, he discovered research that involved the withholding of treatment, sometimes with fatal consequences.

6.8 Confidentiality and anonymity

Although similar in many respects, confidentiality and anonymity are distinct concepts, with different implications. Confidentiality refers to something that is spoken or written in confidence, or with some assurance, whereas anonymity refers to something written or said by a person of unknown name, or to remain nameless. Research involves both concepts; however, there must be certain limits with confidentiality. That is, it is impossible to conduct research that is entirely confidential as the purpose of research is to report findings. If everything that is said or provided to the researcher was done in confidence, not to be shared, there would be no findings. However, 'What researchers can do is to ensure they do not disclose identifiable information about participants and to try to protect the identity of research participants through various processes designed to anonymise them' (Wiles et al., 2008: 1). In other words, a degree of confidentiality can be assured by making participants anonymous.

Ensuring confidentiality and anonymity

Deliberate disclosure of identity may be required in certain cases. For example, the law may require the reporting participants who are at risk of harming themselves or who are about to commit a crime. Also, cases of child abuse must be reported. In the context of this research, these circumstances are not expected to occur. However, that does not mean that protective measures do not need to be implemented to ensure anonymity. Dantzker and Hunter (2006) reported that privacy can be protected by ensuring that links cannot be made between data that is reported and the information that was provided by respondents. An additional step to ensure privacy is to limit the number of people who have access to data with identifying information. Babbie (2008) reported that it is difficult to track the completion of questionnaires when they are submitted anonymously. Therefore, as it was a goal of this research to have a high completion rate, some tracking was necessary. Participants were asked to list their police agency name on the questionnaire and this allowed for a follow-up message to be sent, if necessary. However, once the questionnaires were received, the recommendations of Dantzker and Hunter were followed. More specifically, procedures as suggested by Babbie (2008) were followed. Each questionnaire was given an identification number that replaced the police agency name. Although a file of this association was kept, identifying names were not reported in this research. In 2006, Corden and Sainsbury wrote the paper: *Using verbatim quotations in reporting qualitative social research: researchers' views*. The notion of presenting verbatim quotes in qualitative research reports is well accepted and this was explored, along with techniques that various researchers have used. However, when using verbatim quotations, one must be cautioned about using too many, or more importantly, using those that contain too much personal or unique information, as doing so will jeopardise anonymity. Along those same lines, Wiles et al. (2008: 9) reported, 'The desire to use data in cases where distinctive stories might make individuals identifiable led some researchers to change the identity of participants in various ways'. However, researchers were cautioned about making changes as they need to ensure they do not change, either the ideas presented in or the integrity of the data. This research involved the gathering of some very distinct stories, especially as obtained during the interview phase. As such, the findings were reported in such a manner as to provide anonymity.

6.9   Informed consent

The concept of informed consent has assumed slightly different meanings to different people through the years. Bailey (1987) reported that, 'Informed consent essentially entails making the subject fully aware of the purpose of the study, it's possible dangers, and the credentials of the researchers' (409). Babbie (2008) reported that informed consent formalised the ethical norms for gaining voluntary participation, full disclosure of risks to participants and not harming participants. In many cases, especially in medical treatment, the researcher has to obtain informed consent of the participant in an informed consent document.

However, that is not always the case, as with social science research, which may involve only observation (Babbie, 2008: 69). Although there was no mention of researcher credentials in Babbie's definition, this could be important as it is possible that it would help the potential participant make a 'fully informed' decision. Hesse-Biber and Leavy (2010: 85) provided a definition that is more inclusive than either of the above:

> Informed consent is a critical component in ethical research that uses human participants. Informed consent aims to ensure that the subject's participation is fully voluntary and informed, based on an understanding of what the study is about, what its risks and benefits are, how the results will be used, and the fact that participation is voluntary and can be stopped at any time and that identity will be protected.

The additional components here include information about identity protection, the benefits of the research and how the results will be used, along with specifications that that participation can be stopped at any time. In survey research, respondents may read an informed consent document and then complete the survey. Dantzker and Hunter (2006) called this conferred consent and the logic is that participation must have been voluntary and informed, otherwise respondents would not have participated. Although this research utilised a survey method, a slightly different approach was taken to ensure that participants fully understood and agreed to participant. Recall that questionnaires for Phase I were distributed electronically. The first page that opened for the participants was an informed consent letter. At the bottom of the letter was one question. Knowing the above information, do you wish to participate and complete this questionnaire? There were two possible answer choices: By clicking 'yes', participants were taken to the questionnaire document. By clicking 'no', participants were thanked for their consideration. In other words, the questionnaire could not be taken without acknowledging and agreeing with the contents of the informed consent page. For the interviews, an informed consent letter was e-mailed to each possible participant. They are asked to respond via e-mail.

6.10   Researcher bias/insider research

Kanuha (as cited in Dwyer and Buckle, 2009: 58) explained that 'Insider research refers to when researchers conduct research with populations of which they are also member'. As I work in the field of police management, it was necessary to examine the literature and assess the prevailing thoughts associated with concept. Early in this century, Malinowski suggested that scientists, anthropologists in particular, should 'go native' or act as participants rather than observers when conducting research. The belief was that this was necessary to fully understand the native's life and point of view. Although with benefit, years later this method of research had been challenged as it can lead to bias or incomplete data collection (Kanuha, 2000). 'The most critical aspect of the native researcher role is the need to distance from the project, the participants, and indeed even the process of studying one's own people' (Kanuha, 2000: 442). Although this is not an anthropological research project, nor is this a participative study, insider research is relevant across all fields. As explained by Dwyer and Buckle (2009: 55), 'The issue of researcher membership in the group or area being studied is relevant to all approaches of qualitative methodology as the researcher plays such a direct role and intimate role in both data collection and analysis'. It has been suggested that there can be both positive and negative consequences of being an insider. Dwyer and Buckle (2009) advised that two of the benefits include access to groups that may have been unavailable or suspicious and the ability to acquire a greater depth and understanding of the data. However, bias can exist if not controlled for and perceptions held by the researcher can be less than clear. Additionally, individuals are often so enmeshed in their own experience that the adequate distance required to know their experience is not available; therefore, someone from the outside might more adequately conceptualise the experience. This notion of distance is similar to that as described by Kanuha. For this reason, the police chief interview portion of this project has taken place with someone who is not associated with my department. Mercer (2007) also discussed the subject of insider research and presented advantages and disadvantages as similar to those discussed above. Additionally, the issue of researcher ethics was discussed. For example, there is the issue of what to tell colleagues, both before and after they participate in the research. Therefore, the concept of fully informed consent appears important. However, as Silverman (as cited in Mercer, 2007: 11) advised, a study may be flawed 'by informing subjects too specifically about the research questions to be studied'. For that reason, the informed consent document for this study has provided sufficient information for the participants, but it has not divulged too much about the research questions.

Lessons learned from this research

1. The distance between the locations studied did not present a limitation for this research because of the available technology for communication and because of the resource networks that were already in place.
2. Access to senior police presents its own difficulties.
3. The only worry for this research was that some police chiefs may be concerned about their identification, particularly in the United States.
4. In other words, it was possible that a very small number of chiefs would not want to participate for fear of straining management relations with their police unions.
5. However, that worry was unfounded as evidenced by the response rate.

References

Babbie, E. (2008) *The Basics of Social Research* (4th ed.), California: Wadsworth.
Bachman, R. and Schutt, R. (2008) *Fundamentals of Research in Criminology and Criminal Justice*, Thousand Oaks, CA: Sage.

168   *The Anglo-American Experience*

Bachman, R. and Schutt, R. (2014) *The Practice of Research in Criminology and Criminal Justice* (5th ed.), London: Sage Publishing.

Bailey, K. (1987) *Methods of Social Research* (3rd ed.), New York: The Free Press.

Baker, S. and Edwards, R. (2012) *How Many Qualitative Interviews Are Enough*. Available at: http://eprints.ncrm.ac.uk/2273/4/how_many_interviews.pdf [Accessed 04 January 2014].

Berg, B. (1989) *Qualitative Research Method for the Social Sciences*, Needham Heights, MA: Allyn and Bacon.

Boeije, H. (2010) *Analysis in Qualitative Research*, London: Sage Publishing.

Brown, T., Suter, T. and Churchill, G. (2012) *Basic Marketing Research* (7th ed.), London: Hampshire, Cengage Learning.

Bryman, A. and Teevan, J. (2005) *Social Research Methods*, Oxford: Oxford University Press.

Conrad, C. and Serlin, R. (2011) *The SAGE handbook of Education* (2nd ed.), London: Sage Publishing.

Dantzker, M. and Hunter, R. (2006) *Research Methods for Criminology and Criminal Justice: A Primer* (2nd ed.), Sudbury: Jones and Bartlett.

Dwyer, S. and Buckle, J. (2009) 'The Space Between: On Being and Insider-Outsider in Qualitative Research, *International Journal of Qualitative Methods*, 8(1): 54–63.

Evans, J and Mathur, A. (2005) 'The Value of Online Surveys', *Internet Research*, 15(2): 195–219.

Hagan, F. (1989) *Research Methods in Criminal Justice and Criminology* (2nd ed.), New York: Macmillan.

Hagan, F. (2010) *Research Methods in Criminal Justice and Criminology* (8th ed.), London: Prentice Hall.

Hesse-Biber, S. and Leavy, P. (2010) *The Practice of Qualitative Research*, London: Sage Publishing.

Kanuha, V. K. (2000) 'Being Native versus Going Native – Conducting Social Work Research as an Insider', *Social Worker*, 45(5): 439–447.

Madge, C. and O'Connor, H. (2004) *Exploring the Internet as a Medium for Research: Web-Based Questionnaires and Online Synchronous Interviews*. Available at: http://www.ccsr.ac.uk/methods/publications/documents/WorkingPaper9.pdf [Accessed 04 January 2014].

Mercer, J. (2007) 'The Challenges of Insider Research in Educational Institutions: Wielding a Double-edged Sword and Resolving Delicate Dilemmas', *Oxford Review of Education*, 33(1): 1–17.

Myers, M. (2013) *Qualitative Research in Business and Management*, London: Sage Publishing.

NESH. (2006) *Guidelines for Research Ethics in the Social Sciences, Law and the Humanities*, Norway: Forskningsetiske Komiteer.

Patton, M. (1990) *Qualitative Evaluation and Research Methods* (2nd ed.), California: Sage.

Perone, J. and Tucker, L. (2003) An Exploration of Triangulation of Methodologies. The 'Quantitative and Qualitative Methodology Fusion in An Investigation of Perceptions of Safety Transit', *NCTR*, 416(8): 137–222.

Punch, K. (2009) *Introduction to Research Methods in Education*, London: Sage Publishing.

Shuster, E. (1997) 'Fifty Years Later: The Significance of the Nuremberg Code', *The New England Journal of Medicine*, 337: 1436–1440.

Smith, T. (2004) 'Developing and Evaluating Cross-national Survey Instruments in Methods for Testing and Evaluating Survey Questionnaires', in *Survey Methods in Multinational, Multiregional and Multicultural Contexts*, Presser, S., Rothgeb, M., Couper, J., Lessler, E. and Martin, J. Hoboken (Eds), John Wiley, Hboken, New Jersey, USA.

Swanson, C., Territo, L. and Taylor, R. (2012) *Police Administration Structures, Processes and Behaviours*, (8th ed.), Upper Saddle River, NJ: Pearson Prentice Hall.

Trochim, W. and Donnery. (2008) *Research Methods Knowledge Base*, Hampshire: Cengage Learning.

Wiles, R., Crow, G., Heath, S. and Charles, V. (2008) 'The Management of Confidentiality and Anonymity in Social Research', *International Journal of Social Research Methodology*, 11(5): 417–428.

7
Hard to Reach Groups

Amanda Milliner

Research methods involved

1. Qualitative

Interviews and Focus groups

About this research

This research is concerned with the interaction between the police and disadvantaged groups, focussing specifically on adults with learning difficulties, with a view to gaining:

- an understanding of their day-to-day experiences, with a particular interest in their experiences of incidents of crime, hate crime, disability hate crime;
- their relationship or engagement (if any) with the police; and
- an understanding of whether they would feel able and comfortable to report incidents to the police.

This research was conducted between 2011 and 2014.

7.1 Aim of the research

It is believed that a greater appreciation of the current engagement process between the police and this marginalised and vulnerable section of the community would be gained, as very little was written about this subject. This study will, at the very least, inform and contribute knowledge to the academic arena and will provide ideas for practitioners on ways in which the engagement process can be reconsidered and ultimately improved.

7.2 Social inclusion

I felt that this research was important as it is acknowledged that in almost all social situations people with learning difficulties can feel less powerful than people who do not have learning difficulties. It is the case that adults with learning difficulties often find themselves marginalised or socially excluded from society (Riddell et al., 2001).

The Cabinet Office (1999) suggests that individuals and indeed entire communities are in danger of being socially excluded due to a variety of reasons such as poor skills, low incomes, poor housing, bad health, unemployment, high crime environments, poverty and family breakdown. It is for reasons such as these that the Department of Health (2001) in its 'Valuing People' report states that 'inclusion' is one of the key principles laid out by the government for future service provision for people who have learning or intellectual disabilities.

There has been little research into the social inclusion of people with learning or intellectual disabilities from their own perspective with a view to gaining their perceptions of the barriers that exist in society and their suggestions of remedies (Abbott and McConkey, 2006); this research seeks to provide some insight into this arena.

Abbott and McConkey continue to discuss four main barriers that can prevent social inclusion, the location of the individual's housing, the role of support staff and service managers, a lack of necessary knowledge and skills, and some community factors, such as attitudes of community members and poor amenities.

It is important to understand that, in order to attempt to prevent social exclusion, it is therefore necessary to seek the views and opinions of potentially marginalised members of society, such as people with learning difficulties. In spite of the challenges associated with the engagement of people with learning difficulties in social research (Brewster, 2004), it is very much possible for a researcher to provide an environment of understanding, mutual respect and trust, which can then bring about positive outcomes for the participants (Manning, 2010) and a growing number of adults in our communities are displaying a desire to engage and to become included in community activities (O Rourke et al., 2004).

Emerson and Einfield (2011) advise researchers to be cautious as occasionally people with learning disabilities may exhibit behaviours that may be deemed challenging in an attempt to assert some control and power over situations, and the service providers can ultimately restore the balance of power through medication or restraint techniques. It is suggested that even adults with mild to moderate learning disabilities, who have actively been involved in self-advocacy groups and organisations, may be ultimately aware that the power lies with support workers who do not have learning disabilities and are responsible for the management of the organisation's finances or the interpretation of inaccessible written material (Goodley, 2000).

For this research, I needed to consider various reasons why a participant with learning difficulties may feel reluctant to express their true opinions and views. They may fear repercussions, or have a history of bad experiences in educational establishments, or possibly previous experiences of abuse. They may view me as a person who wields power in their lives, therefore they feel the need to 'do the right thing' or may do anything they can to please me. These factors need to be considered, they can contribute to an unusual research dynamic between the respondents and researcher. There was a real need for me to develop a relationship of trust with people with learning difficulties with a view to developing a research relationship that does not abuse the position of relative power (University of Sheffield, 2013).

7.3 Ethical considerations

Therefore, consideration to ethics was important as this was a sensitive piece of research due to the potential vulnerability of the participants involved. I had a moral duty to ensure all participants and interviewees were treated fairly and ethically.

Diener and Crandall (1978: 19) suggest that there are four main areas that need to be considered with regard to ethical principles in research:

Whether there is harm to participants
Whether there is a lack of informed consent
Whether there is an invasion of privacy
Whether deception is involved

These principles overlap at times. Bryman (2008) suggests that it is difficult to imagine a research project where informed consent could be built into research where the respondents/participants had been deceived. 'Harm' was considered by Diener and Crandall (1978) to include physical harm, stress, loss of self-esteem, inducing respondents to perform reprehensible acts, and harm to the respondents' development.

There is evidence to suggest that research ethics committees have been cautious with regard to the approval of qualitative research studies involving 'vulnerable' adults (Hannigan and Allen, 2003). The role of an ethics committee is to prevent potentially vulnerable people from being harmed by research. However, Boxall (2011) believes that there is potential for participants with learning difficulties to gain positive experiences from being involved in research.

Generally, the concept of the ethical approach is seen as being associated with morality, and giving a researcher the standpoint from which to determine what is right and what is wrong. In effect, what we ought to do or what we ought not do (Rowson, 2006; Babbie, 2011). However, Babbie (2011) poses some questions for consideration. How do we know what is right and what is wrong? How do we ascertain the distinction? The answers to these questions can vary. Each individual will have a different influence, whether it is political, religious or possibly a pragmatic observation of what works or what does not. In order to provide an answer to these questions for the social researcher, Babbie continues to discuss general agreements shared by social science researchers about what is considered proper or improper in the conduct of such research, to include the principles that all participation is voluntary, no harm comes to the participant, and anonymity and confidentiality (Babbie, 2011).

Ethical considerations of this research study included the well-being of the respondents; for example, would they be protected from harm? Extensive consultation with support workers was carried out during the planning stage of the research. It was decided that if the respondents were given detailed information regarding the research, along with time to decide whether they wanted to take part, and the knowledge that they could, at any time during the process, change their mind and rescind their participation with absolutely no consequence. Consideration was also given to ensuring the participants received detailed information to ensure they were able to consent to their participation; the confidentiality and anonymity of the respondents; and concerns over the use of audio tapes.

7.4 Access

Access to this section of our community was given much consideration. The process of gaining and maintaining access to a particular group that may be considered hard to reach, or establishing a meaningful, working relationship with people in order to carry out a research study, can be one of the most difficult steps, but is key to the research process (Bell, cited in Bryman, 2004; Jupp, 2006). If there are any official channels that need to be cleared, these should be addressed prior to the interview or focus group stage of the research process (Bell, 2005). Bell believes it would be unethical to commence any form of interview/focus group/questionnaire without prior permission from the body/people being researched, and if appropriate, a contract established. For the purpose of this research contract was made with the 'People First' organisation, and it became clear that there was no official body to obtain permission from, all support staff and participants alike welcomed the research. Once an agreement had been made that I could obtain access to members of this group, the subject of sampling was given consideration.

7.5   Sampling

Due to the sensitive nature of this research and the requirement to speak to members of a particular population, who may be difficult to locate, i.e. adults with learning difficulties, the snowball technique of sampling was adopted. The use of snowball sampling enables researchers to make contact with a small group of individuals who are relevant to the research and, through these respondents, make contact with other respondents, accumulating more and more people from the target population as the research progresses (Bryman, 2001; Babbie, 2011; Monette et al., 2011). In addition, Monette et al. (2011) suggest that this sampling method is preferable where the respondents may feel hesitant to take part if they are approached by someone they don't know.

It is not possible to make generalisations when using snowball sampling as this technique will only reach members of the population who are involved in the particular social network, missing out those who are isolated from such networks. As this research aims to provide an insight and not make generalisations, this method of sampling was thought to be the most appropriate.

Recruitment of participants for this project was therefore less challenging than I expected. The long-established support network of 'People First' within the geographical area under consideration was approached and invited to take part in the research. A relationship with the first group was developed during the preliminary research phase. Members of this group expressed their interest in taking part in the research, as they wanted their views/feelings/voices to be heard. For the purpose of this research, other branches of the 'People First' organisation from other areas were approached and connections established. Many meetings were held with the support workers in all the areas in order to develop these relationships and determine which members would like to take part. Consideration was given to how participants would be recruited. It could be possible to write to all possible participants, but that would require them to reply in writing, and it was felt that it may compromise the recruitment process as many probably wouldn't reply. It was decided instead to visit the members of these organisations, and make personal contact on a date before the research took place. I had many opportunities to discuss the research with all potential participants to explain what it would entail in detail. The relationship between myself and support workers was extremely important as the support workers effectively became 'gatekeepers' to research participants.

Gatekeepers

Gaining access to desired groups in order to carry out research can be problematic. Often a gatekeeper plays a crucial role, is often in control of the research access, whether they be a senior executive of a company or a person within a certain group who makes the decision as to whether a researcher should be allowed access in order to carry out their research. Without the permission of the gatekeeper, it is unlikely that access to the groups will be permitted in practice (Jupp, 2006).

The identification of the most suitable person to become the gatekeeper within a formal organisation can be reasonably straightforward. It could be a senior executive or manager of the company, or someone else in authority. In contrast, it is more difficult in less formal settings, such as a gang, or a less formal group of people to ascertain the most appropriate person to approach as a gatekeeper. A key characteristic of a gatekeeper is their position within the group, commanding others within the group (Jupp, 2006).

As well as controlling the access to the group, such gatekeepers often become sponsors, championing the value of the research and vouching for the researcher (Bryman, 2001).

Jupp (2006) suggests that a gatekeeper will need to be convinced of the research in order to allow the researcher access, although there may be circumstances where the gatekeeper will decline access despite supporting the research in principle. This may be because of issues concerning confidentiality, the sensitivity of the topic to be researched or a general concern regarding time and resource constraints. If the gatekeeper belongs to a large organisation, they may hold a view differing to the researcher regarding how much time participants should dedicate to the process. I needed to acknowledge and recognise these potential problems and consider them during the access negotiation phase (Saunders et al., 2003). All of the support workers (gatekeepers) involved in this research were extremely positive and supportive of the study. During the relationship building phase of the research, many discussions were held and reassurance provided that the well-being of the participants was paramount. The support workers had sufficient time to ensure the participants genuinely wanted to take part. At no point did any participant exhibit any signs that they did not want to take part, most described a strong desire to have their voices heard.

Buchanan et al. (1988) proposes that some researchers may want to offer something in return for the participation in the research. In the case of a large organisation, this may present itself in the form of a summary report of the research findings. In less formal settings, bargains can be more varied and diverse in nature. However, Bryman (2001) states that not all researchers and commentators recommend this approach to recruiting or securing a gatekeeper as it could cheapen the research that is being carried out and possibly restrict the researcher's activities. The organisation may want to insist on seeing what the researcher is writing.

The nature of the groups to which access was required for this research study was less formal. Consequently, I was able to build relationships with potential gatekeepers with relative ease. It was decided that the support workers who worked for members of the 'People First' organisation would be approached, with full details of the research in the first instance.

A connection was made with a support worker in Area One initially, and once an agreement was made for access to the group, and a relationship of trust developed, this gatekeeper was responsible for introducing me to potential gatekeepers in the other three areas.

Throughout the research, the gatekeepers provided full support and genuinely welcomed me, championing and promoting the research as a topic they felt was important and worthy of inquiry because they have witnessed issues and difficulties that members of their groups experience. They desire to see improvements in the engagement process between the police and adults with learning difficulties, embracing the process, recognising that it could provide significant insight. It was not necessary to offer anything in return for access to the groups, other than to keep the gatekeepers informed of the progress and the research findings and to ensure that continued consideration was given to the sensitivity of the research topic, and potential concerns regarding confidentiality. Continuous reassurance was provided throughout the process to the support workers and participants regarding ethical considerations such as confidentiality to alleviate any concerns before they arose. I had provided written information prior to carrying out the focus groups, and verbally discussed procedures and the process of safeguarding confidentiality and anonymity at regular stages of the process.

Due to the sensitive nature of the research and discussion topics, it was important during the recruitment stage to discuss with all potential respondents the subject of confidentiality and anonymity.

7.6 Confidentiality and anonymity

Sapsford and Abbott (1996: 318–319), when writing about a participant's involvement in unstructured interviews, suggest that

> interviewing is intrusive, but having your personal details splashed in identifiable form across a research project is even more intrusive

Respondents who take part in research often go through a process of negotiation, agreeing terms before the study commences. They may stipulate that any information obtained about them during the course of the research can only be used by the researchers, and only in specified ways. I had to respect that this private information was shared voluntarily in confidence often with no direct benefit to the respondent (Jupp, 2006). The consequences of me breaking a promise regarding confidentiality and anonymity were difficulties with future research efforts as the respondents would have lost trust in them and the possibility that they may damage the prospect of other social scientists who may have considered completing similar research.

Confidentiality

Confidentiality is described by Jupp (2006) as the principle that information regarding respondents and participants in research should be considered as private and only revealed in the research with the participants' consent. Sapsford and Abbott (1996) continue to explain that if a respondent has been promised confidentiality by a researcher, then the information they give will not be presented in an identifiable format and they will not be identified.

Anonymity

If a researcher promises a person their anonymity, not even that researcher should be able to identify the respondent. Therefore, if anonymity is promised, there is no opportunity to carry out follow-up interviews or send out follow-up letters (Sapsford and Abbott, 1996; Bryman, 2008; Babbie, 2011). It is, however, acknowledged that there may be occasions where respondents would prefer not to be anonymous, instead wishing to take credit for work they have done, or for their views and opinions to be recognised and acknowledged. Some commentators suggest researchers must be mindful of the consequences of including names of respondents/participants in research reports, particularly if the report is to be made available on the internet. It is possible that the respondent may be exposed to repercussions if they are recognisable. These issues should be discussed with respondents prior to the inclusion of people's real names in any research study (University of Sheffield, 2013). No respondents expressed a desire to have their names made known in this research study, therefore the assurance of confidentiality was deemed to be most appropriate.

7.7 Justifying confidentiality

There are three main arguments that support and justify the case for confidentiality. The first is the consequential argument, which examines the results of ethical practices, and gives consideration to what would happen during the research process if these ethical practices were not present. For example, respondents may be reluctant to take part in research if the information they provide were to be freely disseminated to other parties. The second argument is rights-based. A person's right to privacy rests on the principle of respect for personal independence (autonomy) (Beauchamp and Childress, 2001). Some things should not and cannot be concealed. However, people have the right, as far as possible, to make the decision as to what happens to them. Within the research arena, participants should be able to maintain private information and secrets, deciding what information people have access to about them (Jupp, 2006).

The third argument is fidelity-based and suggests that researchers should respect bonds and promises associated with research and they should remain loyal to them. A researcher offers a participant to their research a promise of secrecy and, to guard their confidentiality, this promise has to be honoured (Sapsford and Abbott, 1996; Jupp, 2006; Babbie, 2011; Bryman, 2011).

In many cases negotiations regarding the maintenance of confidentiality are relatively straightforward, as researchers can work in predictable contexts where assurances may be included in standard forms that can be included in a covering letter, for example with a questionnaire.

However, other researchers may be working in areas that are less formal and more unpredictable. In such cases, agreements need to be talked through and topics such as confidentiality need to be negotiated and sometimes re-negotiated if the study involves a lengthy piece of fieldwork (Jupp, 2006).

For the purpose of this research, it was decided at the beginning that the geographical areas would not be identifiable. Therefore, it is not possible for anyone to know which area the respondents came from. The respondents are not named, but are referred to as Respondent A, B, C, etc. Further, I did not record myself the names of the individuals taking part in the research. The use of pseudonyms in order to offer a research participant confidentiality is often viewed as a good practice when considering the involvement of adults with learning difficulties in the process, particularly when the topic being researched is of a sensitive nature. The process of providing potential respondents with information regarding confidentiality and anonymity is important if a researcher is to provide sufficient detail about the research to enable them to make an 'informed' decision with regard to taking part and their consent.

7.8 Informed consent

Researchers need to be cognisant of the need to ensure informed consent as a prerequisite of research participation (Marshall, 2007). Key to achieving this is to provide adequate information regarding the research process, the purpose and scope of the research, the types of questions that would be asked during the focus group, how the results of the research will be used, and how the confidentiality of the participants will be protected (Richards and Schwartz, 2002). Further, the ability of participants to retract from the research should be provided.

In all research of this type, participants should not only be provided with adequate information regarding the research, but I needed to ensure that the respondents were capable of understanding the information provided. Participants should be free to decide whether they wish to take part in the research or not. This voluntary participation is crucial (Polit and Beck, 2004; Marshall, 2007). Therefore, obtaining informed consent is important, possibly more so when it's the consent of an adult with learning difficulties at the heart of the research, due to their potential vulnerability (Wiles et al., 2008).

Obtaining the views and perceptions of a person with learning difficulties can be a challenging process, particularly if the person has impaired communications skills. Mansell (2010) suggests that in some cases, where the learning disabilities are more severe, profound or the respondent has multiple disabilities, the researcher may not be able to communicate directly with the individual. In such cases, the use of an interpreter or proxy respondent may be required. This can raise further ethical issues (Stancliffe, 1999; Clements et al., 1999). It is important that relatives and carers are mindful that there is a boundary between providing support during the research process and making decisions on their behalf, a boundary that is often blurred (Lloyd et al., 1996). All the respondents in my research had mild learning difficulties, therefore the use of a proxy respondent or interpreter was not considered necessary.

It has also been suggested that some people with very severe learning disabilities may not possess the ability to consent to the participation in research (Sheffield University, 2013). However, it is important not to assume that that is the case; decisions regarding capacity to consent to research are situation-specific, and while an individual may not be able to consent to one piece of research (Project A for example), they may possess the capacity to consent to another piece of research (Project B for example). The Department of Health (2008) discusses this dilemma of consent, and suggests the use of a 'consultee' who is responsible for advising the researcher about individuals who lack capacity, they should be able to discuss their wishes and feelings in relation to the research study on the respondent's behalf. Such use of formalised procedures for gaining consent of people with intellectual disabilities is relatively new in the United Kingdom, but surrogate or proxy procedures have been in place for obtaining consent for several years in Australia and North America (Iacono and Murray, 2003; Griffin and Balandin, 2004; Iacono, 2006). While these approaches being used appear to be helpful when gaining consent where an individual lacks the capacity to offer consent, in practice they have proven to be complex, and there are concerns that researchers may be relying too much on surrogate or proxy consultees in order to satisfy the ever-increasing stringent requirements of University Research Ethics Committees (McVilly and Dalton, 2006). It had to be acknowledged that this is a complex matter. However, while researchers need to be considerate of the issues discussed, there is a danger that they will perhaps become discouraged from researching topics where participants are deemed to lack capacity to consent to participating in the research process because of the stringent requirements of ethical approval procedures that are in place to protect vulnerable research participants. This, according to the Department of Health (2009), could be an unwelcome and unintended consequence of procedures in place to protect the vulnerable.

For the purpose of my research, relationships were built up over a period of time with respondents with learning difficulties and their support workers in order to develop trust. The research topic was discussed with all participants on at least one occasion before the research took place. People were invited to take part if they wished, and the vast majority of those approached agreed to take part. The support workers were present when the research study was discussed with potential respondents as this was deemed to be vital to me as the support workers had greater knowledge of the participants and their capabilities. The respondents would then be able, and perhaps more comfortable, to ask any questions or raise any queries they may have, with the support workers once I had left the premises. People were made aware that they did not have to feel obliged to take part, and that there would be no 'comeback' if they declined. None of the respondents who are members of the 'People First' organisation had severe learning difficulties, and it was felt by the support workers and myself that all the participants had the ability to understand the process and provide genuine, informed consent. On the day of the focus groups, I outlined once more the aims of the research, the process of the research study, and confirmation was obtained that all the participants were indeed consenting to the participation in the research.

7.9 Research approach discussions

The purpose of this particular research was to gain rich, contextual data surrounding this particular phenomenon and to this end, a qualitative research method would be adopted. It was desirable to reach as many adults with learning difficulties as possible in order to gain a range of differing views within the time frame that this research was afforded.

To inform the decision regarding the most appropriate method of gathering data, the following approaches were considered:

- Interviews
- Focus Groups

Interviews

Interviews are an effective method of gathering data based upon the respondent's opinions, emotions, feelings, perceptions and experiences of a given situation, which require exploration in detail. They can be used when researching topics of a sensitive nature; careful consideration needs to be given if this is the case (Denscombe, 2007). Interviews are one of the most popular methods of gathering data in qualitative research and are generally far less structured than interviews more commonly associated with survey research (Bryman, 2008).

The use of interviews during the data generation phase of the research process can be attractive as they can be viewed as not requiring a great deal of technical knowhow. I needed to possess a set of assumptions and a certain amount of understanding about a situation and this is not normally the case with a casual conversation (Denscombe, 1983; Silverman, 1985).

I needed also to consider whether I could gain access to prospective participants as well as whether this method of gathering data was viable in terms of cost and travel time (Denscombe, 2007).

Denscombe (2007) suggests that there are four types of interview:

- Structured Interview
- One to One/Unstructured Interview
- Semi-structured Interview
- Group Interview
- Focus Group

These important types are discussed below.

Structured interview

A structured interview is in essence a questionnaire that is very much suited to quantitative research methods. It could be carried out face to face with the respondent, or perhaps over the telephone. It consists of a predetermined, tightly controlled and highly structured list of questions with limited option responses (Dawson, 2002; Denscombe, 2007). The responses should be fairly easy to record, summarise and analyse (Bell, 2005).

Gathering data by using structured interviews was not appropriate for this research project because, as there was little emphasis on the interviewee's point of view, the data gathered would be restricted to the topics that the interviewer feels are relevant/important (Bryman, 2008).

Unstructured interview

The one-to-one/unstructured interview is sometimes referred to as 'life history' interview, in which a researcher is able to obtain a holistic understanding of the participant's views and opinions as they are able to talk freely about what is important to them (Dawson, 2002; Bryman, 2008). An unstructured interview is usually placed at the preliminary interview stage of a research where the researcher is perhaps trying to gain an understanding of the topic; this interview would involve one respondent and one researcher. This method, which produces a wealth of valuable data, is only suitable for qualitative research methods (Bell, 2005). This method of data collection is attractive for the following reasons: it presents the researcher with a number of benefits; it is quite easy to arrange since it only has to consider the diaries of two people; it is relatively easier to control as there is only one respondent's thoughts, opinions and views to grasp; there is only one person that the researcher has to guide through the interview process; and it is much easier for the researcher to transcribe, as there is only one voice to recognise (Denscombe, 2007).

However, despite one-to-one interviews offering me greater control, I felt that they would be too time-consuming for this study, introducing limitations on how many respondents could be reached within the timescale of the study and that individual interviews would not allow me to observe similarities and differences of opinion between participants, meaning that these conclusions would need to be drawn at a later stage during the data analysis phase (Litosseliti, 2003; Denscombe, 2007).

Semi-structured interview

This is possibly the most common type of interview used in qualitative research. I was keen for the interview to be fairly flexible while seeking specific information regarding the topic being researched. This information could be compared and contrasted with responses from other participants during the data analysis phase. It was recommended that I prepare a schedule of questions or topics that I would like to discuss. This schedule was taken into each and every interview. In some research studies, this schedule can be updated following each interview to include new topics as they arise during previous interviews (Dawson, 2002).

Group interviews

Group interviews are conducted in a similar fashion as one-to-one, unstructured interviews, the difference being that they increase the number of respondents reached by the researcher thus providing the researcher with a broader spectrum of opinions and views (Bell, 2005; Denscombe, 2007). Usually the researcher remains the focal point of the interview, and they should interact with respondents as individuals, not as a group. If the researcher is interested in how the respondents interact as a group, then a focus group should be considered.

7.10   Piloting the research

Prior to conducting my research, preliminary research took place. Semi-structured one-to-one interviews were the chosen method of gathering data. I felt that the respondents who took part, who all had mild learning difficulties, would have perhaps felt more comfortable talking about their experiences if they were within their support network. Prior to these preliminary interviews, a group of 8–10 respondents were gathered together to allow me to explain the process. Often these respondents expressed their preference to remain in the group, and not take part in an individual interview or the respondents would agree to take part in an interview, but not say very much when the interview took place.

Focus groups

A focus group, according to Matthews and Ross (2010), is a type of group interview. Typically, a focus group will consist of between 5 and 13 participants invited to take part in a discussion that can last an hour or two, the participants would be selected as they share something in common, something that is connected to the topic being researched. The data generated during a group discussion is gathered by a researcher. Although the researcher can do more than gather data from the discussion, they can also gather data from the participants associated with the focus group. It may be of interest to the researcher to analyse how the group interacts, how the individuals respond to each other, and react to a situation as a group, rather than as individuals, allowing the researcher to build an overall picture of perceptions (Litosseliti, 2003).

Focus groups are often the chosen method of data collection when the respondents are viewed as hard-to-reach, including members of our community who are out of touch with services, members of minority ethnic groups, and in the case of my research, adults with learning difficulties (Kitzinger and Barbour, 1999; Krueger and Casey, 2000). Krueger and Casey (2000: 19) suggest that

> participants are influencing and influenced by others just as in real life

It can be a perception that focus groups will save researchers time and cost, but consideration needs to be given to the logistics involved. It can be difficult to bring individuals together at a certain time and place for the research to take place (Barbour, 2008). Krueger and Casey (2000) argue against this perception, stating that an advantage of focus groups is that it can be more economical, as the researcher sees groups of respondents rather than one at a time. For the purpose of my research, members of the 'People First' organisation who met on a monthly basis were invited to take part in the study. Therefore, it was convenient to coincide the time of the focus group session in each area with their monthly meeting. This arrangement followed many months of relationship building.

The focus groups were split within two clear stages. An initial focus group invited support workers who worked with adults who have learning difficulties to take part. This enabled me to gain some further understanding of the issues/concerns that these professionals believed adults with learning difficulties faced. The initial review of literature had highlighted three main areas of concern. First, adults with learning difficulties experience high levels of crime and disability hate crime; second, it identified that these crimes often go unreported; and finally, of the cases that are reported to the police, very few result in a conviction. These issues were discussed with the support workers to gain their thoughts and perspective. This enabled effective planning of the focus groups that were to follow, which would be carried out with adults who have learning difficulties.

Specific thoughts that were helpful in the planning of subsequent focus groups were that the duration of each focus group should not be more than two hours because the groups were to be held at times convenient to the groups. All members of the group needed to have the opportunity to take part in the focus group if they wanted to. The discussions would need to be easily captured on audio tape, as this would be the easiest way to record what was discussed and leave me free to observe the interaction between the participants. The use of visual aids to facilitate discussion was approved by the support workers. These photographs would hopefully prompt feelings/views, and would focus conversation on the topics that I wanted to address.

7.11 Role within focus groups

During this stage of the research study, my role was crucial. I needed to be aware that the purpose of the focus group was the views, opinions and perceptions of respondents, not to inform, teach, resolve conflict or make decisions (Morgan, 1997). It was necessary that I considered potential issues that can occur; for example, the potential for bias and manipulation.

Prior to the focus groups taking place, much thought was given to these potential issues. The conclusions drawn were:

• I could be perceived to hold certain views in relation to the police, which could influence/prompt participants to respond in a certain way.
• I needed to be cautious to avoid the use of leading questions, as these could result in respondents saying what they think I wanted to hear.
• Some people may be more vocal than others, and there is the potential for them to impose their views on the rest of the group.

It was important that I was not viewed as a figure of authority as the participants could feel intimidated and doubt their role within the group, and thus fail to contribute to the discussion (Fraser and Fraser, 2001). It was also necessary for me to reflect upon my own experiences, views and values in relation to the topic to be discussed to ensure they could be identified and bracketed prior to the research taking place, something that Bowling (2002) suggest is important if I wished to minimise researcher bias.

For the purpose of my research, I felt that in order to ensure I did not intimidate the participants with an air of authority, it was necessary for there to be a certain degree of familiarity with the participants, so that they would feel comfortable taking part.

Holding the focus groups at the centres where these adults with learning difficulties met on a regular basis was preferable as travelling to neutral premises would have introduced disruption to the participants' other work, something that it was felt better to avoid so that the participants felt comfortable and familiar with their surroundings (Fraser and Fraser, 2001).

7.12 The use of visual aids

In an attempt to involve and engage people with learning difficulties in qualitative research, a range of approaches have been developed. These include the use of visual data, such as videos and photographs (Banks, 2001; Rose, 2001; Prosser and Loxley, 2008). The visual emphasis of these research studies enabled me to engage participants as they were more accessible than traditional text- or talk-based approaches.

'Photo elicitation' as a method of encouraging respondents to discuss the topic in question has been used in social research for a number of years (Rosenblum, 1997). In some research, cameras were given to respondents and they were asked to take photographs of areas of concern. This was known as 'photovoice' as they had control over both the photographs and the voice. What the respondents had to say about each photograph was an important element of this research (Webb, 2004).

Much reflection was given to the preliminary data gathering interviews and the questions posed at that time. I decided that the use of visual aids during the focus groups would prompt discussion surrounding various aspects of policing without the need for questions, which have the potential to lead the respondents, a method referred to as 'photo elicitation' (Rosenblum, 1997). A careful selection process took place, to ensure that a broad spectrum of images were chosen, portraying the police in various settings and carrying out a variety of policing functions, in order to gain an extensive range of views, opinions, perceptions and feelings.

Careful consideration was also given to the questions and prompts used during the focus group, and I was mindful not to lead the group. Open questions were used during discussions, and the responses I gave were carefully considered in order to ensure that they did not verbally or non-verbally convey my approval or disapproval, which could be seen to lead the group (Evans, 2010). All of the focus groups were audiotaped with the consent of the participants. I myself transcribed the discussions in each of the focus groups, despite being an extremely time-consuming exercise. This facilitated familiarity with the data and assisted me during the analysis phase. The use of audiotapes had of course brought with it further ethical considerations. Leggett et al. (2007) propose that the use of audiotapes may be viewed aversively, especially due to the sensitive nature of the research. First, there is a fear that participants would feel that they were under interrogation by me as their comments were being recorded. Furthermore, respondents may have felt concerned about how the audiotapes were going to be used, their assumption may be that the tapes would be given to the police. During this study, this concern was overcome by me taking time to explain to all respondents the rationale for the use of the audiotape, how the tapes would be stored and how they would be used. All individuals were reassured that only I would listen to the tapes during the transcribing process. At this time of reassurance and explanation of the process, the respondents were invited to verbally give consent to the recording of the discussion. None of the participants objected to their use.

Lessons learned from this research

1. There is a need for marginalised groups to become involved in research, especially if there are groups that can engage with the police on a regular basis.
2. It is essential to use gatekeepers to assist in the research process as a whole.
3. The qualitative method of utilising focus groups and visual aids greatly assisted the research process.
4. The need to explain and apply the ideas of ethical research, informed consent and confidentially were paramount for research of this type.
5. Researchers should not be afraid to engage in research areas involving the police and the so-called hard-to-reach groups.

References

Abbott, S. and McConkey, R. (2006) 'The Barriers to Social Inclusion as Perceived by People with Intellectual Disabilities', *Journal of Intellectual Disabilities*, 10(3): 275–287.

Babbie, E.R. (2011) *The Practice of Social Research*, USA: Wadsworth Cengage Learning.

Banks M. (2001) *Visual Methods in Social Research*, London: Sage Publications Ltd.

Barbour, R. (2008) *Introducing Qualitative Research*, London: Sage Publications Ltd.

Beauchamp, T.L. and Childress, J.F. (2001) *Principles of Biomedical Ethics* (5th ed.), New York: Oxford University Press.

Bell, J. (2005) *Doing your Research Project* (4th ed.), England: Open University Press.

Bowling, A. (2002) *Research Methods in Health Investigating Health and Health Services*, Maidenhead: Open University Press.

Boxall, K. (2011) 'Research Ethics Committees and the Benefits of Involving People with Profound and Multiple Learning Difficulties in Research', *British Journal of Learning Disabilities*, 39: 173–180.

Brewster, S.J. (2004) 'Putting Words Into Their Mouths? Interviewing People with Learning Disabilities and Little/No Speech', *British Journal of Disabilities*, 32: 166–169.

Bryman, A. (2001) *Social Research Methods*, Oxford: Oxford University Press.

Bryman, A. (2004) *Social Research Methods* (2nd ed.), Oxford: Oxford University Press.

Bryman, A. (2008) *Social Research Methods* (3rd ed.), Oxford: Oxford University Press.

Buchanan, D., Boddy, D. and McCalman, J. (1988) 'Getting in, Getting on, Getting out, and Getting Back', in Bryman, A. (Ed.) *Doing Research in Organisations*, London: Routledge, 53–67.

Cabinet Office London. (1999) *Social Exclusion Unit: What's It All About?* Available at: http:www.cabinet-office.gov.uk/seu/index/faqs.html [Accessed on 02April 2014].

Clements, J., Rapley, M. and Cummins, R.A. (1999) 'On, To, For, With –
Vulnerable People and the Practices of the Research Community', *Behavioural
and Cognitive Psychotherapy*, 27: 103–115.

Dawson, C. (2002) *Practical Research Methods. A User-Friendly Guide to Mastering
Research Techniques and Projects*, Oxford: How To Books Ltd.

Denscombe, M. (1983) 'Interviews, Accounts and Ethnographic Research on
Teachers', in Hammersley, M. (Ed.) *The Ethnography of Schooling: Methodological
Issues*, Driffield: Nafferton Books.

Denscombe, M. (2007) *Good Research Guide: For Small-Scale Social Research Projects*,
England: Maidenhead McGraw-Hill International (UK) Limited.

Department of Health. (2001) *Valuing People: A New Strategy for Learning Disability
for the 21st Century*, London: Stationery Office.

Department of Health. (2008) *Guidance on Nominating a Consultee for
Research Involving Adults who Lack Capacity to Consent: Issued by the
Secretary of State and the Welsh Ministers in Accordance with Section
32(3) of the Mental Capacity Act 2005*. Available at: http://www.dh.gov.
uk/en/Publicationsandstatistics/Publications/PublicationsPolicyAn Guidance/
DH_083131 [Accessed on 08 April 2013].

Department of Health. (2009) *Mental Capacity Act Factsheet for Social Scientists*,
London: Department of Health. Available at: http://www.dh.gov.uk/prod_
consum_dh/groups/dh_digitalassets/documents/digitalasset/dh_106006.pdf.
[Accessed on 08 April 2013].

Diener, E. and Crandall, R. (1978) *Ethics in Social and Behavioural Research*,
Chicago: University of Chicago Press.

Emerson, E. and Einfield, S.L. (2011) *Challenging Behaviour* (3rd ed.), Cambridge:
Cambridge University Press.

Evans, L. (2010) *A Critical Appraisal of Patient and Public Involvement in South East
Wales*, Pontypridd: University of Glamorgan.

Fraser, M. and Fraser, A. (2001) 'Are People with Learning Disabilities Able to
Contribute to Focus Groups on Health Promotion?' *Journal of Advanced Nursing*,
33(2): 225–233.

Goodley, D. (2000) *Self-Advocacy in the Lives of People with Learning Difficulties*,
Buckingham: Open University Press.

Griffin, T. and Balandin, S. (2004) 'Ethical Research Involving People with
Intellectual Disabilities', in Emerson, E., Hatton, C., Thompson, T. and
Parmenter, T. (Eds) *The International Handbook of Applied Research in Intellectual
Disabilities*, Chichester: Wiley.

Hannigan B. and Allen D. (2003) 'A Tale of Two Studies: Research Governance Issues Arising from Two Ethnographic Investigations into the Organisation of Health and Social Care', *International Journal of Nursing Studies*, 40:
685–695.

Iacono, T. (2006) 'Ethical Challenges and Complexities of Including People with
Intellectual Disability as Participants in Research', *Journal of Intellectual and
Developmental Disability*, 31: 173–179.

Iacono, T. and Murray, V. (2003) 'Issues of Informed Consent in Conducting Medical Research Involving People with Intellectual Disabilities', *Journal of Applied
Research in Intellectual Disability*, 15: 41–52.

Jupp, V. (2006) *The SAGE Dictionary of Social Research Methods*. Available at: http://
lib.myilibrary.com/?ID=124045 [Accessed 10 April 2013].

Kitzinger, J. and Barbour, R. (1999) 'Introduction: The Challenge and Promise of Focus Groups', in Barbour, R.S. and Kitzinger, J. (Eds) *Developing Focus Group Research: Politics, Theory and Practice*, London: Sage Publications Ltd.

Krueger, R.A. and Casey, M.A. (2000) *Focus Groups*, London: Sage Publications Ltd.

Leggett, J., Goodman, W. and Dinani, S. (2007) 'People with Learning Disabilities' Experiences of Being Interviewed by the Police', *British Journal of Learning Disabilities*, 35: 168–173.

Litosseliti, L. (2003) *Using Focus Groups in Research*, London: Continuum.

Lloyd, M., Preston-Shoot, M., Temple, B. and Wuu, R. (1996) 'Whose Project Is It Anyway? Sharing and Shaping the Research and Development Agenda', *Disability and Society*, 11: 301–315.

Manning, C. (2010) ' "My Memory's Back!" Inclusive Learning Disability Research Using Ethics, Oral History and Digital Story Telling', *British Journal of Learning Disabilities*, 38: 160–167.

Mansell, J. (2010) *Raising our Sights: Services for Adults with Profound Intellectual and Multiple Disabilities*, London, Department of Health. Available at: http://www.dh.gov.uk/en/Publicationsandstatistics/Publications/PublicationsPolicy AndGuidance/DH_114346. [Accessed on 08 April 2013].

Marshall, P.L. (2007) *Ethical Challenges in Study Design and Informed Consent for Heatlh Research*, Cleveland: World Health Organisation.

Matthews, B. and Ross, L. (2010) *Research Methods. A Practical Guide for the Social Sciences*, England: Pearson Education Ltd.

McVilly, K. and Dalton, A. J. (2006) 'Ethical Challenges and Complexities of Including People with Intellectual Disability as Participants in Research', *Journal of Intellectual and Developmental Disability*, 31(3): 186–188.

Monette, D.R., Sullivan, T.J., DeJong, C.R. And Hilton, T.P. (2011) *Applied Social Research: A Tool for the Human Service* (9th ed.), USA: Brooks/Cole Cengage Learning.

Morgan, D.L. (1997) *Focus Groups as Qualitative Research*, London: Sage Publications Ltd.

O Rourke, A., Grey, I.M., Fuller, R. and McClean, B. (2004) 'Satisfaction with Living Arrangements of Older Adults with Intellectual Disability: Service Users' and Carers' Views', *Journal of Learning Disability*, 8: 12–29.

Polit, D.F. and Beck, C.T. (2004) *Nursing Research: Principles and Methods* (7th ed.), London: Lippincott Williams & Wilkins

Prosser J. and Loxley A. (2008) *Introducing Visual Methods, Esrc Methods Review Paper NCRM/010*. Southampton, University of Southampton, National Centre for Research Methods. Available at: http://eprints.ncrm.ac.uk/420/ [Accessed on 01 April 2013].

Richards, H.M. and Schwartz, L.J. (2002) 'Ethics of Qualitative Research: Are There Special Issues for Health Service Research?' *Family Practice Journal*, 19: 135–139.

Riddell, S., Baron, S. and Wilson, A. (2001) *The Learning Society and People with Learning Difficulties*, Bristol: The Policy Press.

Rose, G. (2001) *Visual Methodologies: An Introduction to the Interpretation of Visual Materials*, London: Sage Publications Ltd.

Rosenblum, N. (1997) *A World History of Photograph*, New York: Abbeville.

Rowson, R. (2006) *Working Ethics: How to Be Fair in a Culturally Complex World*, London: Jessica Kingsley Publishers.

Sapsford, R.J. and Abbott. (1996) 'Ethics, Politics and Research', in Sapsford, R. and Jupp, V. (Eds) *Data Collection and Analysis*, London: Sage Publications Ltd.

Saunders, M.N.K., Lewis, P. and Thornhill, A. (2003) *Research Methods for Business Students* (3rd ed.), Harlow: Financial Times/Prentice Hall.

Silverman, D. (1985) *Qualitative Methodology and Sociology: Describing the Social World*, Aldershot: Gower Publication Company.

Stancliffe, R.J. (1999) 'Proxy Respondents and the Reliability of the Quality of Life Questionnaire Empowerment Factor', *Journal of Intellectual Disability Research*, 43: 185–193.

University of Sheffield. (2013) *Doing Research with People with Learning Disabilities*, Sheffield: University of Sheffield.

Webb T. (2004) *Photovoice: A Starting Point for Social Action?* Available at: http://www.cpe.uts.edu.au/pdfs/starting_point.pdf [Accessed on 09 April 2013].

Wiles, R., Crow, G., Heath, S. and Charles, V. (2008) 'The Management of Confidentiality and Anonymity in Social Research', *International Journal of Social Research Methodology*, 11(5): 417–418.

8
Researching Vulnerable Children, a Multi-agency Perspective

Louise Skilling

Research methods involved

1. Qualitative

In-depth interviews, Focus groups and secondary data analysis

About this research

This research was conducted in 2005. The primary objective of this research was to investigate 'street girls' vulnerability to HIV/AIDS infection, and to suggest ways in which the public health community can inform and educate these young vulnerable women about HIV/AIDS. The research aims were as follows:

1. To assess this group's understanding of the transmission of, and protection from, HIV/AIDS and how this understanding is transmitted through information networks.
2. To determine attitudes towards HIV/AIDS and actions taken to avoid infection.
3. To investigate their lifestyles and how their 'vulnerability' impacts on their sexual activity.
4. To investigate the barriers to reducing HIV infection amongst this group.

This research was conducted in 2005.

8.1 Introduction

Although not directly related to the police, this research considers the important work carried out by wider partnership agencies that work and engage with vulnerable and often hard to reach groups dealing with crime, and the underlying causes and consequences of criminality. This chapter discusses the qualitative multi-method approach that was adopted to gain data for this study. The involvement of street girls in this research was imperative to ascertain how their lifestyles and livelihoods placed them at risk of HIV infection. Both the target group and key informants were able to provide advice on the flaws of previous HIV/AIDS public health campaigns and suggest appropriate approaches to adopt for future promotions.

8.2 Stages of the study

Following the literature review, the fieldwork commenced in Freetown, Sierra Leone. There were four methods adopted to collate the data required for the study: semi-structured key informant interviews, focus group discussions, in-depth interviews and visual methodology utilising disposable cameras. Information was gained from key informants on HIV/AIDS public health campaigns, sexual information networks for female adolescents, condom usage, and the street girls' lifestyles and livelihoods. The three remaining methods were conducted (in English) with the street girls to obtain information regarding condoms, HIV/AIDS, sexual behaviour, pregnancy, public health campaigns, their backgrounds, lifestyles and livelihoods. On completion, all those involved in data collection were provided with a report stating the preliminary research findings, and were invited to a workshop to discuss and provide feedback on the findings. This process validated the research data, and provided informants and participants with an opportunity to network and share ideas.

8.3 Adopting a multi-method approach

For complementary purposes, interviews, focus group discussions, in-depth interviews and visual methodology were employed for this research. The different qualitative techniques used for the multi-method approach assisted me with validating information and triangulating data.

8.4 Qualitative research

Micro theory

To thoroughly understand street girls' vulnerability to HIV/AIDS, research using humanistic philosophical underpinnings was undertaken.

In order to adopt this micro approach, it was essential to use qualitative research because the data collection involved personal and intimate information. Graham (1997) believes a study of people must involve recognition of humans as emotive beings, and not numbers or statistics.

According to Holloway and Hubbard (2001), the inclusion of human experience allows a richer picture of knowledge to be attained. Through understanding the intricacies of street girls' lives, I was able to view their susceptibility to HIV infection from another perspective. Focus group discussions and in-depth interviews (with the aid of visual methodology) were adopted to accomplish this. Through these methods, the street girls were given the scope to provide expression of feeling as well as thought, which other approaches, such as quantitative, would have failed to achieve. Tuan (1977) believes that the ability to know how others see and think has the capacity to encompass a greater depth of knowledge. Ascertaining the views of various street girls helped to inform the research about their lifestyles and livelihoods, and their attitudes towards HIV prevention.

Macro theory

The methodologies discussed above established a clear perceptive of the girls 'place in the world', but did not necessarily provide a full explanation of their vulnerability. For instance, Johann's (1996) research on street children in South Africa recognised that the participants were able to interpret the immediate causal factors for their situation, but failed to identify the deep causal issues.

Therefore, for my study, it was also imperative to consider the macro approach, so that the social systems and structures that influenced the street girls' susceptibility could be analysed. This was established through interviews with key informants who provided various 'outside' perspectives. As Sayer (1999) points out, when the two approaches are utilised, they can be synthesised and all points of discussion can be incorporated into the research.

8.5   Research design

While informants required for the macro perspective of the study could be located through organisations, the sample population needed for the micro perspective proved to be more challenging. First, there were definitional differences that needed to be debated in order to ascertain exactly who the sample population were. Once this was known, measures had to be put in place to gain access to the group.

The sample population

Within the society of Sierra Leone, the ideology of a 'street girl' is different from the UN perspective: the local definition for the phrase is

'street girl' means a prostitute.

Although there were differences between the international and national meaning, there was a close correlation between the street girls (prostitutes in Freetown) and 'street children' (as per the UN definition). The majority of the street girls involved in this study had spent a period of time living on the 'street' before a pimp or madam recruited them. In most of their cases the only alternative other than living under the control of a pimp or madam would have been to move back and live 'independently' on the 'street'. In many respects, the street girls (who had not reached adulthood) fitted the UN definition of a 'street child', as they all worked in a public location and most resided in a public area, whether that was a shack or a derelict building.

The sample frame

Taking this into consideration, the sample frame for this research could not be 'found' from girls who just lived and slept on the street. However, the street girls could have been located through using 'local knowledge' to locate the area where child sex workers (CSWs) operated. Although this was not considered acceptable, as the study would have interfered with the girls' 'business' and potentially aggravated them, plus my own safety had to be taken into consideration. Therefore, other means of locating street girls had to be identified.

There were numerous projects operating in Freetown, which specifically targeted 'vulnerable girls' who were likely to be engaging in CSW. The intention of many of the projects was to find an alternative method for the girls to obtain money. They attempted this by teaching the young women new skills, from which they could potentially make a living. The mission statements for two of those organisations are stated as:

Women in Crisis (WIC):

To improve on the status of women and young girls in extremely difficult socio-economic circumstances, through skills and vocational training; the promotion of gender issues including better access to reproductive health services including STDs/HIV/AIDS messages and related issues.

(Author's fieldwork, 2005)

COOPI:

> Providing quality services for vulnerable women to help rebuild their lives through psychosocial counselling skills, training and medical services.
>
> (Author's fieldwork, 2005)

Due to time constraints, the group being marginalised and the desire to access the participants through a trusted and well-established network, I decided that the most appropriate way to contact the girls would be through organisations already operating with them, although this was not straightforward. The sensitive nature of the work undertaken by these organisations led to complications in contacting the girls, as some organisations denied me access in an effort to protect their beneficiaries.

However, I was able to contact 'vulnerable girls' through the following organisations: COOPI, Women in Crisis, Handicap International (HI), Camp Hill Vocational Skills and Gracelands. Through contacts made from these establishments, 'snowballing' occurred, and I was introduced to three other groups of street girls who are referred to in the study as the 'Bus Station', 'Tower Hill' and 'Sawpit' groups; these new groups provided a second category of respondents. Being introduced to the new groups by personal contacts known to the groups instantly gave me credibility.

The selection of the participants from the sample frame was usually carried out by either a staff member from the respective organisation, a dominant member of the group or in some cases whoever was in the vicinity at the time of the data collection. While the participants used for this research were a non-representative sample, the study specifically targeted groups of different ages, geographical living and working locations, in an effort to encompass the broadest the scope of this study. A further 'contrasting group' was also incorporated into the research. In addition to the sample groups previously mentioned, two groups of secondary schoolgirls were also used. Table 8.1 displays the different types of interviewees involved in the research, and the number of respondents from each category.

School girls

Girls from a school called Educaid were used to compare and contrast the lifestyles of street girls. The majority of the pupils that attended Educaid considered themselves to be fortunate, as they were amongst the small minority in Freetown who received free education. Most of the

Table 8.1 Table displaying the categories of interviewees

Categories of interviewees	Number of respondents
Participants connected to an organisation	30
Street girls	18
Schoolgirls	12

students from the school would otherwise not have been able to afford to complete their secondary education. Therefore, the sample used from the school could not be considered 'privileged'.

The 'schoolgirl' participants involved in the research were aged between 15 and 19 years. All lived with a relative or a guardian, a large proportion stated they lived with their grandmother. Prior to and after school, the schoolgirls engaged in income-generating activities such as selling coal, necklaces or attending to vegetable gardens. With regard to relationships, the participants explained that schoolgirls were known to have had up to six boyfriends at one time. Therefore, in one respect some of the schoolgirls' 'livelihoods' were similar to that of the street girls.

8.6 Method overview

In addition to researching the sample population, key informant interviews have proven to be a valuable aspect of the multi-method approach, during previous studies with street children. In Young and Barrett's (2001b) research, the use of organisations working with street children in Kampala was used to triangulate information gained from the children, as it provided a different perspective of the street children's lives. McKay and Mazurana (2004) claim that their understanding of ex-girl soldiers' situation was enhanced through discussions with key individuals who were working with these adolescents.

Key informants

The first phase of this research methodology was in the form of semi-formal interviews with key informants. These informants included policy-makers, health workers, UN agencies and NGOs/CBOs (Community-Based Organisations) working with young 'vulnerable women' in Freetown. Initially, the key informants were identified through advice and knowledge provided from CGG. These initial connections led me to contacts of contacts (snowballing).

The interviews with key informants took place at their place of work, and each lasted approximately one hour. During discussions, the participants were asked to refer to their organisations' point of view as opposed to their own personal opinions. The interviews generally revolved around issues relating to street girls, in the following five main themes: public health awareness campaigns, sexual information networks, condom usage, access to sexual health (including HIV/AIDS) services and information, and finally 'street girl' lifestyles and livelihoods. However, many key informants had specialised knowledge (such as the Family Support Unit – FSU), therefore a number of interviews were focussed on the relevant field of the interviewee. Below is a brief explanation of the general themes that were explored during the interviews.

Public health campaigns

Public health campaigns relating to HIV/AIDS were discussed in general and with specific regard to street girls. The successes and limitations of projects were highlighted, and suggestions for future campaigns were often volunteered.

Sexual information networks

Obtaining information on this theme involved enquiring with the organisations, where they believed street girls gained information about sexual health, the reasoning for this thinking, and the flaws in the street girls' knowledge networks. This information was required in order to recognise current networks and assist with identifying new methods for disseminating HIV/AIDS information.

Condom usage

This topic gained knowledge about the organisations' perspective of condom use, both within the general public and street girls, creating an image of those who use condoms and those who do not. Condom use amongst street girls was then explored further, questioning why many of the girls do not use condoms, and where the girls get their information about them. Accessibility and cost of condoms was ascertained, plus any known stigmas or myths associated with them. Suggestions from key informants were encouraged regarding how campaigns could successfully encourage street girls to use condoms.

Access to services and information

Information was obtained relating to STD clinics and VCT (Voluntary Counselling and Testing) centres. Information was sought on issues such as their location and number of clinics/centres and the services they provide.

Lifestyle and livelihood

Data was sought from informants on the lifestyle and livelihoods of the street girls. Information on these issues was required to build up a picture of the lives of the girls and establish how they are placed at risk of HIV infection.

Although the key informant interviews commenced in the initial stages of the research, due to time constraints of both myself and the informants, many of the interviews were held intermittently with focus group discussions. However, it is believed that this benefited the research as new data gathered from both methods was validated by cross-checking.

Focus groups

Past research has confirmed that focus groups are beneficial to a researcher who wishes to explore sensitive topics, in a non-personal or threatening manner. As Preston-Whyte (2003) states, focus group discussions enable participants to define the situation in their own terms, while highlighting important points relating to perceptions, beliefs and attitudes. Brink's (2001) research demonstrated that group discussions with street children could provoke information from various aspects of children's lives.

During the course of this research, a total of ten Focus Group Discussions (FGD) were held, with approximately six participants in each. Within all of the focus groups, there was always a mixture of mother and non-mother participants. Utilising participants from different geographical locations of the city, and accessing them through dissimilar means (as discussed earlier), ensured that different perspectives of street girls would be incorporated into the study. The topics debated in this phase focussed on young street girls' knowledge of and attitudes towards HIV/AIDS, knowledge networks, condom use, sexual behaviour, health support networks, access to health services and information, lifestyles and livelihoods.

The sessions began with a story about a fictional girl who lived on the streets of Freetown. I initiated the tale, setting the scene, and then invited participants to contribute to the story. The tale was used as the framework for the group work, building on the story using probes. Questions were asked about the character and her situation, pictures were also shown to the participants to direct the discussions and elicit information on specific issues. For example, the participant's knowledge of condoms and their attitudes towards them were ascertained through showing them a picture of a condom, then asking questions in an abstract context. The participants were queried about what it was, its use, who they are used by, where they can be obtained, and at what cost. Issues such as HIV/AIDS, information networks, sexual behaviour and access to health services were also explored through the use of further pictures and additions to the story. For example, the scenario of the fictional street girl becoming pregnant initiated a debate about where the girl might get assistance, advice and support. Discussions also took place about how young street girls are educated about sexual health issues (i.e. pregnancy and STDs), and how they learnt about topics such as menstruation. The participants were also invited to provide their own suggestions on the most appropriate methods through which street girls could be educated about sexual health.

Sensitive issues were dealt with; participants were asked directly not about their personal experience but about their knowledge and attitudes towards the issues. However, once the participants trusted me, the majority began referring to their personal experiences and volunteering their own opinions and attitudes.

During one of the discussions, a Sierra Leonean member of staff from Handicap International was present. She was amazed at the amount of personal information the participants were disclosing. She believed the girls would not have provided the intimate information without the use of the 'story'. The girls began by discussing the situation from a non-personal perspective, and then chose to include their personal experiences. The staff member from Handicap International believed that if I had asked direct questions about their personal life, very little, if any, personal data would have been provided.

Recording information

During the majority of FGDs and interviews, information was recorded by means of a dictaphone. However, for some FGDs the use of a dictaphone was considered inappropriate for the environment in which the discussion took place. On these occasions, a written record of the data was made. Both recording methods had advantages: using the dictaphone allowed discussions to flow without disruption, while the written method gave me time to consider the dialogue and in some cases provoked new lines of enquiry. Even though two different recording methods were used to gather data, I did not feel it had an impact on the findings.

Locality and time of research

The locality of the focus group discussions took place either at the participant's living area or at their affiliated organisations. Both the focus group discussions and the in-depth interviews primarily took place in the mornings as this was deemed the most convenient for those girls who worked during the night, and often traded or attended vocational skills training during the day. I was mindful not to intrude on their 'working time'.

The areas used to carry out the data collection for these methods were generally successful, although on one occasion a focus group discussion could have been influenced by the presence of a staff member from the organisation from which the participants came. I was aware of this situation but did not feel in a position to request privacy with the girls, due to their vulnerability and the organisation's obligation to protect them.

8.7 In-depth life histories

Through combining group interactions, and individual discussions with street children, an accurate impression can be gained about them (Brink, 2001). McKay and Mazurana (2004) successfully utilised in-depth interviews to gain knowledge about the lives of female ex-soldiers during and after the civil war in Sierra Leone.

In-depth life histories were the final phase of this research; a total of ten were conducted. Following the conclusion of each of the focus group activities, a volunteer was requested to partake in in-depth interviews, which involved discussing their life histories. 'Selecting' participants by this method seemed the most appropriate method because it was conducted on a voluntary basis but only those girls who were confident enough to speak English put themselves forward. A certain level of English was advantageous because it meant an interpreter was not needed, and therefore, the interview could be conducted on a one-to-one basis and remain completely confidential. However, it was acknowledged that this 'criteria' would have excluded the less confident English-speaking street girls from being involved.

Previous research with street children has highlighted the desire of these children to discuss their personal situations with an adult (Gunther, 2001). Although this had been the case for previous research, I was aware that the majority of the participants involved in this study were likely to have been subjected to horrific atrocities that they may be reluctant to discuss. Fortunately, the relationships that developed between myself and the individual participants over a period of time, and meetings, seemed to alleviate this problem.

Crucial information relating to the methods of intervention was obtained through discussing the street girls' life histories. The basic themes for the in-depth histories included the street girls information networks (e.g. initiation ceremonies), issues relating to reproductive health, womanhood, their knowledge and attitudes to STDs and HIV/AIDS, their sexual networks, events that have impacted upon their lives, their attitude towards health professionals, public health provisions and information, and their lifestyles and livelihoods.

8.8   Visual methods

Some of the in-depth interviews were complemented by the use of disposable cameras. Four of the participants involved in the interviews (from four different localities) were provided with disposable cameras. Those involved were shown how to use the camera and were informed to take 'significant' photographs, it was then left to their own discretion as to what they took pictures of. After a few days, at pre-arranged times the cameras were collected and two copies of each film were developed. During confidential follow-up meetings (conducted on a one-to-one basis), participants were provided with a copy of their pictures and were invited to discuss the photographs they had taken.

This method acted as a useful tool as it allowed me, 'the outsider', to view the participant's life from the 'insiders' perspective, without altering the dynamics of the situation. Knowledge was gained about areas that would not have been accessible to me, areas such as the locations where the street girls had sex with their clients. In addition to this, the photographs often acted as catalysts for discussions on issues previously not mentioned. This method proved to be particularly useful to obtain information about their home and work life.

8.9   Data analysis

The analysis of the data for this study began as soon as the fieldwork commenced in Sierra Leone, and became an ongoing process. All four methodological tools were analysed using framework analysis. As Kenneth (2000) recognised, framework analysis is a versatile tool that can be utilised for analysing a variety of methods.

The procedure for analysing data using a 'framework' involves categorising the material into themes, then interpreting the data incorporated within the particular theme. In the case of this study, the research objectives provided the structure in which the data was themed; this ensured that the material gathered was relevant to the aims of the study.

Although framework analysis was used for all of the methods, the participants undertook the initial analysis of the visual methodology. This process took place during discussions with me, when the photographers were providing explanations for each of the photos they had taken.

The qualitative data collection adopted allowed responders to discuss the themes interchangeably. This assisted with data analysis, by helping to discover 'relationships', and develop explanations for the data (Huberman and Miles, 1994). Although the manual process of 'framing' takes time, the consistency of the in-putter ensures that the material is reliably categorised, plus it was apparent that tabulating range of street girls possible within the results facilitated the task of identifying reoccurring data, which clearly enhanced the reliability of the material.

On completion of the data collection in Freetown, the preliminary research findings were distributed in a report, and during a workshop that was held for all those who had contributed to the research. Presenting and discussing the findings during the meeting acted as a validation process for the research data, as well as allowing responders and informants to network and initiate plans of actions for future public health campaigns. In addition to this, information was also validated throughout data collection by extensive triangulation and researcher observations.

8.10 Ethical issues

Due to the vulnerability of participants, and the sensitive nature of the topic, many ethical issues arose during the research. Concerns relating to gaining formal consent from the participants, expectations of remuneration, and the positionality and the power dynamics between the researcher and the researched had to be considered.

Consent

As Young and Barrett (2001a) state, UK guidelines for carrying out research with children about 'sensitive issues' are not always appropriate or practical when working with street children in developing countries. Many of the participants involved in this research were illiterate and it was, therefore, impractical to ask them to sign to give their consent. In addition, it was impossible to obtain the permission from their parents (or guardians), because most were orphaned or estranged from their families.

All participants who consented (verbally) to be involved in the research were informed that they could withdraw their involvement at any time, and were made aware that they could refuse to discuss any issue, or answer any question. During the research, many of the street girls supplied personal and sensitive information. It was made clear to the participants that even though the information they had provided could be used as part of the study, identities would remain confidential and anonymous. To ensure the participants thoroughly understood these issues, a responsible and trusted adult (usually a member of staff from an organisation working with street girls) always explained this in the Creole language Krio (the language spoken by the majority of the population). These individuals were usually accessible during the discussions in case any issues needed clarification.

Key informants were also advised that even though the data they provided might be utilised for the research, their identities would remain anonymous but if consented to, their position and name of organisation would be cited.

Visual method

During the visual methodology, ethical issues arose when participants took photographs of other individuals. It was unknown whether all those photographed were aware of the purpose of the pictures, and had consented for them to be used as part of this research. This became evident by some participants taking pictures of their clients. It is unlikely that these men would have agreed to be documented as 'men who use prostitutes'. To overcome this problem, only consented photos have been used, and the faces of those 'consenting individuals' have been covered to ensure their identities remain anonymous.

If this method is going to be adopted in future research, the ethical issues would have to be considered more fully if the photographer's pictures were to be included in the paper. Although, it is apparent from this study that valuable data has only been obtained because both the environment and the photographer were natural. Should additional actors have been introduced to acquire 'formal consent', the dynamics of the situations are likely to have been altered.

8.11   Remuneration

The issue of remuneration was a difficult dilemma to overcome. It was acknowledged that within Sierra Leonean society, a white, Western researcher, gaining information from an underprivileged group, would be expected to pay participants. Many NGOs have 'accepted' this predicament, and have gone to the extent of paying participants to attend workshops. However, I was aware that payment might affect the data provided and complicate the power dynamics further. These issues were taken into account, and it was recognised that participants were giving their time to the research, instead of potentially earning money. Therefore, whenever possible I reciprocated by acts of kindness such as buying interviewees drinks and food during meetings, and assisting street girls resolve medical problems. Gratitude was shown to pimps and madams for allowing me access to 'their girls', by providing them with condoms and HIV/AIDS awareness posters.

8.12 Positionality

It would be virtually impossible for me to be completely objective, as all researchers will take their own 'frame of reference' to a study. Our own understanding is a precondition of our own research (May, 1993). Therefore, different data collectors or data analysers will come to varying conclusions, even if they have similar data. May (1993) states that as researchers we need to understand and acknowledge these influences in our own thinking, and that of society, and understand how it may affect our research. As a white, British, young female, my positionality is likely to have influenced the results of this research. However, the positionality of all researchers irrespective of their culture, age or gender will affect the outcome of any study.

There are other dimensions that also need to be considered, dimensions that are 'hidden from view', such as the power relationships. It was evident that there were power dynamics between me and the participants. On many occasions, I was asked questions that insinuated that 'the researcher was in the know'. As a consequence of the power relationship, the responders may have modified their answers according to social norms or to their perceptions of the interviewer's expectations.

8.13 Conclusion

The philosophical underpinnings of the methodologies adopted ensured rich and diverse data was collated through qualitative means. These methods included semi-structured key informant interviews, focus group discussions, in-depth interviews and visual methodology. The macro and micro approaches allowed both the 'insiders' and 'outsiders' perspectives be considered, in addition to acting as a triangulation and cross-checking devise.

Ascertaining the 'identity' of the 'insiders' was complex and involved definitional debates on street girls. This resulted in the local meaning of the phrase being adopted for the purpose of this research. Once this was established, the sample population was contacted through three means. These were organisations working with 'vulnerable girls', a school and 'contacts of contacts' that allowed me access to groups that were not connected to organisations.

Lessons learned from this research

1. Overcoming ethical issues was difficult when undertaking research of this nature.
2. Using photographs/cameras offers researchers a unique opportunity to gather valuable research data while limiting the 'observer effect'.
3. Although such devices/technological developments offer such opportunities, they do bring with them other methodical and ethical considerations that need careful exploration and consideration.
4. Snowball sampling in research such as this offers a real valuable way of obtaining access to participants.

References

Brink, B. (2001) 'Working with Street Children: Reintegration Through Education', *Support for Learning*, 16(2): 79–86.

Graham, E. (1997) 'Philosophies Underlying Human Geography Research', in Flowerdew, R. and Martin, D. (Eds) *Methods in Human Geography: A Guide for Students Doing a Research Project*, Longmans, 6–30.

Gunther, H. (2001) 'Interviewing Street Children in a Brazilian City', *The Journal of Social Psychology*, 132(3): 359–367.

Holloway, L. and Hubbard, P. (2001) *People and Place – The Extraordinary Geographies of Everyday Life*, London: Pearson education limited.

Huberman, A.M. and Miles, M.B. (1994) *Handbook of Qualitative Research*, Thousand Oaks, USA: Sage.

Johann, L.R. (1996) 'Street Children in South Africa: Findings From Interviews on the Background of Street Children in Petoria, South Africa', *Adolescence*, 31(122), 423–431.

Kenneth, J.R. (2000) 'The Unsolicited Diary as a Qualitative Toll for Advanced Research Capacity in the Field of Health and Illness', *Qualitative Health Research*, 10(4): 555–567.

May, T. (1993) *Social Research Issues, Methods and Process*, Buckingham: Open University Press.

McKay S. and Mazurana M. (2004) *Where Are the Girls? – Girls in Fighting Forces in Northern Uganda, Sierra Leone and Mozambique: Their Lives During and After the War*, Montreal, Canada: Rights and democracy.

Preston-Whyte, E. (2003) 'Contexts of Vulnerability: Sex, Secrecy and HIV/AIDS', *African Journal of AIDS Research*, 2(2): 89–94.

Sayer, A. (1999) *Realism and Social Science*, London: Sage.

Tuan, Y. (1977) *Space and Place – The Perspective of Experience*, London: Edward Arnold.

Young, L. and Barrett, H. (2001a) 'Ethics and Participation: Reflections on Research with Street Children', *Ethics, Place and Environment*, 4(2): 130–135.

Young, L. and Barrett, H. (2001b) 'Adapting Visual Methods: Action Research with Kampala Street Children', *Area*, 33(2): 141–152.

9
Summary

Colin Rogers

9.1 Conclusion and discussion

The recently published Independent Commission into the Future of policing had as its starting discussion points such topics as the challenges facing the police in the 21st century, how best to develop the work force of the police and equip it, to cut crime and increase public confidence as well as considering governance and accountability and the management of resources in difficult economic times.

Such a review demands a new approach to providing police resource and a new way of thinking about policing, which of course needs to be based within a solid foundation, that being based within excellent scientific research and evaluation. It is, therefore, no accident that the rise in evidence-based practices has been so prominent in the police as well as in other public agencies.

Indeed the newly formed College of Policing has stated its aims to include access to evidence about what works in policing and crime reduction, with the aim of helping those involved to make better evidence-based decisions (www.college.police.uk/20996.htm accessed 8 January 2014).

A substantial amount of its website includes much reference to research and evidence-based practice and decision-making. Clearly, we may be on the frontier of a new era of police research, fuelled by the need to provide policing services in an economical, efficient and effective manner.

The future of policing appears to be based therefore upon sound research that can be applied to the pragmatic world of policing in a changing society. A sound knowledge and understanding of research techniques and the problems associated with them are therefore vital if this new era of police research is to be successful. Learning lessons from previous researchers' work and attempting to improve upon them will be an important part of the future of police research.

Throughout this book, therefore, which is not primarily a research methods book, the authors have highlighted the fact that the journey of researching the police organisation and other criminal activity is not a straightforward one. It requires a sound knowledge of the police and other organisations to an extent, as well as appreciating political and structural nuances of such an agency as the police, as well as an understanding of the wider criminal justice system in whatever country the police are situated.

However, the authors have provided valuable insights into how to engage with the police organisation and other aspects of policing, and by employing different research methods and approaches, have been able to effectively research into such seemingly difficult circumstances.

What has become clear throughout this book is that despite the topics being researched in several different countries, such as the United States, Germany, Africa and the United Kingdom, there are commonalties in terms of actually undertaking research. In particular, access for many of the researchers proved problematic initially, while the problem of what Punch (1985) refers to as going native for those regarded as outsider/insiders was always hovering in the background.

The topic of access, for example, was problematic for most of the researchers. Why this should be is open to discussion. It may be that the police and other organisations are suspicious of those who wish to pry into their business, or may have in the past allowed access to researchers who subsequently unfairly criticised them. Further, it may be that they do not wish to allow sensitive or secret information regarding security to be compromised, or at least be potentially compromised. Whatever the reason, apart from those researchers actually situated as insiders/insiders, access has, in the main, proved to be problematic. Yet, in most democratic policing models, the claim of transparency and openness would suggest that access for researchers would be an easy task to negotiate. As we have seen in the chapters of this book, each researcher has had to negotiate that particular task in line with their own location either within or outside the organisation being researched.

In a very practical sense, as more and more surveys are being undertaken, topics such as how questionnaires were formulated, piloted, adjusted and distributed, along with associated ideas such as sampling and representativeness discussed in the chapters, will be invaluable for those working in research units or about to undertake such research as part of their studies. In particular, with the rise in social websites and increased mobile technology, the utilisation of online surveys as opposed to older methods of postal or face-to-face surveys is of interest to readers of this book. Similarly, the function of interviewing and observing, as carried out by the individual authors, will be of great benefit to those who wish to undertake similar research.

The use of Brown's typology applied to each separate chapter will, it is hoped, enable the reader to understand some of the problems faced by the authors in conducting their research while also helping future police and crime researchers to understand and plan their research. The lesson learned section by each author, highlighted at the conclusion of each chapter, will also assist future researchers engaged in this field of research.

Further, the diverse range of research topics that were studied illustrates how wide the policing mandate can be. From community safety partnership work, community engagement techniques, use of community intelligence, management problems and dealing with vulnerable groups such as street girls and educationally disadvantaged people illustrates just how wide the scope of research actually is when considering policing and its impact upon society.

In a very practical sense, this book has illustrated some of the problems associated with research in general and so with the police and criminal activities in particular. The chapters have included not only an appraisal of these problems but have also shown how individual researchers have attempted to overcome these problems. It is hoped that these experiences will enable the reader and potential police researchers to understand and learn from the work discussed in the chapters in this book.

As police and other criminal justice organisations across the world face an uncertain journey, research at all levels will play a growing and significant aspect in their ability to continue to perform their functions satisfactorily and to improve to meet the challenges that surely lie ahead of them. This book will, it is hoped, provide some important information, learning and insights that will help researchers, whether professional or amateur, academic or student, to carry out that function more effectively.

References

College of Policing Research. (2014) Available at www.college.police.uk/20996.htm, [Accessed 05 February 2014].

Punch, M. (1985) *Conduct Unbecoming*, London: Tavistock Publications.

Appendix A1: Preamble –
An Interpretation of the Brief

'Why do the police ignore research findings?'
'Why don't researchers produce usable knowledge?'
'Why do the police always reject any study that is critical of what they do?'
'Why do researchers always show the police in a bad light?'
'Why don't police officers even read research reports?'
'Why can't researchers write in plain English?'
'Why are the police so bloody defensive?'
'Why are researchers so bloody virtuous?'
'Why are the police unwilling to examine their own organisational performance?'
'Why are researchers unwilling to produce information that a practical man exercising power can use to change a limited aspect of the organisation instead of theoretic and explanatory structures of no use to the problem-solver?'
'Why do the police insist that they know better, when the researchers are the experts in knowledge construction?'
'Why do researchers write recipes when they can't even cook?'

(MacDonald, 1987: 1)

Appendix A2: List of the Six Research Categories and 27 Subject Sub-categories

Organization of police

Police and society
Organizational change
Training
Hiring and retention
Militarization
Privatization
Media relations*

Attitudes and behavior

Attitudes of police
Occupational stress
Minority issues

Accountability and misconduct

Accountability
Police violence
Discrimination and profiling
Control of police powers
Corruption

Police strategies

Community policing
Investigative tactics
Technology and equipment
Targeted groups
Patrol
Drugs and alcohol
Domestic violence
Intelligence-based
Sexual assault

Terrorism*
Computer crime
International/global concerns*

Citizen satisfaction

Measurement

*Category did not exist in 2000
Adapted from Mazeika et al. (2010: 522)

Index

Note: A page reference in **bold** indicates a table; figures are shown in *italics*.

Printed and bound in Great Britain by
CPI Group (UK) Ltd, Croydon, CR0 4YY

CEN Jurnal Riset
Computer Room 126
Item # 25182
[barcode]

CPI Antony Rowe
Chippenham, UK
2016-12-27 12:38